HOW TO MAKE DISCIPLES

A SIMPLE, PROVEN MODEL FOR MAKING
SELF-SUSTAINING FOLLOWERS OF GOD.

DOUG BURRIER

DIFFERENT.LY PRESS

Published 2019 by Different.ly Publishing
PO Box 176
Cave Spring, Georgia 30124
www.different.ly

ISBN: 978-1-7334021-0-1
First Edition .
Printed in the United States of America

Sustainable Discipleschip® is a registered Service Mark of Doug Burrier

For the immigrants and the lost ones of Christianity,
who came to this great faith full of hope,
who long to know how to follow God,
who want to understand His words,

but who live on the streets of Christianity,
neither prepared, confident, nor skilled
to find abundant life or live their dream

because they found no experienced guide
to teach them the language,
to provide clear direction, and
to show them the ropes along the way.

We should have been ready for them . . .

CONTENTS

PART I

INTRODUCTION

I came that they may have life and have it abundantly.

— JESUS

1

THE STATE OF DISCIPLESHIP

We make followers of churches, musicians, pastors, and authors all the time. It is easy. What seems difficult and time-consuming is making followers of a God that cannot be seen. What if making disciples of God could be easy too? It is.

How would you define "discipleship"? What is a disciple? Most of us will quickly identify a disciple as a follower and discipleship as the process of making a follower. But are those answers correct? Are they useful? Do you really know what a disciple looks like? How do you measure success in your disciple making? What does it mean to follow God? What is a clear, simple way to make disciples?

You are not alone if you struggle to answer these questions. A joint Barna Group and Navigators research project[1] revealed confusion among leaders and followers regarding discipleship. Worse yet, the data indicates that most discipleship efforts are impotent, with only 25 percent of Christians saying they were in a discipleship relationship.[2]

The report concludes:

> *Churches are in need of new models for discipleship. Current programs capture only a minority of Christians, and most believers do not prioritize an investment in their spiritual growth. At the same time, church leaders desire a clear plan and lack systems to evaluate spiritual health.*

The study showed little agreement among Christians about what was and what was not a discipleship activity. Church leaders did not fare much better. They could not agree on any particular definition of discipleship, and only 1 percent of leaders said, "Today's churches are doing very well at discipling new and young believers."

There is also a significant gap between the perceptions of church leaders and the people in their churches.

- Sixty percent of the leaders believe that churches are not doing well at discipleship, while nearly 90 percent of attenders say that the church does or probably does a good job of discipleship.
- Eighty-eight percent of church leaders believe that small groups will have a significant impact on developing disciples, while only 31 percent of the people say that small groups have been helpful to them.
- Church leaders say that lack of commitment (87 percent), too much busyness in the people (85 percent), and sinful habits (70 percent) are the top three barriers to discipling people. The people disagree, with only 23 percent of them saying that busyness is the problem. The people's second and third barriers were "it will take hard work" and "their friends are not interested in spiritual things."

Neither leaders nor attenders have a clear definition of discipleship. Only one in four Christians are in a discipleship relationship and only one in five leaders are attempting to disciple someone else. Do you see the implications? The great commission[3] instructs Christians to "make disciples," but over three-quarters of active Christians are not carrying out the great commission. Over three-quarters of Christians are settling for something less than God's best for them.

How did we get here? Most of the churches we encounter long for their people to be "fully devoted followers of Christ," but few have a comprehensive process for making disciples. They struggle with results, and most of them equate assimilation into the church or biblical education with making disciples. Nothing could be further from Jesus's great commission! He wants us to make followers of Him. Confusion about what discipleship is and how to make disciples may be the single greatest contributor to the impotence of discipleship—and to the struggles of believers who really want to follow God. I was one of those lost ones.

The Church failed me by failing to understand what it means to make disciples. The lack of a discipleship process focused on me, as an individual, created a massive void in the early years of my faith. The busyness of being a Christian instead of being a follower caused me to be a spiritually deficient doer.

My discipleship journey was so lonely at first. Everyone wanted me to become a Christian, but no one wanted to walk with me after I became one. Someone handed me a "First Steps Book" to help me understand my faith. The first chapter warned me that, although I was excited now, I would soon become discouraged. It encouraged me to "hang in there." What a start! I got saved with a bunch of twenty-something misfits who also needed help. We did what all twenty-somethings do when the establishment fails us: we started a Bible study in our apartment. It was a mess. A bunch of reformed yahoos and ex-addicts led each other in circles. We really tried. We really believed. But we had no idea what we were doing. We had no depth and no experience. We needed old guys.

We were open to anything or anyone who would give us attention. A crazy Pentecostal guy (not all Pentecostals are crazy) told me if I spoke in tongues, I would be filled by God and everything would change. I remember being trapped for hours in a prayer room while everyone prayed that I would "get it." Yes, I even muttered a few words out of exhaustion. That failure led me to question what was wrong with me. Another time, I was invited to a Bible study by a cute girl, who introduced me to their teacher. He was so interested in helping us. I went and chomped at the bit for the first few Bible studies. On my third visit, we were getting ready to take communion, and the girl who brought me said, "Do you want to make love now?" What? She went on to explain that making love was the greatest demonstration of the love that we all shared in God. You got it —I was attending a cult. I was smart enough to remember Paul[4] telling me to stop making love outside of marriage. I left, but others did not. How sad for us.

I wandered from conference to conference. My Christian walk went on from fad to fad. I got with the wrong girl— everyone knew it, but no one stopped to help me. I needed an honest, experienced guide. My first discipleship relationship was with Milam Beasley. He explained the scriptures to us, gave us books to read, and taught us the basics. He taught me to give a thankful gift back to God for all God gave me. Milam was just a regular guy. I never had a pastor, church leader, or anyone with credentials offer to disciple me until I met Joe Durham. Joe was my boss at one of my first ministry jobs. He was not much older than me, but he cared and he had years' more experience. He pumped me full of resources and challenged me. Then there were Reymundo and Orlando in Nicaragua. These two men piled on tons of chopped-up, translated learning and guidance. I had a few mentor types but still had no peers to walk with daily. Day to day, I was on my own. But I tried. I went to Bible studies and even approached two successful senior pastors in my community. That did not work! The first pastor listened to my troubles and then told everyone. The second allowed me to make one appointment with his secretary.

Starving for answers, I consumed the Bible cover to cover a few times. I read every Christian book I could find. I read and read. I went to seminary and learned a lot of information, but still, no one discipled me. I found a monk who walked with me in discipleship for a while. I learned much about following from Bob Coder (a rock-star well driller for God), but my discipleship process remained the school of hard knocks and accidental meetings.

Years after I had been a pastor, a dear friend said, "It has been so great seeing you grow up as a leader all these years." I was torn between being happy and being a bit offended. But she was right. I knew nothing when I started, and no one should have made me a pastor. I was not "who I should have been" to get the job done. Thankfully, I was just bullheaded enough not to give up. I just kept trying. I finally hit a point where I was a follower and developed ongoing discipleship relationships with people smarter than and different from me. These relationships continue to this day. These wonderful people are patient, push, and champion me to experience my best next day as I follow God.

If anyone owes me any debt in this Christian life, it would be for all the years of screwups, regrets, bad memories, and wasted time that is now a part of my story. My story could have been cleaner, better, and far more profitable if someone had a plan to intentionally disciple me along the way. God knows, I wanted it. It just was not there. The Barna survey proves this point, with over half of the people who responded saying, "No one offered them discipleship."

I believe, more than ever before, it is time for church leaders to take a long, hard look not only at the state of discipleship but, more importantly, the state of the Church. The single most important thing we can do is make disciples (followers) so that they can enjoy all that God has for them. People need the opportunity to make great life decisions, survive the storms of life, and most importantly, have a deep relationship with God. We need to have a clear plan that actually delivers these objectives to the people we lead to Christ. We need to execute this plan for the Christians who wander in the door. We cannot ignore this wonderful task. Making disciples is every Christian's privilege and responsibility.

It is time to clear the confusion about what discipleship is. It is time for a simple, successful plan to make disciples. It is time to be intentional, intimate, and invested in people's success. It is time to model being a disciple, to pitch it out of successful practice, and to provide healthy discipleship for others. The church must return to a culture of discipleship where success is measured based on people choosing and succeeding with God daily. Large, medium, and small churches need to make sure they are not winning people to a shallow, regretful, insecure, and shaky faith.

But we need to be clear on what a disciple is, what discipleship is, and how to effectively "make disciples" before we can succeed.

Do you have questions about what discipleship is? Would you like a simple, proven model to make disciples? There are simple answers so universal that everyone can agree on them. And I will share our proven model that adapts to and works in any culture. But first, let me share the secret sauce to our disciple-making success story.

2

THE SECRET SAUCE

Making disciples is entirely about who someone is and becomes. It is not about what they do or how they do it. Doing is the natural result of being.

I have spent my life solving problems: personal problems, corporate problems, leadership problems, manufacturing problems, transition problems, and church problems. I focus now on helping people avoid problems by helping leaders think differently and make better decisions. How cool is that? I have this crazy, beyond-me track record of solving most of the problems that I have been asked to solve. My secret sauce is prayer. When people invite me to help, I listen while I am praying. My discipleship journey has taught me that God knows everything, that he wants us to succeed, that we must endure, and that we are gifted uniquely. Those truths fuel my belief that God can inspire beyond my education or experience. I have leveraged this secret sauce again and again to solve problems far beyond my experience.

One of those times was solving KRC Power Steering's sales and profitability problems. KRC is the only US manufacturer of a racing power-steering pump. Though I had no experience in production, engines, racing, or manufacturing, KRC was desperate and called me solely because of my track record. I took the job because I was hungry and childlike enough to believe that God would come through again. We solved many things, like sales processes, departmental communication, and production flows. I used my usual process: listen, pray, solve the easy things, listen, pray, look for the unseen things, and repeat. I also worked alongside the staff performing all of the relevant jobs for a couple of days each. I kept hearing about how repairing pumps cost the most money, lost the most sales, and caused the most downtime. So I learned how to rebuild, test, and adjust power-steering pumps. It took no time to see the problem. There was this one little spring that just would not perform consistently over time. I listened, I googled, and I prayed. The engineers took me through what was supposed to happen. They showed me how to add micron spacers to adjust the tension of the spring. The owner and I were talking, and he told me how he had even tried to temper the spring by cooking it in oil. I googled "metallurgy" and prayed, and then, beyond myself, I had one of those moments where I thought, "What if we did this in a different order?" Long story short, we tempered that little spring after it was adjusted instead of before it was adjusted. The combined solutions quadrupled KRC's profits in ninety days. We made a bunch of money. I still know very little about engines.

There is no doubt that my training in decision sciences, problem-solving, accounting, finance, and business management helped in the process. But it was my secret sauce that led to success beyond my training and experience. It has happened again and again, and it will keep happening.

Every successful thing has a secret sauce. Our model has a secret sauce, and it can be illustrated in the story of my problem-solving life. Two things make me the problem solver that I am: I am a decision scientist; and I am a disciple of God, who knows everything and is willing to share it.

I started college as an English literature major with a philosophy minor. I loved it—Lord Alfred Tennyson, Plato, all of it. Then I was forced to take a business elective. I registered for "An Introduction to Decision Science." That class became the end of my future in literature and philosophy. I was captured. I became lost in the mystery of how humans make really good and really bad decisions. I studied and continue to study the science of decision-making and problem-solving, but my study is not what made me a decision scientist. Decision sciences resounded in me, and I chose to become a decision scientist. Study just added preparation, confidence, and skills to my "call" to become a decision scientist. Choice made me a decision scientist. Learning makes me a more successful decision scientist. Decision science pervades my thinking, my dreaming, and my desires. I do not solve problems because I know how. I solve problems because I am a decision scientist.

I am also a follower of God, but I was not always a follower. There was a time when I just knew about God. I wrote a commentary on the book of Romans when I was sixteen and not a Christian. I went to countless Bible studies, but I struggled with living most of what I learned. It was not until an older man quietly shared what it really meant to be a follower that I got it. I heard God call me deep down inside that day, and I answered. I prayed that he would never let me be complacent and that he would never let me stray. I needed Him, I believed in Him, and I wanted Him. I was captured. I became lost in God's truths. That day, I became a follower—a disciple. You have read how hard it was for me to learn how to follow, but all that learning did not make me a disciple; it just made me a more successful follower. Each experience drew me nearer to God's incredible ways, promises, and truths. Each decision to find and apply a God answer to my life prepared me, made me confident and skilled to follow. I do not follow because I know how to follow. I follow because I am a follower. Finding God and following Him pervades my thinking, my dreaming, and my desires. I do not follow God because I know how. I follow God because I am a disciple. I do not make disciples because I know how. I make disciples because I am a disciple.

Therein lies the secret sauce to discipleship:

 Making disciples is entirely about who someone is and becomes. It is not about what they do or how they do it. Doing is the natural result of being.

That's it. It should resonate with most of you. You know that salvation is about who we believe in and who He makes us to be. Salvation is not about what we do. The focus of any discipleship effort should be who the person is: a follower. People will never follow (do) unless they are already followers (be). Nothing they do will make them a follower. Learning, applying, and doing will only make them a successful follower. Discipleship adds the preparation, confidence, and skill to be what we already are: followers of God.

It feels revolutionary, but it is an old truth that God taught us. You will see the secret sauce spilled on every page and in every paragraph of this book.

3

THE BURGER

"Anyone who listens to my teaching and follows it is wise, like a person who builds a house on solid rock. Though the rain comes in torrents and the floodwaters rise, and the winds beat against that house, it won't collapse because it is built on bedrock."

— Jesus, in Matthew 7:24–25

McDonald's Big Mac, with its secret sauce, is the company's all-time, best-selling burger.[1] Its secret sauce is, no doubt, the thing people talk about, but the Big Mac would not be successful without a good burger. The bun, the beef, and the other ingredients are the foundation of the Big Mac. The secret sauce is just what makes a Big Mac a Big Mac. Discipleship is no different. Successful discipleship has a secret sauce, but it needs a solid foundation.

I shared the secret sauce to successful discipleship:

Making disciples is entirely about who someone is and becomes. It is not about what they do or how they do it. Doing is the natural result of being.

Now let me share the burger:

Successful discipleship will always embrace certain biblical principles about how God designed us, His desires for us, and His way of making followers.

There are so many ways that people make disciples. Our team[2] reads about, asks about, and studies every model we can find, hoping to increase our odds of success. We have noticed that several methods appear in all of the successes. All of the successes embrace, knowingly or unknowingly, basic biblical principles about humanity, following, and being made a follower. Likewise, key elements are missing when discipleship fails.

We can discover (or rediscover) how to successfully make followers by understanding how God designed people, how God interacts with people, who God says people are, and who He knows they can be. Fundamental biblical truths of disciple making run cover to cover, from the beginning of mankind to today, and are observable in everything from anthropology to economics, from physiology to psychology. Each of these truths form a solid foundation for successful, sustainable disciple making.

The Fuel Is God's Words

Discipleship must be based on His truth, and the most significant record of His truth is found in the Bible. The Bible provides the history of God interacting with humans. It provides endless examples of good and bad choices. It records the truths of God to us through prophets, visions, and Jesus. It records straightforward direction, instruction, commands, and warnings. The Bible contains the universal truths of God and eternal principles communicated in different ways to different people in different times. It is a treasure trove of how to follow (or not to follow) God.

Paul reminds Timothy that the word of God is good to prepare us for every good work.

All Scripture is inspired by God and is useful to teach us what is true and to make us realize what is wrong in our lives. It corrects us when we are wrong and teaches us to do what is right. God uses it to prepare and equip his people to do every good work.

— 2 TIMOTHY 3:16–17

The writer in Psalm 119:103–105 sings,

"How sweet your words taste to me; they are sweeter than honey. Your commandments give me understanding; no wonder I hate every false way of life. Your word is a lamp to guide my feet and a light for my path."

In Proverbs 22:6, we see the importance of God's words in making disciples of our children:

Direct your children onto the right path, and when they are older, they will not leave it.

Again and again, the record of God's eternal truths is found to be the sure foundation of being disciples and making disciples. There is nothing greater than knowing His truths so that we can live the best life ever. The history of humans' good and bad decisions strengthens the foundation of following. There is nothing better than learning by example. Ironically, less than 20 percent of Christians (including those in discipleship) have read the Bible cover to cover. Almost half of all Christians have either never read or only read a few verses of the Bible.[3]

God's words also come alive in many challenging, life-stretching, topical resources and books. These resources complement the Bible and really help us follow God, apply His truths, and understand exactly who we are. *The Search for Significance* by Robert S. McGee is a classic at helping with our new identity and self-confidence. *Piercing the Darkness* by Frank E. Peretti will open the eyes of many to the reality of spiritual warfare. *Mere Christianity* by C.S. Lewis and *Sit, Walk, Stand* by Watchman Nee help us understand what it means to be and live as a Christian. The list of enduring works goes on and on. The impact that they can have on our discipleship goes on and on as well.

God's words are the fuel for being a disciple, but His words are also the fuel for creating a sustainable disciple-making model. When we apply His eternal truths about making disciples, discipleship becomes successful. Disciple making is modeled for us throughout the Bible. The making of disciples is part of God's recorded history. We see how great disciples were made in the Old and New Testaments. Biblical history even records two irrefutable models for making disciples.

Sustainable discipleship is biblically based. Everything that we do while making disciples—every how and every why—is found within the context of the Bible and based upon those two irrefutable models. We will explore the two biblical models, two key discipleship concepts, and an expanded definition of discipleship in the next section, "What Is Discipleship?"

Making Disciples Is Intentional

The Bible also reveals that making disciples is not done accidentally. Making disciples is done with intent. Making disciples is a priority to those who do it successfully. The greatest discipleship successes are found in the masses of unknown, passionate individuals who followed God to a thriving life and pass it on through one-on-one or small-group, nonprogrammed relationships. These disciple-making machines are the people we remember when we think about who helped us follow Christ well. Milam Beasley was one of those men to me. He was intentional. His venue was a small group. His work went unpaid and untracked. His life and passion were his tools. He only taught God's word. He cared. He did it intentionally, year after year, for group after group. He could not be stopped.

Organizations and churches that succeed at making disciples are intentional as well. Making disciples is the heartbeat of their mission. Doing ministry is simply a result. Successful organizations pour their people, their people's time, and their people's money into making disciples. These organizations are passionate about people thriving in their personal walk. These churches are solely motivated by what "can be" for each individual. They make disciples intentionally and passionately. They cannot be stopped.

Jesus made disciples. He trained them, sent them out, debriefed them, and right before he left them, said, "Go. Make followers of God." He left them with a single, intentional priority—God's priority. Successful disciple makers make disciples intentionally and with priority. They also know what they are doing. They know the end goal.

The Definition Is Simple

You can be as intentional as you want, but if you do not know what you are trying to accomplish, you will just fail intentionally. Part of my life's work has been traveling the world and training incredible teams to achieve great goals. I always open up with this question: "What is the first and most essential thing to achieving great goals and doing something big in this world?" I get all kinds of expected answers, such as have a great team, have the resources, have passion, or have a great plan. But I am fishing for one answer:

To do anything great, you first have to know what needs to be accomplished.

I know it is obvious, but think about the simplicity. You have to know what the work is before you can succeed at the work. How can you make a follower of God if you do not even know what a follower looks like? If we cannot define what discipleship is, how will we ever get the work done? What is it that we will do?

If you want to succeed in making disciples, you need a simple definition of discipleship. You need a simple definition of the work. The Barna study revealed that both leaders and followers struggle with a simple definition of discipleship. I believe the problem is that most of us are trying to define the wrong thing. I believe that every leader can easily define discipleship.

Discipleship is the process of making disciples followers of God.

The definition of discipleship is simple. It just is not the answer that we want. We want to define the process, but when we attempt to define the process, we begin to see there are so many ways to make disciples. If we want a simple definition of discipleship, we need to step back to the original question: what is the work that needs to be done? We need to make disciples. So what is a disciple?

A disciple is a follower of God.

What does it mean to be a follower of God? What does a follower look like?

A follower of God believes in God and has accepted the unconditional forgiveness, love, and grace of God and now has a relationship with God. He has decided to do life "God's way" because he believes that God created him. She is hungry to learn, apply, and synthesize God's truths for living so she can thrive in her God-given design. He is becoming prepared, confident, and skilled to live his best life ever on earth.

There we have it. Now that we know what a follower looks like, how can we get people there? What is the work that needs to be done? We need to help people learn and apply God's truths so that they will be prepared, confident, and skilled to live full lives. Here is our practical definition of how to make disciples based on the end goal of our work:

Making disciples introduces people to God, who loves and understands them, helps them understand who they are and what they can be, helps them apply God's transforming truths, and releases them as prepared, confident, and skilled to live their best life ever on earth.

There are two essential elements in discipleship: evangelism and teaching. Evangelism is easy to define and necessary for making followers. No one will follow God daily if they do not choose Him. We need to tell people about Christ. Evangelism is essential to making followers of God. Every disciple-making process needs to make sure that followers know how to share the Good News about Christ with others intentionally. Each of us needs to have a good, quick answer for our thriving lives.[4]

Few of us struggle with understanding this first element of making disciples (evangelism). The struggle of making disciples usually begins as we try to figure out our role in the second element of making disciples: teaching people how to follow. How exactly do we do it?

We help them understand who they are and what they can be. We help them apply God's transforming truths, and release them as prepared, confident, and skilled to live their best life ever on earth.

Successful disciple makers are just matchmakers getting people to God. The proper relationship will always be between God (the one to be followed) and the disciple (the follower). Disciple makers are just guides taking people down the path that they themselves have walked. Disciple makers are just teachers intentionally teaching biblical truths they have learned and applied. Disciple makers are the accelerant to what anyone could do on their own. Disciple makers help followers of God avoid needless disasters and navigate needed trials.

Discipleship adds the preparation, confidence, and skill to be what we already are: followers of God.

Successful discipleship is all about transforming individuals. We need to use the Bible, be intentional, and know what we are trying to accomplish, but we will fail if we do not reach our target audience.

The Focus Is Individuals

Discipleship has to reach the individual, as an individual, solely for the benefit of the individual. The goal is to allow individuals to encounter God (and His truths) so that they can be transformed. We are not trying to make the masses into disciples. Mass discipleship does not work. God's people are each unique, different, and individual. One size does not fit all in disciple making. The truths of God are enduring, eternal, and universal, but the application and methods come in different ways in different moments for different people.

Making disciples requires that we watch, pray, and lead people from where they are to the next closest place to God. Every successful disciple-making model is focused on individuals. Making disciples needs to be done interactively and intimately regardless of group size. Our research and testing show that the effectiveness of discipleship increases as the distance decreases between the leader and the follower. The effectiveness also increases as the time spent together increases. Discipleship is all about people, and real-life lessons learned while doing life together.[5] Making disciples requires you to live, work, walk, sail across stormy lakes, and push those you make disciples. This is what Jesus did.

Disciples follow God. The proper relationship will always be between God and his disciple. He miraculously invests individually and intimately with every follower simultaneously. He reaches people where they are. He reaches people precisely as they are. He customizes his discipleship of us, to us, with his infinite wisdom and ability. We will never be able to do what God does. We do not have the same capacity. We will only be able to disciple a certain number of people at a time.[6] We cannot reach into the hearts of those we make disciples. We cannot even know what is going on inside them without God inspiring us.

What we can do is disciple individuals as individuals. We can use a fluid model of discipleship that allows us to successfully make individual disciples. We can intimately disciple multiple people simultaneously. We can customize discipleship to the culture and to each individual. We can treat them as if they are the only person in the world.[7]

We can also reach them solely for their benefit. Successful disciple making has nothing to do with our churches, missions, or needs. God will use each of us in His great work, but He did not choose us, save us, and transform us to be workers. He saved us because we are His creation. He saved us because He loves us. He saves us so that we can have a real relationship with Him, our creator. Jesus came that we might have life abundantly. Disciple making is about individuals finding the real them and living as the real them. We can and should make disciples for their own benefit.

The secret sauce to McDonald's Big Mac is nothing without the Big Mac.

Though I never set out to develop a discipleship model, we have one. It works, but it is hopelessly dependent on these four foundations. We know this from our failures to nurture all four principles. We know this from our forgetfulness to instill all four principles in those we train. We know this from watching and measuring the success of others.

- The model uses God's truths to fuel the process.
- The model requires intentionality.
- The model has a simple definition of the work to be done.
- The model entirely focuses on individuals.

Sustainable discipleship, at its core, rests on these four principles that none of us own. These principles are God's principles. Solomon said it best:

> *Sometimes people say, "Here is something new!" But actually it is old; nothing is ever truly new. We don't remember what happened in the past, and in future generations, no one will remember what we are doing now.*

— ECCLESIASTES 1:10–11

Successful disciple making was done generations before Jesus ever walked the earth. We rediscovered it as He walked the earth. Each time God interacts with people, each time He draws them back to a thriving life, He teaches them to follow in the same simple way.

These four founding principles, along with the why, how, and value of making disciples, are there for us to rediscover.

PART II

WHAT IS DISCIPLESHIP?

4

TWO IRREFUTABLE DISCIPLESHIP MODELS

Dear friends, I am not writing a new commandment for you; rather it is an old one you have had from the very beginning.[1]

— The Apostle John

Discipleship is not a new thing. Discipleship has been going on from the beginning of the Old Testament, through the New Testament times, and on into our current day. We see God disciple Adam and Eve. We see God disciple Cain. We see God disciple Noah. The list goes on and on. Discipleship is an ancient journey between followers and God.

Sustainable discipleship is actually a rediscovery of God's model of discipleship. The methods may be new, and we may use new resources, but the model is ancient. It can be adapted for generations to come as it has been for generations before us. Sustainable discipleship is merely a reflection of how God has discipled His followers since the beginning of our time on earth.

And God's way to make disciples is concisely preserved for us in two irrefutable, biblical models. What better place to go for a discipleship model than the Bible?

From the Old Testament

A concise, Old Testament discipleship model is found in Deuteronomy 6, where God calls his people to be disciples and then shows them how to make disciples. Deuteronomy 6:3–4 not only calls the Israelites to follow God but reveals the value in humans following God.

> *Listen closely, Israel, and be careful to obey. Then all will go well with you, and you will have many children in the land flowing with milk and honey, just as the LORD, the God of your ancestors, promised you. "Listen, O Israel! The LORD is our God, the LORD alone.*
>
> — DEUTERONOMY 6:3–4

God had promises for Israel and all of those who would follow him. God knew who they should be. He created them. He watched them fall away from the glory of His original plan. He longed to return them to their glory, and like a loving father, He reached out with a plan. He showed them how to live. He showed them how to thrive. And he showed them how to help others thrive.

> *And you must love the LORD your God with all your heart, all your soul, and all your strength. And you must commit yourselves wholeheartedly to these commands that I am giving you today. Repeat them again and again to your children. Talk about them when you are at home and when you are on the road, when you are going to bed and when you are getting up. Tie them to your hands and wear them on your forehead as reminders. Write them on the doorposts of your house and on your gates.*
>
> — DEUTERONOMY 6:5–9

Straight from the mouth of God comes the instruction. Follow and then teach and remind your children of God's wonder, truths, and commands. First, be a disciple (follower, student) and then make disciples (followers, students). I love the practicality of this model. I abandon myself, I surrender, and I follow God's life-giving directions; then I pass these on to my family in very practical ways.

How incredible would life be for kids if moms and dads discipled them from day one? God is so efficient that his model does not require a children's church staff. I have a radical believing friend whose church has no children, youth, or other programs for kids. I personally think he is a little over the edge. I believe there is value in a variety of teachers and value in kids being kids together in kids' environments. But he has a point when he says, "It is my responsibility."

My kids teased me when they got older. They got tired of me during their teenage years too. I sent them off each day, saying, "Choose God. Every decision counts. Have a great day. Love you." I can hear our daughter, Jordan, saying, "I know, I know." I hear fourteen-year-old Isaac echoing me, "Choose God, blah blah." Every day, every moment was an opportunity to show them God's wonder and to teach them life lessons from God and the history of His people.

I started out when they were born, "Hey. Who gave you that head of hair? Do you know? I do. God. God gave you that head of hair." It worked its way into their early years. I remember the first time each of them found money in a parking lot. I made them take it to the nearest store and turn it in. The storekeepers would try to give it back, saying it wasn't theirs. We would tell them, "Well it isn't ours. Maybe the person will come in looking for it. We just know it isn't ours." "Do unto others" was one of the many Bible lessons. Application continued when they erred as preteens: "You know the Bible says an eye for an eye and a tooth for a tooth when it comes to punishing people for doing wrong. God is saying that the punishment should fit the crime.

So let me ask you, what do you think is a punishment that fits your crime?"

We had a three-strikes discipline method based on God's truths. The first time they did something wrong, we assumed they did not know anything. I would teach them why the action was not good for them and their future. The second time they did the same thing, I reminded them of the values we learned the first time and clearly communicated the discipline that would come if they did it again. The third offense brought discipline that fit the offense. Jordan was a talkative little girl. When her name got on the teacher's board the third time, she was not allowed to have fun talking time with the kids in her youth group. The third time she did not take care of her toys brought a week of no toys.

Discipleship and modeling also included me being honest with them. It included never having rules that did not have a biblical basis. Our kids were allowed to run around being loud in our house because kids are designed to run around and be loud. There was no scripture telling them to be quiet so I could watch TV, so I turned it off and ran around with them. There were verses for that.

Because of Deuteronomy 6, we never had family devotions or Bible studies. I just taught the entire Bible for eighteen years "along the way." It was so effective. It was such a privilege. It was awesome as other leaders reinforced those truths. Marshall Segal, a staff writer for DesiringGod.org, writes,

> "The reality, though, is that we have always been involved in disciple-making, even from birth — just not always disciple-making for Jesus. You *are* a disciple. The question is: Who are you following?"[2]

Marshall is right. My children were going to follow someone, something. The question was "Who and how good would those leaders or ideas be?" Marshall also wrote,

"You *have* disciples. The question is: How are you influencing the people watching you?"

I was not trying to make robots. I was offering eternal, life-giving truths to these little people so they would have a choice. They eventually tested those truths and the teachings. All teenagers do this. In fact, kids should test what they have been taught. If it is good, it will last. My kids would one day decide on their own whom to follow. My goal was to give them an excellent opportunity to choose wisely.

This goal required that I model these truths as well. I had to be honest with my failures. I had to model forgiveness and grace, and how to recover from failure. I had to apply God's truths to my life and share that process with them.

I was also doing something else that I learned from this great Old Testament discipleship model. I was teaching them along the way, as they rose up and lay down. Did you notice the method of discipleship that God recommends?

Repeat them again and again to your children. Talk about them when you are at home and when you are on the road, when you are going to bed and when you are getting up.

— Deuteronomy 6:7

Blue's Clues was one of the single most effective early-child-hood-teaching television shows. It is said that *Blue's Clues* beat out *Sesame Street* by improving on their model.[3] How did they do it? There was only one episode a week. The same episode aired Monday through Friday each week. *Blue's Clues* repeated important teaching again, and again, and again, becoming the most successful children's show ever. The episodes were engaging and interactive, and the kids never tired of the content.

Teaching truths over and over along the way illustrates a few incredible points.

- We may not always "get it" the first time.
- Some truths apply to many situations and will get repeated in new ways.
- Culture is built through many little lessons.
- Truth is much more applicable when immediately applied.
- Answers and direction are needed along the way.

It is important for disciples to know that no people are the same or have the same experiences; yet God's truths apply to both of them along the way. God's model of discipleship customizes universal, unchanging truth to the experience and temperament of each follower. God's model of discipleship is based on eternal truth, not on any derivation of it. Our models should mimic His model.

Learning along the way frees us from hour-long sermons on topics that do not apply to us. God's model of discipleship is not about lectures, education, or rules. It is about real-time instruction on how to get the most out of life. God's model teaches and inspires the student to see the value of choosing God's way. It reveals the value of following God through history, promise, and application to the immediate situation. God's model does not make robots, impose rules, or exasperate[4] followers. God's model of discipleship is all about the best, most incredible, long-term result for the child and the student.

This Old Testament model also reveals the most effective way to be a disciple maker. Effective disciple makers are present. Discipleship is not a class, a message, or a once-a-week event. Learning to be a disciple, and making disciples, is an all-in, down-and-dirty, on-the-job experience. Effective disciple makers live life with the ones they lead. They are there in the service, in the success, and ever-present and empathetic in the challenges and failures. Effective disciple makers model adjusting to and applying God's truths. Effective discipleship is intimate and involved.

Sustainable discipleship has such incredible results that people from other churches ask us to help them become disciples. It is humbling. (If they only knew!) We receive request after request for distance discipleship. We have tried several distance groups, but none of them have been as successful as discipleship along the way. There are methods and science to "along the way" involvement. Discipleship is interactive.

I love the practicality of Deuteronomy 6. Even more, I love that the Old Testament model is reflected in the way Jesus made disciples.

From the New Testament

The New Testament model for discipleship is, of course, the way Jesus made disciples. Jesus did not leave a step-by-step guide on how to make disciples, but His methods are easily observed. He modeled making disciples for us.

The Old Testament model is seen as we study one passage that is reflected throughout biblical teaching. The New Testament model is seen as we explore how disciple making was done over time in a specific situation. We observe the New Testament model directly in how Jesus discipled His twelve followers. All Jesus did was not recorded in the New Testament.[5] Likewise, the vast majority of Jesus's disciple making is not recorded. We do not see the long nights, the jokes around the campfire, the correcting along the way as Peter told a questionable joke, and Jesus's guiding as the disciples judged others who were not following well. There is so much that we do not know, but what we do know is that every parable, every situation, every challenge, and every truth was based on God's truths. We know that Jesus

- called them to surrender,
- discipled them along the way,
- asked tough questions,

- put them in residency,
- released them,
- took three years to make disciples,
- discipled them as individuals, and
- discipled them often in smaller groups.

The beauty of the New Testament model (as contrasted with the Old Testament model) is that it is a perfect fit for "not my children" discipleship. The New Testament model entirely applies to me making a disciple out of another adult or non-family member. Jesus was a model, teacher, and mentor to those who followed Him. We are wise to watch and imitate Him as we make disciples. Of course, we are leading others to follow Him, not us. That's important.

Surrender Is Essential

Jesus's first call was for the disciple to surrender everything, choose him, and follow him. From the first call,

Jesus called out to them, "Come, follow me, and I will show you how to fish for people!" And they left their nets at once and followed him.

— MATTHEW 4:19–20

and through every disciple-making moment, Jesus made it clear that you can only follow if you surrender to what you are following. You may follow the world, sin, or God, but you will only follow the one to whom you surrender.

If any of you wants to be my follower, you must give up your own way, take up your cross, and follow me.

— MATTHEW 16:24

Jesus did not make disciples out of those who did not want to follow Him. He could not. His call was to follow Him. That is our call to people: follow God. If they follow God, we can make disciples.

Along the Way

The disciples spent some three years, day in and day out, walking with, learning from, serving alongside, doing ministry with, and living in community with Jesus. They were literally following Jesus. Disciples can still do this. They can follow moment by moment through the Spirit. Disciples were made along the way. If we are to make disciples, we must do the same.

Jesus did this with Peter when Peter doubted. He did this when they fed the five thousand. He did this when He was called to Lazarus's funeral. He did this when Peter wanted to defend Him against the soldiers who arrested Him. Jesus discipled along the way. Sometimes He taught them ahead of time (proactive) and sometimes in the moment of need or opportunity (reactive), but Jesus was always there along the way.

Tough Questions

Jesus also asked tough questions as He made disciples. He made them think. He called them to be taught, to learn, and to synthesize God's truths. He asked things like,

> *"Can you drink the cup I am going to drink?"*
>
> — Matthew 20:22 (NIV)

as he expanded their understanding of their position and responsibility. They could not do what He could do. They did not need to do what He would do. He was God. They were followers.

Jesus called those He made disciples to go beyond education into application. He called them to be transformed by applying God's beautiful, life-enhancing instructions. In His last moments, He revealed the ultimate model of maturity in a tough question.

> *For who is greater, the one who is at the table or the one who serves? Is it not the one who is at the table? But I am among you as one who serves.*
>
> — LUKE 22:27–28 (NIV)

Jesus did not just teach. He caused learning. He caused application. This is perhaps one of the most undersold aspects of discipleship. We tend to educate rather than cause learning and cause application. Tough questions cause the application and synthesis of God's transforming truths.

Challenging Situations

Jesus put his disciples in challenging situations. Some of those situations were proactive, while others were reactive. Jesus may have had a grand plan, but the miraculous feeding of thousands with an endless, small basket of food was a reactive, challenging situation to the disciples. It started with a challenging question:

> *Turning to Philip, he asked, "Where can we buy bread to feed all these people?" He was testing Philip, for he already knew what he was going to do. Philip replied, "Even if we worked for months, we wouldn't have enough money to feed them!"*
>
> — JOHN 6:5–7

"Pass the basket around," he said. Can you imagine how

much faith it took? Hilariously, after everyone ate, Jesus told the disciples, "Now gather the leftovers, so that nothing is wasted."

Another example is the first time he sent out the twelve disciples to evangelize and physically heal people. He sent them out with nothing—no money, no food, nothing.[6] The list of proactive and reactive challenging situations for the disciples goes on and on. We can model and create challenging situations as we make disciples. We can stretch their faith as they do far more than they ever thought by applying God's truths and finding hope in who they are in Christ. The opportunities are endless. From evangelism to missions to praying for crazy miracles, God is still in the challenge business.

Residency

Jesus pushed the disciples out of the nest as they learned and began to apply God's truths. They were not entirely on their own yet. He was still there to help and teach. He was still there helping them to synthesize and apply. Jesus was very real and present to guide, to model, to mentor, and to teach, but He made them do the work. Jesus sent them out. He gave them the power of His Spirit. He told them to go, and they did. His disciples met with incredible success as they did the work of ministry. They also faced the learning, failure, and trial of residency. Mark 9 tells how a crowd had brought a demon-possessed boy to be healed by Jesus. The boy's dad began,

"So I asked your disciples to cast out the evil spirit, but they couldn't do it."

Jesus taught the crowd and healed the boy in that moment. The disciples had cast out demons. Jesus had given them power. The crowds had seen it. The disciples had seen it. But this time, they could not heal the boy. After Jesus healed the boy, they asked,

"Why couldn't we cast out that evil spirit?"

Jesus was there to keep teaching.

"This kind can be cast out only by prayer and fasting."

Jesus sent them to serve, to teach, to heal, and to do ministry. They had walked along the way with Him, watching and seeing God work. Their faith and confidence were grown. In residency, He had them do the work with a safety net.

He Released Them

The culmination of the New Testament model is releasing the disciple to lead, to serve, to minister on their own. The disciple is prepared. She is confident and skilled. She is ready for the front lines. In 1933, a man named Dawson Trotman founded a worldwide Christian organization called the Navigators. The Navigators was tremendously successful at making disciples.

It started when Trotman was asked to visit a sailor, Les Spencer, and share God's word with him. When one of Spencer's shipmates asked him the secret of his changed life, Spencer brought the man to Trotman: "Teach him what you taught me."

"You teach him!" Trotman responded.[7]

The book of Acts came alive in that moment. Spencer's life was so transformed by following God that a shipmate noticed and wanted to be like Spencer. Trotman trusted the work of God in Spencer and released Spencer to do the work. Jesus got the disciples ready and then told them,

"Go and make disciples."[8]

He completed his work, leaving them to do their work. They were now the hands and feet of God on earth.[9] If they did not do the work, it would not get done. He sent them to make disciples.

It Took Time

The Old Testament model took the first part of a lifetime as parents modeled, taught, and mentored their children along the way. The New Testament model took about three years as Jesus did the same thing for anyone who would follow.

Discipleship is not a quick fix, but it provides a fix for a lifetime. Discipleship takes time because it takes time to consume the truths of God. It takes time to learn on your own. It takes time and work to learn to apply the truths to varying situations. It takes time to practice. It takes time to experience.

Discipleship is the long game of a Christian's success.

Individual Discipleship

Jesus spent time with his disciples in different ways. There were times when they were taught along with crowds. The number of disciples varied from twelve to hundreds and back to twelve at times. He pulled two or three aside for experiences, challenges, and teaching. He taught one-on-one alone. He addressed one or two in front of the others. He addressed the disciples as a group, answering their questions (reactive) and opening the scriptures to them (proactive).

He taught the universal truths of God in so many different ways, but Jesus watched His disciples along the way, and He taught them as individuals. He showed them how the truths of God were relevant to their individual lives. He addressed their spiritual needs. He answered their individual issues even when He responded to their group complaints.

Jesus did this for potential disciples as well. He spoke directly to the individual tax-collector.[10] He called to Zacchaeus in the tree.[11] He spoke to individuals in their situations. He customized the where and when of disciple making, even though the universal truths applied to all. When the rich young ruler came to Him, asking what else he should do to follow Jesus, Jesus told him,

> *"If you want to be perfect, go and sell all your possessions and give the money to the poor, and you will have treasure in heaven. Then come, follow me."*

> — MATTHEW 19:21

Clearly, Jesus did not and does not call everyone to sell all they have in order to follow, but the rich young ruler needed to let go of his security to follow. His submission required letting go of all his money. The universal truth of surrender to follow had a specific application for this man.

Discipleship is, at its best, a real, interactive investment in helping individually created humans in diverse situations learn to follow right where they are.

Two Models, One Purpose

Both the Old Testament and New Testament models have the same purpose: to show us how to live the best life ever by living according to our design. God's laws, commandments, truths, culture, and directions are meant to give life, not to take life away. The way of God is actually a return trip back to our original relationship with God and His plan for living completely.

Following God and being made a disciple are entirely about being transformed inside. Following God allows people to embrace the best way to live so that they can thrive. Jesus said,

> *"My purpose is to give them a rich and satisfying life."*

> — JOHN 10:10

There is no doubt that a follower of God will want to share with others how to follow, but that is not God's express purpose for us when we become His disciples. God rescues us so that we can restore our relationship with our creator and be returned to abundant living. God wants to transform us as we follow His way.

Who we are comes first. Our relationship with God comes first. If we are not transformed, there is little hope that we will ever transform anyone else. The goal of discipleship is all about who we are.

If we are not complete in Him, it is unlikely that we will suffer well the trials of reaching others and changing the world. If we are not full, there will be nothing to give others. Simply put, being comes before doing.

5

"BE" COMES BEFORE "DO"

Getting people to do the right thing is not the goal of disciple making.

I shared how I raised my kids and decided to teach them God's truths along the way. Whether I was teaching them not to run with scissors, to put my tools back, to be quieter in class, or to treat their friends nicely, I always had a single goal and a single method in mind. The goal? I was totally focused on who my kids would be when they were thirty-five years old. I was not focused on them having a complete understanding in the moment. I was totally focused on them having the best life possible at thirty-five. I taught them truths far beyond their years (proactively) while teaching them how to deal with every silly situation along the way (reactively). I taught them the immediate truth and then expanded it to the future by saying things like, "I want you to have incredible friends when you are thirty-five. If you are selfish like this, you will not have any friends. You want friends who will share. You need to learn to share."

I taught them the immediate consequences, but my focus was on future results. I was teaching them that who they are will impact positively or negatively what their life is like in the future. And I chose to teach them the enduring truths of God, every time along the way.

I taught them why truth was important. Knowing truth is first. Applying truth is second. However, truth is rarely applied well if we do not see the value in its application. The value is the "why." I shared the why along with the "what" for their present and their future.

My goal remains for them to be as complete as possible when they are thirty-five. There is no way I can predict what they will go through on their way to thirty-five, much less what they will be facing when they are thirty-five. I cannot address things that I do not know, but I can help them "be" complete, wise, prepared, and skilled to face those unknowns. Here it is again, the secret sauce of successful disciple making. Successful disciple making is all about the "be."

Jesus said that "You can love because I first loved you."[1]

I am loved and then I love—simple. I am a disciple before I can make a disciple—simple. I am surrendered before I can follow—simple. I can go on and on, but it is always true that "be" comes before "do."

The goal of discipleship is not making people who do the right thing. The purpose of discipleship is precisely what Jesus's purpose was: to give people a rich and satisfying life,

"My purpose is to give them a rich and satisfying life."

— JOHN 10:10

That purpose is only fulfilled if they "be" Christians, if they "be" followers, and if they "be" filled with His Spirit. The goal of making is all about the "be." I promise you, if we get this right, the "dos" will follow. We were created in the image of God, and then the garden and the rest of life happened. The goal of discipleship is

to be conformed to the image of his Son.

— ROMANS 8:29 (NIV)

Being God's child, being his follower, being complete, being wise, being peaceful, being like Him is the goal. Being is the crown jewel of a relationship with God. Being is the target.

If I am going to make disciples, my goals and purpose should line up with God's goals and purpose. I am wasting my time if I am just trying to get people to do what they should do. If, instead, I teach, model, and mentor people to "be" who God designed them to be, they will conquer the world, recover from their failures, and be able to fish instead of waiting for the next worship service to be fed.

The goal of discipleship is to teach those who want to follow and, while teaching, show the why and value of God's truths. We need to show them who they can "be" and how that can change their world. We also need to show them along the way, who they already "be." Discipleship is about the transformation of people, not the education or conformation of people.

Take the example of a butler. A real butler is about who you are, not what you do. A butler has no purpose without someone to serve. A butler has nothing if he does not have a "mister." Now, before anyone gets cranky and says, "No one should have to serve another person," I agree with you. Making someone serve is making them do. But a person who is a true servant chooses to serve. If I am the best butler ever, I want to buttle. My purpose in life is to buttle.

A true servant is not defined by what he does but who he is. A person who is a servant is content to stand by the doorway, awaiting the next need of the person he serves. It is his life, his passion, and his purpose. A servant is a servant deep inside, so he serves with class, precision, and excellence. A servant does not need to be reminded to serve. A servant lives to serve. A servant is living for the opportunity to meet the next need. It is all about being and little about the doing. The doing is the result of the being.

Just like the true servant chooses to serve, the first step in being a follower (disciple, student) of God is choosing to be a follower. A true follower has chosen to follow, wants to follow, longs to follow, and loves following. When I become a Christian, God affects a mysterious and spiritual transformation of me. He forgives me, justifies me, reconciles me, fills me with His spirit, and so much more. God changes my identity from being an orphan to being His child. He makes me (be) an heir to all of his riches. Peter wrote these inspiring words (all focused on being):

> God the Father knew you and chose you long ago, and his Spirit has made you holy. As a result, you have obeyed him and have been cleansed by the blood of Jesus Christ.
>
> — 1 PETER 1:2

Paul stresses the idea of being before doing—of who we are in Christ and who we are becoming on earth.

> And the Lord—who is the Spirit—makes us more and more like him as we are changed into his glorious image.
>
> — 2 CORINTHIANS 3:18

> Instead, let the Spirit renew your thoughts and attitudes.
>
> — EPHESIANS 4:23

The goal of discipleship is to show people who they are as

followers and help them embrace that identity. A rich and satisfying life will produce rich and satisfying doing.

I was a youth minister long ago, and God blessed us with influence. One by one, students came to Christ just as they were —scared, with baggage, messed up, and with little morality. It was a motley crew, but they loved God, and they were understanding bit by bit. The more they embraced their new being, the more their dos changed and fueled further transformation of their lives. The old guard was not happy with me. They wanted me to get these kids cleaned up quickly and make them look like Christians. They wanted me to focus on the dos of life. I was called into the pastor's office to meet with an angry mom. She was concerned that her son kept looking at the breasts of one of the new girls. "She wears those leotard things. They are tight, and they show off her chest. You need to do something. My son is getting distracted. You need to tell her how to dress." I said a few dumb things, like, "Really! Have you looked at this girl? She doesn't even have boobs," and, "Your son's lust problem is your son's lust problem," before I said one smart thing that changed me forever.

"How about we give this girl some time to learn more about God and give her time to be transformed outwardly like God has already done inwardly? We can force her to change the way she dresses, but how she dresses will never affect who she is inside. How about we focus on who she is, let her get it. She will."

And that is exactly what happened. She made friends with other girls who were followers and got into discipleship. In no time, she dressed more modestly without anyone saying a word about how to dress. She was learning how precious she was to God, how He loved her, and how much dignity she had with Him. She valued herself more, and much more than how she dressed changed—she became a woman of God.

Again, disciple making is the long game of Christianity. I am not sure we ever reached the son or the mother. They just never got it. Mom wanted me to change the outside of this young girl to meet her need. She wanted us to improve the outside before the inside. When we focus on changing the outside first, we drive people into shame, into hiding, and into feeling bad about who they are. When we focus on changing the outside first, we further the lousy theology that righteousness is based on works.

Christians make the error, again and again, of focusing on the doing of life rather than being that brings life. Discipleship is about who we are in Christ. Showing a person her new identity is a great privilege. Showing her God's love and respect for her is incredible. It gets better as we walk alongside people, pushing them, teaching them, and watching them become who they already are without ever writing one rule for them.

One of the early lessons in discipleship must be comparing the old and the new life. In the old life, we adjusted God truths to us, but as followers, we adjust who we are to God's truths. We adjust our self-view to God's view of the new us. We adjust our behaviors to God's directions so we can enjoy more of the new us and the new life we have been given. Who we are in this world becomes transformed to look more and more like who we already are inside.

When people follow God, they become something new. It is a simple, small truth that will change everything you do when you make disciples. Focus on who they are, and are becoming, instead of what they are doing or will do.

6

THE EVERYTHING ANSWER FOR CHURCHES

Discipleship is the long game of Christianity.

Our team has the privilege of working with many different churches and ministries. We work with independent, denominational, para-church, big, little, new, innovative, stalled, active, and old ministries. Again and again, their concerns seem to fall into the same categories.

- Finances
- Twenty percent doing 80 percent of the work and giving
- Human barriers to change
- Exhausted volunteers
- Burnt-out staff
- Stalled ministry effectiveness
- Confusion and division

Ironically, there are hundreds of ministries and consultants out there to help with these issues, but the issues remain.

Churches are dying, which means the impact of Christ is waning in communities all around the world.

It gets worse. Junior staffers are not cared for and are pushed beyond their calling. They are pushed beyond their limits without receiving the education and personal leadership they need. The church is so busy doing ministry to others that it often misses covering, protecting, and championing the leaders. Boards are possessive. New ideas cannot get heard. People want a powerful church but are not open to self-awareness and change. Hundreds of frustrated leaders head off, ill-prepared, starting new ministries that consume them and rarely succeed.

I have a heart for small and midsize churches where these struggles are more apparent and magnified. But even larger organizations struggle. Larger churches struggle to make a personal impact at the individual life level. It is frustrating for all. Conference solutions, staff swapping, ministry revamping, building enhancements, and marketing just do not seem to be solving the problem.

Hope, however, is not elusive. Individuals can be impacted and drawn closer to God. Finances can get better. Human change barriers can be turned into catalysts. The entire community can invest their time, talent, and treasure. Exhausted volunteers can become rested, excited, fresh volunteers. Staff can become steadily burning instead of being burnt-out. And confusion? Well it can become unity. What is the answer? You already know it.

✳ *Making disciples is the answer to all of it.* ✳

The church is God's natural outcome of people becoming disciples. Healthy churches are the natural outcome of healthy disciples. A building full of vibrant, complete people is a vibrant, complete church. Crappy churches are the natural outcome of crappy disciples. I know it is so simple, but it has to be said: the church is made up of people. Christians naturally gather and make churches. It just happens. Whether you are the disastrous church of Corinth or the more stable, fun church of Thessalonica is determined by the people.

Making disciples is the answer to all of it.

I am so proud of the church where we gather to worship, serve, and live.[1] We have been part of starting three schools, four churches, four para-church ministries, and innumerable mission campuses. We run a community daycare, a professional recording studio, and a consulting agency, and sponsor a really cool Christian theater group that helps kids have fun and gain confidence. We have eighteen full-time staff, four part-time staff, and ten bi-vocational staff. We have participated in two church plants. We gave over a quarter of a million dollars to missions and mission leaders last year. And there are only a hundred of us.

Of that one hundred people, about eighty would call themselves partners in the ministry. About 90 percent of the partners tithe, serve in a ministry, and participate in a mission effort each year. We work with a principle of unanimity. There is no division. There is little drama. There is no gossip. Our staff loves being staff and report that they are supported, championed, and cared for well. We provide coaching and college benefits. Our volunteers love what they are doing. Our lead teacher is backed up by four capable teachers each headed toward leading a church plant. Our band has some incredible songwriters, and they do not bicker on Sunday mornings. Almost every ministry leader has a fully trained replacement ready for the next church plant. Is it easier because we are smaller? Not really, most small churches struggle. We struggled more before we started making disciples.

But let me be clear, do not make disciples so you will have a strong, growing, funded ministry. If that is your goal, you will be brought down to worse depths. All of us should make disciples because we want each and every person to have the most incredible life that they can have. The fact that incredible people make incredible churches is just the gravy.

I do not live for the church. I live for the people. I will not die for the church. I will die for the people. When I say, "I love the church where we gather to worship," I am saying, "I love who the people are and not what they do." All of the dos can go away and I will be fine as long as we are who we are today: followers.

Look again at the list of challenges that our team has observed while working with various ministries. What is the biblical answer to each of them?

- **Finances are tight**. Either we are spending unwisely or people are not tithing, or both. Nonetheless, the Bible tells us how to manage money and that we should all give a thanks offering of a tithe to God. Why are people not tithing? Why do we make poor decisions? We are not following God's truths.

- **Twenty percent doing 80 percent of the work and giving.** Either we are doing too much or people are not working and giving. The Bible clearly tells all of us to serve one another and put the work of ministry on high priority. But the ministry described in the Bible is nothing like the busy, event-oriented ministry that we do today. The Bible tells us to rest. Why are we doing too much? Why aren't people serving? We are not following God's truths.

- **Human barriers to change.** Either we are proposing worldly changes to the ministry or someone is being a barrier to what God wants. The Bible tells us to submit to others, tells us what our leaders should look like spiritually, tells us to embrace new ideas, tells us to respect old truths, and tells us that the church is God's. So why can't we make those changes that are needed? We are not following God's truths.

I could go on, but you get it. God's truths need to be applied to every situation that the church encounters (reactive) and His truths need to be the foundation of our culture and practice (proactive). We, the people, need to adjust our ministry lives to God's truths in everything from rest to effectiveness.

Many use Acts chapter two as the classic definition of the ministry of the church. There is probably a heading in your Bible just above this passage reading, "The Believers Form a Community/Church." Here it is, the classic quote:

> *All the believers devoted themselves to the apostles' teaching, and to fellowship, and to sharing in meals (including the Lord's Supper), and to prayer. A deep sense of awe came over them all, and the apostles performed many miraculous signs and wonders. . . . They worshiped together at the Temple each day, met in homes for the Lord's Supper, and shared their meals with great joy and generosity—all the while praising God and enjoying the goodwill of all the people. And each day the Lord added to their fellowship those who were being saved.*
>
> — ACTS 2:42–43; 46–47

And so develops the ministry model that you and I have learned throughout time. The five purposes of the church are as follows:

- Fellowship
- Discipleship
- Worship
- Ministry
- Evangelism

Interestingly, no one includes verses 44–45 in this purpose statement:

And all the believers met together in one place and shared everything they had. They sold their property and possessions and shared the money with those in need.

Those two verses illustrate the absolute surrender and sacrifice of those early followers. These five purposes outlined by so many leaders are excellent outcomes of followers coming together. They are great goals for individuals, but did you notice they are all about "do" and not at all about "be"? It is no wonder that so many of us view church as something that we "do" rather than something that we "be." Let us expand the context of this new church by looking backward a bit to verses 37–39:

Peter's words pierced their hearts, and they said to him and to the other apostles, "Brothers, what should we do?" Peter replied, "Each of you must repent of your sins and turn to God, and be baptized in the name of Jesus Christ for the forgiveness of your sins. Then you will receive the gift of the Holy Spirit. This promise is to you, to your children, and to those far away—all who have been called by the Lord our God."

Do you see it? The outcomes (the dos) of verses 42–47 are entirely based on those people being convicted. What the followers did was the direct result of who they became: followers of Christ. They were pierced to the heart when they heard God's truths, they cried out, they adjusted themselves to His truth, and they became Christians. They became absolutely sold-out, abandoned, convicted, repentant followers of Christ. These radically transformed people (transformed at a high cost in their society) gathered together and "did church."

Their sacrifice, dedication, worship, gathering, abandonment —all of it—was preceded by who they became. A church is a collection of believers. If they are followers of God and if they have taken up their cross to follow Jesus, then they will be a church that will naturally do great church.

Can you imagine being part of a church that lives peaceably and in harmony with one another? As Paul puts the dream,

> *Is there any encouragement from belonging to Christ? Any comfort from his love? Any fellowship together in the Spirit? Are your hearts tender and compassionate? Then make me truly happy by agreeing wholeheartedly with each other, loving one another, and working together with one mind and purpose.*
>
> — PHILIPPIANS 2:1–2

The pathway to a model church (the one everyone dreams of) is not found in Paul's "do" statements but in his "be" questions. If we belong to Christ, if we live in His love, if we are partners together in the Spirit, if we are humble, then we can be in agreement when we come together. The individual effort comes first. The community life comes second. When we all follow one leader, we become unstoppable.

How about church growth? The church has so many barriers to overcome because of the bad reputation that church has in this world. The only way to overcome reputation barriers is to change the reputation. And that transformation comes one encounter at a time as individuals model being a follower to the world. Without the transformation of individuals, and thus the church, no one will see the Lord.

> *Make every effort to live in peace with everyone and to be holy; without holiness no one will see the Lord.*
>
> — HEBREWS 12:14 (NIV)

Discipleship is the answer for the individual to have a full life, and it is the answer that will bring about a naturally great church. It is also the answer to reaching new people and making disciples. The single purpose of every Christian (and then, by extension, the purpose of the church) is to make disciples. Disciple making is the culture, the goal, the objective—not so we will have great churches, but so each individual will have a full life on this earth and in the age to come. Making disciples precedes everything in Christianity.

Making disciples is the answer to all of it.

This everything answer, however, is not a quick fix. We have to invest in the long game of leading people to a fully devoted life—for their good. The Old Testament model took the growing up of a child. The New Testament model took as short as three years and as long as twelve.[2] We cannot help ourselves, help others, and build healthy churches quickly. Discipleship is a long game and, unfortunately, many people adapt or bypass the long journey for a shorter path.

I believe that all of us want to participate in transforming lives. I believe with all my heart that most Christian leaders want to see people be true followers. There is just so much noise. We are so busy doing ministry that we cannot conceive of stopping "doing" to fix "being" problems. We have a heart for making disciples, but we do not have the time. What if we could change the church culture to make discipleship a top priority without abandoning good projects? The North American Mission Board (NAMB) has done a great job facing a similar challenge. The NAMB leadership recognized that there was a shortage of quali-fied pastors to reach the millions of unreached people in the United States. They faced the brutal facts and took on the chal-lenge of preparing those future leaders. Instead of stopping their core work, they have expanded it by trimming off non-core work and refocusing resources to their core. The problem is not solved today, but their Pipeline process for preparing pastors is gaining ground and more pastors are being better prepared for the future. Making disciples needs to be our primary directive because . . .

Making disciples is the answer to all of it.

Making disciples is a simple, ingenious, natural, biblical plan focused on individuals. It builds up the Church. It honors God. It focuses on who believers are and cheers on the dos that naturally result. The journey draws each of us closer in relationship to God and blesses us richly.

7

WHAT DISCIPLESHIP IS

What we do in discipleship is not discipleship. Discipleship is making disciples.

Making disciples introduces people to God, who loves and understands them, helps them understand who they are and what they can be, helps them apply God's transforming truths, and releases them to live their best life ever on earth.

Discipleship adds the preparation, confidence, and skill to be what we already are: followers of God.

Discipleship is leading another person to life-changing truths and experiences with God. Discipleship is the process where knowledge becomes wisdom, prayer becomes a conversation, and people are called to be who they are designed to be.

The process and practice of discipleship are "dos," but doing is entirely focused on who we are and who we are becoming in Christ. The **process** of formal discipleship has a term. The **practice** of discipleship never ends. The process fades into a practice as we become prepared, confident, and skilled followers.

The practice is a lifestyle of learning and choices—each one a decision to adjust to God or foolishly think that we can adjust Him to us. The practice of discipleship leads us to moments where we must accept our humility to receive His glory.

The process of discipleship brings us to a knowledge of who we have committed to follow. It brings us knowledge of who we are, what resources we have, and how we can live full and complete lives. The process changes as we move from being taught to learning on our own. Truth makes us steady and solid in our faith and in God's truths. Steadiness leads us to a life that thrives on this earth through thick and thin. The process leads us to an understanding of unity.

Disciples, predictably, join the communal work of being light to the world. We, as capable hands, feet, and heads (and even butts to sit on), become the body of Christ. Everyone is of critical value. Maturity in Christ and unity are the natural end to formal discipleship. Paul wrote about this to the Ephesian Church:

> Now these are the gifts Christ gave to the church: the apostles, the prophets, the evangelists, and the pastors and teachers. Their responsibility is to equip God's people to do his work and build up the church, the body of Christ. This will continue until we all come to such unity in our faith and knowledge of God's Son that we will be mature in the Lord, measuring up to the full and complete standard of Christ.
>
> — EPHESIANS 4:11–13

The intentional process of discipleship equips each follower to do God's work and to build up the body of Christ. But do not miss the end goal of discipleship: "that we will be mature in the Lord, measuring up to the full and complete standard of Christ."

Discipleship matures us, provides fuel for sanctification, and brings us to maturity. Discipleship conforms us to the image of Christ. The end goal is who each believer, and then the church, becomes. But this formal, intentional process fades into a lifestyle of practice.

> *Then we will no longer be immature like children. We won't be tossed and blown about by every wind of new teaching. We will not be influenced when people try to trick us with lies so clever they sound like the truth. Instead, we will speak the truth in love, growing in every way more and more like Christ, who is the head of his body, the church. He makes the whole body fit together perfectly. As each part does its own special work, it helps the other parts grow, so that the whole body is healthy and growing and full of love.*

— EPHESIANS 4:14–16

Do you see the points Paul makes about us?

- We are prepared.
- We are steady.
- We have developed faith.
- We have become a needed piece of the body.
- We are healthy, and the body is healthy

Every follower has a special work that inwardly benefits believers and outwardly benefits the world, but discipleship remains all about who we become individually and then as a body. Discipleship is being taught, learning independently, synthesizing, applying, and then teaching or leading others. It all happens along a clear, identifiable, and biblical path.[1] The path may begin with a formal process, but it fades into a lifelong practice of growing and maturing. Notice Paul's last sentence: "so that the whole body is healthy and growing and full of love."

Discipleship should get us to a healthy place, full of love and growth. From the moment we are saved, we are complete in Christ. However, there is another moment where we find ourselves prepared, confident, and skilled in living with God on this earth. An older mentor said, "The closer you get to God, the bigger the little truths and errors will seem." As we draw closer, following with endurance and regularity, we will find plenty of opportunities to keep growing. We will apply seemingly new truths to our current life. We will reapply old rules brought to the forefront again by the Spirit in us. John writes,

Dear friends, I am not writing a new commandment for you; rather it is an old one you have had from the very beginning. This old commandment—to love one another—is the same message you heard before. Yet it is also new. Jesus lived the truth of this commandment, and you also are living it. For the darkness is disappearing, and the true light is already shining.

— 1 JOHN 2:7–8

We will go deeper as we "live it." We will explore. We will chase even more moments with our Father. We will actively and independently follow our God. Our relationship with God will be Father to son or daughter, teacher to student, and guide to one seeking to thrive as a human on earth. We are disciples. We have passed some mysterious point of "no return"[2] and are all in by our own choice. We find ourselves living the practice of discipleship.

Being a disciple is a lifelong journey of failure, success, falling, rising up, and learning.

The practice of discipleship finds us in mutual discipleship. We are all students with one teacher. The mentors of our discipleship process become our peers in the practice of discipleship. We follow together. We draw closer together. We complete each other as we commune with God.

Discipleship, as a practice, focuses on sanctification on this earth. Sanctification is like bathing. It is about taming the flesh, conforming our lives to the truths of God, and becoming more like Christ. It is like washing the spiritual dirt off of our lives whenever we find it. Discipleship as a practice is ever aware of God's truths—praying without ceasing, taking every thought captive, evaluating, adjusting, and applying so that we can be on this earth who God has already made us inside.

Discipleship as a practice is about every moment of our lives. The practice is us continually chasing who we really are, where we are, in that moment. Peter and James got it when they wrote,

> *For you know that when your faith is tested, your endurance has a chance to grow. So let it grow, for when your endurance is fully developed, you will be perfect and complete, needing nothing.*

> — James 1:3–4

> *There is wonderful joy ahead, even though you must endure many trials for a little while. These trials will show that your faith is genuine. It is being tested as fire tests and purifies gold—though your faith is far more precious than mere gold. So when your faith remains strong through many trials, it will bring you much praise and glory and honor on the day when Jesus Christ is revealed to the whole world.*

> — 1 Peter 1:6–7

Our goal must be making disciples who can stand on their own. The initial process takes effort and requires much adjustment. It takes time and dedication to read, to listen, to watch, to talk through applications, to apply, to be tested, and to learn. But we need to get disciples to the tipping point where they have read and learned enough so they can quickly assimilate God's truths and apply them on their own. The goal of process is that disciples become prepared, confident, and skilled to independently live out the practice.

Once I learn to walk, I have more time on my hand for other things, like helping others to learn, serving others, or enjoying my walk with God.

These new activities actually reflect my transformation from being selfish and self-driven to being a follower of God and being servant-driven. Discipleship as a practice is ongoing. I will never stop growing, learning, and expanding if I keep following. We will all return, at times, to the first steps of repentance and illumination.[3] We will always be learning. A few weeks ago, I was having coffee on the back stoop of our home.

"You want the church to grow for your success," God said.

"I repent," I said, broken to my very core.

Our church is a smaller but strong church. We have a few empty chairs. We do not seem to be too good at evangelism. Several of my friends are incredible evangelists, reaching thousands at their churches. I long to have that impact, but sometimes the desire is more about numbers equaling success than numbers equaling people who have returned to their father. God knows my heart—I love people. He loved me enough to tell me I was going off course and getting a bit performance oriented. It was a tough moment, but I am thankful that God is invested in me following Him.

The cycle of discipleship never stops. Often, it brings you back to moments of conviction and repentance. Those you have led to God will hold your feet to the fire. Those you walk with will challenge you. I am thankful for my peers and pals who push me to be my best. I want to be the best that I can be—that is what the practice of discipleship is all about.

Discipleship is at first focused on making disciples (a formal startup), and then discipleship becomes a practice that is ever ongoing. But whether in process or practice, some characteristics will always be present in sustainable discipleship.

Discipleship Is Practical

There is a practical side to discipleship. Jesus was a servant, so we should learn to be servants. He was the announcement of God's love for man, so we should learn to be that announcement. Discipleship was never meant to be theological, philosophical, or heady. God wants us to enjoy life and a full relationship with Him. His ways and His guidance are always practical for us.

Sustainable discipleship focuses so much on the "be," but there is nothing wrong with the "dos" that come out of being. Dos are practical, helpful, and life-changing. Last night, Amber (my wife) and I were sitting with some new friends in our house. Amber was tying a prayer rope. Katie Beth, age nine, asked, "What are you doing?"

"Tying a prayer rope," Amber replied.

"What is a prayer rope? Is it like a rosary?" KB's mom asked.

We explained that it was nothing like a traditional rosary. In fact, the prayer rope is the precedent of the rosary by more than a thousand years.[4] I learned about prayer ropes from Partheneous, an Orthodox monk. He taught me about the prayer rope and the benefits of meditative prayer for my daily life. The Bible is full of instruction for us to pray for one another, to pray for the saints, to pray and meditate. A prayer rope is a practical tool coming from a practical call by Paul to "pray without ceasing." Partheneous also taught me the traditional way to use a prayer rope—to sit quietly and pray one hundred prayers. Those moments of prayer launched me from one who said he was praying and listening to one who was actually "doing it" with a bit of structure. Very practical.

Another example of the practicality of God's truths came from Bob Coder. I got to know Bob while learning to drill water wells for those in need. Bob discipled me, and as part of that investment, Bob had me read one chapter of Proverbs a day for several months. On day twenty-two of the first month, I read,

*Don't agree to guarantee another person's debt or put up security
for someone else. If you can't pay it, even your bed will be snatched
from under you.*

— PROVERBS 22:26–27

Have you ever cosigned a loan? Have you ever regretted it? I
have done both. How simple is this proverbial truth about
cosigning? It is so practical. On day six of the second month, I
read this,

*My child, if you have put up security for a friend's debt or agreed
to guarantee the debt of a stranger—if you have trapped yourself
by your agreement and are caught by what you said—follow my
advice and save yourself, for you have placed yourself at your
friend's mercy. Now swallow your pride; go and beg to have your
name erased. Don't put it off; do it now! Don't rest until you do.
Save yourself like a gazelle escaping from a hunter, like a bird
fleeing from a net.*

— PROVERBS 6:1–5

Again, a practical truth about cosigning. The next time
someone asked me to cosign a loan, I could simply say, "No way.
God has taught me not to cosign." The evidence and warning
were clear. God wanted me to have the best life, and cosigning
was an opportunity for stress, division, and trouble that I did
not need. As I moved from being taught to learning and synthesizing God's truths on my own, I learned there was even more
practical truth on this matter. I found Proverbs 22:7 years later.

*Just as the rich rule the poor, so the borrower is servant to the
lender.*

— PROVERBS 22:7

Later, I learned about the dangers of "having to have it now" throughout the New Testament. I learned how lust to have things can consume us and draw us away from God. I learned how I should not participate in the possible destruction of others. Now there were deeper reasons not to cosign. It was not my place to decide if someone should have that thing or not. Nor was it my place to endanger them or our relationship. Discipleship became a practice for me, and I began to say no. At the same time, I also learned to give them a few lifesaving verses to look at along their journey.

From prayer to finances, both in process and in practice, in every phase, discipleship will always be practical as it exposes and applies God's truths to daily life. Discipleship allows God to transform my life in very practical ways. Making disciples should always focus on applying self-evident truths in simple ways to our lives. As we lead others, we should help them discover how each truth of God usefully applies to their life on this earth.

Discipleship Is a Community Effort

The process of becoming prepared, confident, and skilled was designed by God to be a community effort. Paul teaches,

> *Now these are the gifts Christ gave to the church: the apostles, the prophets, the evangelists, and the pastors and teachers. **Their responsibility is to equip God's people to do his work and build up the church, the body of Christ.** This will continue until we all come to such unity in our faith and knowledge of God's Son that we will be mature in the Lord, measuring up to the full and complete standard of Christ.*
>
> — EPHESIANS 4:11–13

God's design uses equipped leaders to build up his church, one by one. In the Old Testament, we see God using prophets, leaders, kings, and perhaps most importantly, parents. The community of leaders is responsible to disciple new followers, but discipleship continues in a broader community as each of us becomes more prepared, more confident, and more skilled. We see it in the communities of believers who raised children in the Old Testament times. We see it in the New Testament as well.

> *Instead, we will speak the truth in love, growing in every way more and more like Christ, who is the head of his body, the church. He makes the whole body fit together perfectly. As each part does its own special work, **it helps the other parts grow**, so that the whole body is healthy and growing and full of love.*
>
> — EPHESIANS 4:15–16

Everyone who is being prepared helps others become prepared. The confident instill confidence in those who are growing in confidence. How to apply the truths of God passes from those applying to those learning. The community of followers disciple one another in formal processes and in daily practice. Peers and pals take part in ongoing discipleship. From the classic iron verse,

> *As iron sharpens iron, so a friend sharpens a friend.*
>
> — PROVERBS 27:17

to the encouragement to have many wise advisors,

> *Plans go wrong for lack of advice; many advisers bring success.*
>
> — PROVERBS 15:22

we see that everyone who follows God is part of our discipleship. Giving and receiving, we mutually push each other toward a transformed, thriving life. Examples go on and on, but there is no doubt that discipleship, in process and practice, is a community effort in which each of us participates. We need to champion, build, and sustain a community culture of discipleship.

 ## Discipleship Is for Everyone

In the same way that discipleship is a community effort, discipleship is for everyone. Discipleship should never be restricted to a chosen few. Everyone should have access to the process of discipleship. Every individual should be our target market. Everyone should be able to play.

Many articles and texts about making disciples include references and instruction on how to select disciples. Most of those references lead back to Dr. Robert Coleman's enduring work on how to train evangelists.[5] Discipleship, as a process and practice, is different from training up leaders or training up evangelists. Paul taught Timothy how to pick leaders for the church:

> *You have heard me teach things that have been confirmed by many reliable witnesses. Now teach these truths to other trustworthy people who will be able to pass them on to others.*

> — 2 TIMOTHY 2:2

Dr. Coleman's work is focused on selecting and training the next leaders of the Church—specifically, those who will evangelize the world. Discipleship precedes that selection. Sustainable discipleship cannot be limited to those who are qualified because it is the process of becoming qualified. We are called to go to the entire world and make disciples.

Model churches have a culture of discipleship. If you asked a member of a model church, "What is the most important thing that believers should do in that church?" they would reply, "Discipleship." Bill Hull, who has devoted his life to furthering discipleship, says it this way: "God has not promised to bless our good motives, dreams, and innovation. He has promised to bless his plan; that plan is that disciples make other disciples—everything else is a sideshow."

Discipleship focused on each person having the best day ever results in a church that has the best day ever. Complete, devoted followers of God are the pool from which we can select leaders, but everyone gets to swim. Everyone gets the opportunity to be discipled and to become prepared, confident, and skilled at enjoying this life God has given us. We must be open to walking with anyone willing to follow God in the discipleship process or practice.

 ## Discipleship Is Intimate

Following Him along the way and making disciples requires that we make the time, have the enduring passion, and walk with those we disciple in the messiness of life. Sustainable discipleship is intimate in process and practice, and its intimacy is built upon

- transparency,
- trust,
- humility,
- empathy, and
- interaction.

It takes transparency to tell someone exactly where you are in life. It takes transparency to allow God to transform you. It takes transparency to share an "I've been there" moment. The hardest moment in life so far has been suffering through a divorce. My friend Mark says that he believes the brokenness and hurt of it all allows me to reach people whom other church leaders will never reach. Tom[6] had been in discipleship for about six months when he called late one night. "I can't live with her

cheating anymore. It isn't healthy for the kids. I know you probably don't want to talk about this, but I need to know if I am the
worst person ever for considering divorce." Thank God for transparency and Waffle House. We talked about what God had said
about divorce, marriage, and love from cover to cover. We
explored what God had to say, and I pushed Tom to apply God's
truths to his situation. We cried. It tore me up inside to have to
relive the memories. But the biblical truths and lessons I learned
could help. Transparency is the first building block of intimacy.
Trust is the second.

Disciples need to be able to trust you. They need to know
that you will always work for their best. We need to be depend-
able. We need to never abandon. We need to keep things
private. We need to work for each other's best. I have heard
confession after confession: "I am having trouble with pornogra-
phy"; "We had sex last night"; "I am not sure if I even believe in
God anymore"; and the list goes on. Those you lead will not
trust you to help them find and apply God's truths to their situation if you are not trustworthy. They need to know that you,
like God, will not abandon them, will not share their ugly
things, and mostly, believe in who they are and who they can
become.

Humility is the third building block of intimacy both for us
and for those we lead. My favorite definition of "humility" is
found in *The Message* Bible, where they paraphrase "humble" as

And don't take yourself too seriously—take God seriously.

— Micah 6:8 (MSG)

It takes humility to think that you might be worthy of
leading someone. You are going to need humility to push
someone in an area where you failed so many times. Humility
will also help you avoid the dangers of judgment. Disciples need
humility to learn from someone. They will need humility to

adjust their choices to God's truths. Humility of leaders and followers also opens the door to empathy.

Empathy builds intimacy. Judgment builds distance. Jesus modeled empathy instead of judgment.[7] People who are wrong know they are wrong. They need more salvation and less judgment. Those you lead must know that you know that God is the only judge. You have to be able to put yourselves in the middle of their angst and humiliation when their performance does not measure up to who they really are in Christ. You have to feel for those you lead. You have to identify with where they are and help them apply God's truths to get them to see his love, forgiveness, grace, and hope for their lives. Intimacy requires that we believe those who follow us. It requires that we strive to save, guard, and protect those who are already complete in Christ,[8] helping them discover their best life ever.

Intimacy also requires interaction because intimacy fades with distance and disconnection. Interaction requires that we give time to those we lead. Interaction demands that those we lead serve, laugh, and live alongside us. Successful discipleship involves interaction. The leader, the peer, and the follower must invest energy in the process. There must be communication. There must be time to pray, explore, and discuss. My favorite discipleship groups never want to go home. Their discipleship goes far beyond the regular meeting time. These people love hanging out, sharing life, doing stuff together—they have become comrades. And they have let me be a comrade. Late, long nights are not an inconvenience when people are healthily interacting.

Intimacy is exercised differently during the process and practice of discipleship. When making disciples, it is the intimacy of a leader to a follower as we lead them to a place that we have already been. When practicing discipleship, the submission, intimacy, and interaction are much more like a brother to a brother—boundless and widely open. However, both the process and the practice of discipleship require intimacy.

Sustainable discipleship models transparency, trust, humility, empathy, and interaction. We must provide each of these to those we make disciples. We must push them to embrace each of these qualities so that they can get the most out of discipleship.

 ## Discipleship Is Relentless, Ruthless, and Risky

Making disciples and being made into a disciple requires that we face ourselves, lean into the challenge, and choose God. My brother used to run marathons and now runs ultra races (fifty-plus miles). Dan shared this about endurance during one of my weaker life moments:

> *When you run long, you feel like you are running out of energy. First, your body seems to go. You don't feel like you can go one more step. Your legs burn, your lungs hurt, and your body tells you that you cannot go one more step. But you know you can. Your mind pushes you through, and your body follows. You find more energy. It is like your mind overrides those initial signals from your body. But then your mind starts to go. You begin to wonder if you can make it. You begin to think that you cannot go one more step. You are running out of mental energy, but somewhere deep inside, you know that you can push more. Your heart kicks in, and somewhere deep inside, strength and energy surge. Now you are running, and you keep running.*

Discipleship is like running that marathon. Your flesh, that all-too-human part of you, fights you and comes to the point of breaking. God's truths and promises rise into your mind, and you know that you can go one more step. And you do until your mind starts to go. You question those truths and promises. You reach another breaking point. If you endure, your spirit kicks in. God's Spirit deep inside you kicks in, providing the energy and endurance that you did not even know you had. You are now running on something beyond you, transformed, step after step. You are running sustainably.

This, of course, is the great path of becoming a disciple that Paul outlines in Romans 6–8.[9] He teaches us to run with endurance, to endure and win the prize of our faith, and to run in the Spirit. Relentlessness is why Watchman Nee teaches us first to be complete and sit in Christ before we ever walk in this life or stand against the enemy.[10]

Discipleship is relentless. Discipleship requires that we evaluate every thought and measure it against the truths that we have learned about living our best life ever. Paul wrote this to the believers in Corinth:

> *We are human, but we don't wage war as humans do. We use God's mighty weapons, not worldly weapons, to knock down the strongholds of human reasoning and to destroy false arguments. We destroy every proud obstacle that keeps people from knowing God. We capture their rebellious thoughts and teach them to obey Christ.*
>
> — 2 CORINTHIANS 10:3–5

It is an every-moment choice to follow Him. It is learning to hear the Spirit remind us of truths and encourage us to follow them. It is risky as we push the relationship with those we "make disciples."

We need to remember that the process of learning, adjusting, and being transformed is mentally, physically, and spiritually tiring. It takes time to grow strong. We need to cheer on those we lead. We need to crew "aid stations." We need to provide them rest, encouragement, and sometimes a break.

Discipleship is also ruthless. It takes no captives. We face our greatest fears and guide others to face theirs during discipleship. We push "what is right" without fear so that each of us can have the best life ever. No nook or cranny is safe, hidden, or reserved in the process or practice of discipleship. Discipleship is ruthless because we have a common enemy who will attack with increasing blows as we become who God has already made us. Our enemy attacks with regrets and memories as he assaults our self-worth. He raises doubts and continues as he attacks our destination of being prepared, being confident, and being skilled. When things get ruthless, empathy and hope are the greatest gifts we can give to those we disciple.

Discipleship in process and practice is risky business. The intimacy and interaction required in discipleship bring feelings of risk. How difficult is it to share what you really think about a verse? How risky is it to submit to and follow another who is leading you to God?

I fell off a cliff when I was twenty-two. Falling is not a big deal. You are not a climber until you have fallen. Falling is part of climbing better. You have to try new things. You have to leap. You have to push yourself to improve. You will fall. You just want to have controlled falls. My fall was not controlled. The devices placed in the rock failed me, and I dropped some sixty feet onto a slab of granite. People ask me if I am afraid of heights now. I am not afraid of heights. I am not even afraid of falling. But I feel risk the moment I am perched high and find myself not in control—risk that freezes me. It can be terrifying.

Feeling risk in discipleship is real. Disciples may wonder if their transparency is going to burn them like they have seen others burnt. They may have scars from their last moment of intimacy and openness. We need to remember the risk that people feel. The feelings are real even if we know that they are not at risk. Feelings of risk can cause us to freeze up and isolate us from the very community that is part of our discipleship. Discipleship in process and practice feels risky even when it is not.

Sustainable discipleship is a relentless, ruthless, and risky journey. We need to have endured before we champion someone to run long. We need to have faced ourselves before we ask others to face themselves. We need to have risked ourselves before we ask others to risk themselves. We need always to remember how it felt when we started this practice of discipleship.

Discipleship Is Easy

Discipleship is easy. Jesus did it without a single book. Moms and dads can do it day by day and moment by moment. It does not require a college degree. Discipleship is the simple process and practice of following God. It is the process and practice of adjusting to His life-giving, empowering, incredible truths. Discipleship is getting cake for breakfast instead of gruel. It is winning the spiritual lottery.

Discipleship only requires saying yes, dropping your net, and following God.

Discipleship should not be made more difficult than it needs to be. Perhaps there is a bit of irony with this section following the section "Discipleship Is Relentless, Ruthless, and Risky," but despite the challenges we may face, discipleship is simply about saying yes. Yes to blessing. Yes to trial. Yes to challenges. Yes to refinement. Yes to my best life ever.

Mike[11] was in discipleship. He was so uptight. He was so performance oriented. He was so focused on the "do" and not the "be." His leader asked him if his daughter was going to camp with their church. Here is how the conversation went:

"I am not sure we have the money," Mike said.

"I hear they are giving away free camp to any kid who reads the Bible cover to cover before camp."

"My daughter can't do that."

"Why not? I bet she can read it just a few pages a day."

"How can she do it if I can't? How can she understand and process all of this if I can't?" Mike responded.

"Hey, you know you are just supposed to be reading, right?

Like, you don't have to get everything the first pass. Just read it and see what you see."

Mike sighed.

Mike's daughter is a smart teenager. She could easily read the Bible cover to cover, but Mike held the irrational belief that she could not because he did not feel he could. Mike was making his discipleship difficult. All he needed to do was follow the instruction of his leader. All he needed to do was to read, but he was overthinking everything. Mike felt that he had to understand everything. He was struggling with the same performance issues that so many of us have had to put aside so that we could follow God (be disciples).

His leader did his best to work through these issues. His leader tried to show him the easy path of following God—be who you are, where you are at the moment, and just follow to the next place. Mike never stopped making following about him. He never stopped making it difficult. Interestingly, his daughter simply followed her leader and continues to read the Bible.

Making disciples is easy if we, as leaders, follow God's simple models of discipleship. We walk with them, lead them to God's truths, cheer them on, explain what we know, and push them to say yes to God. Being a disciple is easy too. You just follow. We need to transfer the idea that following is simple.

Sustainable discipleship is not a marine boot camp. It is learning to ride a bike with training wheels. Discipleship is not just for the elite. It is for everyone, and it is an easy, enjoyable process. Discipleship is not being thrown in a pool to learn to swim. It is learning to swim with a great instructor who is there every step along the way. Discipleship doesn't need to be made hard for the ones following. We do not need to make discipleship this superhuman, superhero process. Likewise, those who are being made disciples need to lighten up and just walk through the process. (How many times have I said this to new followers!) There will be challenges, it requires intimacy, and it is ruthless, but discipleship is just a moment-by-moment process of learning and applying God's truths.

 ## Discipleship Is the Application of Eternal Truth

Discipleship is all about God's truth applied to our lives; thus, God's eternal truths are the basis of successful discipleship. His truths are what people follow. Following Him is about applying his directions and principles for incredible living to our every moment.

Sustainable discipleship focuses every moment, every meeting, and every interaction on application. We guide disciples to read the Bible cover to cover three times during the process. The first pass is like diving in a pool for the very first time. The disciples have no idea how to swim. Discipleship focuses on what catches their attention, what they understand, and what confuses them. Their experience drives the process as they discuss part of the Bible each week. The second pass is like learning to swim laps. The disciple, now experienced at swimming, sets off to explore the pool, beginning to answer their own questions and ask more complex questions. The third pass assimilates all they have learned and focuses on the ability to communicate those truths to others and to use those truths in leadership.

There is nothing greater than God's words to transform humans. Paul writes to the Romans,

> For I am not ashamed of this Good News about Christ. It is the power of God at work, saving everyone who believes—the Jew first and also the Gentile. This Good News tells us how God makes us right in his sight.
>
> — ROMANS 1:16–17

The writer of Hebrews teaches,

For the word of God is alive and powerful. It is sharper than the sharpest two-edged sword, cutting between soul and spirit, between joint and marrow. It exposes our innermost thoughts and desires. Nothing in all creation is hidden from God. Everything is naked and exposed before his eyes, and he is the one to whom we are accountable.

— HEBREWS 4:12

Disciples are pushed to apply God's truths to their past, present, and future. They are taught to

- face the truth,
- measure themselves against it,
- adjust themselves to it,
- store it away for future use, and
- connect it to the entire context of the Bible.

Reading the Bible cover to cover provides context that keeps us from misunderstanding and misapplying "truths." Reading cover to cover synthesizes the principles and truths of God throughout time. Reading cover to cover is not about what I want to learn—it is about what I can learn. It is about learning things that I never knew existed. Reading cover to cover challenges things we have been taught by others. It raises questions. Where does the Bible say that getting a tattoo is a sin? Is it found in the verse about marking our bodies like the pagans when they mourn? Or is that passage about not mourning loss like those without hope? Or is it about not looking like the world? Do we look like the world when we do not have tattoos? These are all great second- and third-pass discussions. These are tough questions that cause us to learn, apply, and grow.

The greatest gift we can give people is cover-to-cover, application-based exposure to the mystically, spiritually powered, life-changing words of God. No one is too young. No passage is too dull. There is life cover to cover. Boredom flees when we search for applications. Sure, I struggle with being excited about reading the lists and the counting of all the families in Numbers. I get depressed when I read Jeremiah. However, I have seen great truths arise as I connect this guy or gal in this history to this incredible statement in another place. I was so amazed and excited at God when I realized that Rahab, a lying prostitute turned believer, was in the lineage of Christ. How many lives have been inspired by the prayer of Jabez found amidst seemingly endless, boring history? We need to show this beauty and these connections to those we disciple. We need to encounter them ourselves as we learn about the success and failure of humans over the years.

Discipleship in process and practice is all about application that leads to transformation.

Discipleship Is about Transformation

The most common mistake in making disciples is thinking that discipleship is about education. It is an easy mistake to make. After all, how are you going to follow unless you learn the rules? And wouldn't knowing everything about God be the best way to get started? How can you follow a God you don't understand? Every bit of following involves some kind of learning.

But education can derail us. Education can lead us very quickly to pragmatism, legalism, and a measurement system that judges ourselves and others based on performance rather than relationship.

Discipleship isn't about education—it is about transformation. Jesus did not tell us to make scholars. He told us to make followers.

Making disciples involves teaching. Being a disciple requires learning. Education is not bad; it just is not the end goal or the measure of success. Education should fuel the fire of transformation. Education is like eating. There is nothing wrong with enjoying great food. There is nothing wrong with wanting to eat incredible delights. But the end goal of eating is growing up, staying alive, and being healthy (well, at least it should be).

Education for the sake of education is like gluttony. Education that does not transform is like a fat man eating cake. Education for the transformation is like pasta to an ultra runner. Education for life and health is like a balanced diet consumed in reasonable amounts. Eating alone cannot save a man, but eating well may save a man. Education alone may make you smart, but if it is not useful, it is wasteful.

Focusing discipleship on education is like putting a doctor into practice right out of medical school. Medical school is important, but residency is more important. Residency is the time where young doctors learn to apply their education under the watchful eye of experienced doctors. Medical students do not become doctors without successfully applying and proving their education in real-life situations. Being transformed by what we learn is like residency.

The application of what we learn should lead to the transformation of our lives. Knowing does not change us. Our response to what we learn changes us. We become followers of God each time we respond to conviction and adjust our lives to God's incredible, eternally profitable truths.

Education is the fuel to the transformational fire. Choice is the match that sets it ablaze. Transformation is completed by God's Spirit. Applying God's truths to guide choices empowers the Spirit to transform the "who I am."

Choice is both the first and the last step in following God. Education helps us know what to choose so that we may be transformed. Sustainable discipleship not only pushes the application of God's truths, but it also focuses on the transformation of the individual. We need to long for the transformation of those we lead, and we need to ask them again and again, "What are you going to do now that you know this truth? What do you do with this?"

From Theory to Execution

"Since making disciples is the main task of the church, every church ought to be able to answer two questions: what is our plan for making disciples of Jesus; and is our plan working?"

— DALLAS WILLARD

Up to this point, we have covered the big picture of successful, sustainable discipleship. Followers and leaders need a simple definition and a comprehensive understanding of discipleship. Regardless of the methods,

> *Making disciples introduces people to God, who loves and understands them, helps them understand who they are and what they can be, helps them apply God's transforming truths, and releases them as prepared, confident, and skilled to live their best life ever on earth.*

We have rediscovered God's pure, irrefutable models for making disciples. The Old Testament model focused on knowing and passing along God's life truths along the way, reminding us of five important discipleship truths:

1. We may not always "get it" the first time.
2. Some truths apply to many situations and will get repeated in new ways.
3. Culture is built through many little lessons.
4. Truth is much more applicable when immediately applied.
5. Answers and direction are needed along the way.

The New Testament model revealed Jesus's method when He made disciples.

1. He called them to surrender.
2. He discipled them along the way.
3. He asked tough questions.
4. He put them in residency.
5. He released them.
6. He took three years to make disciples.
7. He discipled them as individuals.
8. He discipled them often in smaller groups.

Making disciples is entirely about who someone is and becomes. It is not about what they do or how they do it. Doing is the natural result of being when it comes to life. "Be comes before do" is the secret sauce to making self-sustaining disciples. We have also seen that successful discipleship will always embrace certain biblical principles:

1. Discipleship must be based on His truths.
2. Discipleship must be done intentionally.
3. Discipleship is about making followers of God, not man.
4. Discipleship must be focused on individuals.

We have expanded our understanding of the value of discipleship, seeing that it is the "everything" answer for individuals and the Church. And we have explored the characteristics of discipleship to understand better what sustainable discipleship looks like.

1. Discipleship exposes people to practical truth.
2. Discipleship is a community effort.
3. Discipleship is for everyone.
4. Discipleship is intimate.

5. Discipleship is relentless, ruthless, and risky.
6. Discipleship is easy.
7. Discipleship focuses on applying useful, eternal truths.
8. Discipleship is about transformation.

Now we face Dallas Willard's two questions:

• What is our plan for making disciples of Jesus?
• Is our plan working?

Dallas gave his life to championing discipleship. Long ago, he faced the same challenges that the Barna Group has recently identified. He identified the need for sustainable discipleship when he wrote,

> *A mature disciple is one who effortlessly does what Jesus would do if Jesus were him.*

Bill Hull has also given his life to championing discipleship. He, too, identified the need for sustainable discipleship and wrote,

> *Success should not be measured by how many disciples are made, but by how many disciples are making other disciples.*

Bill is also quoted saying,

> *Discipleship is the only hope for the world—it hasn't worked because it hasn't been done. It hasn't been done because we are too distracted—we are an impatient lot who have been more interested in ourselves and our kingdoms than Christ and His.*

What is our plan for discipleship? Will it work? Do we have the time? These are powerful questions. I attended a one-day panel on evangelism and discipleship put on by the North American Mission Board. Hundreds of us showed up to discuss and share about discipleship. The five-member panel (and the moderator) were all successful evangelists. They had personal lives of evangelism. Their churches excelled at reaching people. Their experience ranged from ten to forty years. These inspiring leaders rekindled a desire for evangelism in me. It was humbling. However, when each was asked about discipleship, they said they had not had much success.[12] They were transparent as, one after another, they shared that they struggled with discipleship. There were some stories of one-on-one walking with a few men over the years. One leader shared how he always mentored two or three men a year, but none had a clear plan for discipling the masses of people they had won to the Lord.

I empathize with them. I have faced the same challenge in my responsibility for smaller numbers, but we have discovered an answer, and it is working. I wanted to jump up and say, "Wait! I have the answer." Everything in me was yearning to share what God has taught us—to share the straightforward, successful model that is exponentially creating disciples. That moment fueled me to share an answer. That moment fueled me to get back to this book and finish the rewrites.[13]

It is time to move from the concepts and foundations to the specifics of sustainable discipleship. The next section, "The Sustainable-Discipleship Model," explores the model and lays out seven action items. It includes

- The Evolution of a Plan,
- Plan on Four Years,
- Deploy Comprehensive Discipleship,
- Leverage the Predictable Pathway,
- Use the Seven Core Practices,
- Customize the Process, and
- Understand Your Role.

Sustainable discipleship makes disciples in three phases. The "Step-by-Step Guide" section follows with detailed guides for making disciples in each phase. It gives step-by-step instructions about how to

- Launch Your Discipleship-One Group,
- Continue Leading Disciples in Discipleship Two, and
- Finish Discipleship Well with Discipleship Three.

This section shares our recruitment and assessment process in each phase. It expands the "how-tos" of creating sustainable disciples with detailed examples and applications for each phase. We will explore the requirements of discipleship and the transitions between phases. "Launch Your Discipleship" opens with our most concise review of the model. "The Step-by-Step Guide" is the ultimate guide to executing sustainable discipleship.

We will conclude by taking a look at the great privilege we have in making disciples. "Our Privilege" is one of my favorite chapters. It is the one I read when I am tired. It is the one I read when I am trying to figure out the next step. It reminds me, inspires me, and helps me to endure in this great task of making sustainable disciples.

As we head toward the practicals, I want to remind you that sustainable discipleship is not a program, a set of materials, or a class. Sustainable discipleship is simply a practical reflection of God's model for discipleship. It works. Those we have led are leading others. We are five generations deep and beginning to see exponential power. There is a plan. It works. You have the time. Those you make disciples will make disciples. I promise.

PART III

THE SUSTAINABLE-DISCIPLESHIP MODEL

8

THE EVOLUTION OF A PLAN

Do you have a plan for making disciples? I did not. I was not focused on God's call to make disciples. I just wanted people to be transformed. I had no time or patience with standard Christianity. My life was meaningful, my prayer was a conversation with God, and my decisions had solid reasoning based on eternal truths that were as sure as gravity. I had been pushed by God, and I had pushed myself into situations that were bigger than me. I learned on the job through accidental successes and needed trials. I just wanted people to follow, and I wanted them to have help along the way. Not only did I not have a plan, but I also had no model, template, or mentors to follow. The apostles did not face these two challenges. Jesus told them to make disciples, and he showed them how to do it. The apostles had it easier.

Jesus modeled making disciples by making them disciples. Jesus taught them. They actually had something to teach. The apostles were there. They knew the sacrifice and beauty that they were leading people toward. They knew the challenges, trials, and persecution that new followers would face. They also knew the value of having a relationship with the God of the universe.

They had a direct call and a model to mimic. I wish that had been my journey.

The apostles had it easier.

I wanted to expose people to God's truths and majesty. I wanted to win people to the same full and meaningful life that I had found. Like most leaders, I started teaching. We studied the Bible together. We had classes on just about every classic topic from marriage to evolution. We even hosted seminary classes on campus. People ate it up. Our classes were full, and people were learning, but we still experienced all those classic issues of doing "church."

- Finances
- Twenty percent doing 80 percent of the work and giving
- Human barriers to change
- Exhausted volunteers
- Burnt-out staff
- Stalled ministry effectiveness
- Confusion and division

I struggled with feeling ineffective. The numbers were there, and people were getting educated, but only a small percentage of the participants looked like followers. People were not moving toward unity. People were not applying the truths consistently. Worse still, I was not really looking like a follower. Time and stress were taking their toll. We tried all kinds of things.

We started a thirteen-week intensive discipleship experience for men: Upsilon Mu Chi. It was like a men's fraternity, with the thirteen weeks resembling the pledge process to a life of following God together. The intensive part worked great. We spent every week together, became transparent, pushed basic truths, challenged each other, and held each other accountable to follow. Every week had interaction, activities, and fellowship. But the process failed again and again as the thirteen weeks came to a close. The life change did not seem to endure much beyond a couple of years. The truths did not stick. The lifestyle failed in the face of challenges and trials, and it became just another program. It was discipleship, but the process was not sustainable.

I started taking people on mission trips, using a specific plan to leverage the trips to make them apply God's truths. The preparation time for a trip was one hundred days. We met five or six times before the trip for training, biblical learning, and prayer. The trips were incredible. Each trip was full of life, learning, and adjusting to God's truths. We discipled people to believe in the incredible, to be great servants, to pray, to praise, and to study God's word. It was very successful with small groups but pretty much failed with larger groups. It worked for people who kept going on missions but did not have lasting power for the one-time traveler. It never worked with people who were not from our church and still does not work when we take guests. Prayer, time, and a bit of research revealed that mission-trip discipleship only worked as part of a comprehensive discipleship plan. Guests from other churches did not get the discipleship culture we were building every week. It looked attractive, but the buy-in curve was too steep for one trip.

We revamped our retreats to be encounters with God. Without knowing it, we did what everyone started doing: we did youth ministry to adults. Learning became kinetic with activities, interactions, and well-planned teaching. Fellowship was important, but we entirely capitalized on jump-starting discipleship by pushing, prodding, cheering, and challenging adults to make specific decisions to apply God's truths. We challenged small-business owners with the principle of tithing off their gross like the farmers in the Bible. We had intensive prayer times. We even got them to do a few skits. Each retreat had an intentional focus based on making disciples. Men and women rose to the challenge and adjusted their decisions to God's truths. This strategy faced the same problem as the mission-trip strategy: it worked for people who kept going on retreats but did not have lasting power for the one-time traveler. It never worked with people who were not from our church and still does not work when we take guests. Prayer, time, and a bit of research revealed that special events and retreats only worked as part of a comprehensive discipleship plan. The strategy did not affect sustainable transformation.

We tried small groups as a replacement for the education model of Sunday school. The goal was for the groups to do life together and to cooperatively make disciples among themselves. Small groups did not work for us because we did not have enough prepared, confident, and skilled leaders who could make disciples. The best of our groups ended up as dinner clubs with devotions. There was some change but more disaster. The blind led the blind to places that our church wishes we had never gone. It almost destroyed us.

Interestingly, we have no record of the apostles trying any of these ideas or facing any of these challenges. Their disciple-making journey started with a clear call, a model, and they had the experience. They had something to teach from experience.

The apostles had it easier.

The tipping point[1] came when someone asked me if I would disciple him individually. "Sure," I responded without thinking. I would have the opportunity to lead someone to God's life-changing truths and show them what I had experienced. How cool is that? But I found myself stressing and a bit panicked before our first meeting. I had no idea how to spend our ninety minutes. Should I teach? Should I listen to him and answer his questions? Should I use a "discipleship guide"? I had longed to show others how to experience what I was experiencing, but I realized I had no idea what I was doing. So I prayed and faked the first meeting, asking, "So what do you expect to get out of discipleship?" He wanted to get closer to God. His vague answer and my vague desire were going to lead us nowhere. I prayed desperately for direction from God and followed my heart. "Here is what I want you to do. I want you to read the entire Bible this year. Each week, we will cover one week's worth of reading. Let's start there." It was the greatest inspiration ever. God's word is powerful and provided plenty of discussion and application to his life. He began thriving. I began adding some of the resources that had changed my life. People heard about it, and more requests for individual discipleship came in. I was spending ten hours a week discipling others. It was a dream come true, but I still had no idea what I was doing. I still had no plan.

I quickly learned I was not the best fit for discipling women. It got awkward, and some wives clearly were just looking for a spiritual dude to lead them. But I had no women ready to lead. Some of those I discipled applied truth, and others just faded. Some made it over the humps, but others could not follow a man, much less God—they imploded and exploded. I refined and I retooled, trying all kinds of things along the way. I succeeded and I failed.

I exposed myself to a wide variety of disciple makers, humbling myself and following them. Phil, a senior disciple maker, taught me that I was not alone. It was common for people to buck the system at specific points. He taught me his system. Partheneous taught me that the young in faith could not process the mysteries without grave danger. Coder taught me to have a spine and have some requirements. The Bible backed it all. I was being transformed as a disciple maker. The three-phase approach evolved. The steps became evident. The breaking points were learned. But it was not until I had to pass the torch to another would-be disciple maker that I actually saw how biblically based this accidental model was.

I began to research discipleship. I began to look for it in the Bible. Light bulbs came on all around me. The Bible was full of how to make disciples. The history was full of examples of success and failure. For instance, I could have saved myself some trouble by hearing the words of Paul instructing women to teach women.[2] I tested out new pushes and methods. I integrated what I was learning about personal discipleship to group events that had nothing to do with discipleship. I was won over by Deuteronomy 6 that we should always "disciple along the way." Every moment became an intentional moment of discipleship for me and for others. I pushed forward and began to understand why some of our larger-group disciple making had failed.

Comprehensive discipleship would never have a chance of working until I had mastered individual disciple making.

I began to focus on truly understanding individual discipleship from a biblical perspective. The biblical concepts and principles are covered in the first part of this book, but our journey also taught me many practical things about individual discipleship. I learned that there is a very natural, biblical pathway of discipleship. People begin their walk with God by being convicted and then repenting. Disciples continue in this back and forth of "being" and "doing" until they reach maturity. Disciples become enlightened and then hear God's call. Those who are called then serve. The pathway to maturity is predictable, and we can and should disciple people differently along that pathway.

I learned that making disciples takes much time in two different ways. First, the disciple maker and the disciple have to invest time weekly. They both have to go along the way together. Discipleship is an intimate journey. Second, it takes time to become a prepared, confident, and skilled follower. It simply takes time for us to process all of God's truths. A thirteen-week program will never make disciples. It takes time to grow up. We practice adjusting to and apply God's truths in experiences that happen over time. The first disciples spent roughly three years in discipleship, and they still did not feel prepared.

I also learned that making disciples is a replicable process. In fact, we are supposed to make other disciple makers. Becoming a disciple maker is part of being a disciple. Multiplying disciple makers is the only way we will ever meet the needs of exponential growth. If one new convert reaches ten people for Christ, then what we need are enough prepared, confident, and skilled followers to reach ten people for Christ. Our experience shows that a teacher-to-student ratio of 1:3 is the most potent method of disciple making. So if we want to reach three hundred people in the first year of ministry, we would ideally need one hundred skilled disciple makers. How do you get one hundred disciple makers? Could we plan to find thirty-three people and spend one year preparing them to reach one hundred? Then in year two, we can reach four hundred. In year three, we can effectively reach 1,700 new converts, and we will have thirty-three leaders capable of being upper-level leaders and church planters.

> The apostles had it easier, but it could have been easier for me too.

Yes, my journey was more difficult than it needed to be. I tried to reinvent the wheel, I had no mentors, and it took a long time before I was driven to the Bible to really understand discipleship. I could have stopped and made a plan. I could have done the work, done the research, and read everything I could find.

> *Just like being comes before doing, a discipleship plan should precede discipleship.*

You do not have to make the same mistake. Sustainable discipleship is a biblical model. It is adaptable. It is customizable to your culture. It works—that I can promise you. You can start with God's plan for making disciples. You can start with realistic timelines and expectations. You can avoid discouragement and see measurable success. Making sustainable disciples is the everything answer.

9

PLAN ON FOUR YEARS

"No matter how great the talent or efforts, some things just take time. You can't produce a baby in one month by getting nine women pregnant."

— WARREN BUFFET

Sustainable discipleship is a highly successful and replicable process. But be prepared, making disciples who endure and stand on their own takes time. Becoming prepared, confident, and skilled takes time. The formal process of sustainable discipleship is carried out in three phases over four years:

- Discipleship One - 1yr
- Discipleship Two - 2yrs
- Discipleship Three - 1yr

Each phase leads disciples further down the predictable pathway. Disciplaships one and three each take one year. Discipleship two takes two years. The first year of discipleship two ends at the residency step. Disciples are ready to begin leading others, and with your help, they invest a year making disciples. Leading others reinforces what they have learned. It causes them to think, integrate, and better understand the truths of following. Leading others also supercharges their journey through discipleship three. The whole process works, but it takes four years. Trust me. We have spent years studying, testing ideas, and trying virtually everything to make the process as efficient and timely as possible. There simply are no shortcuts in making sustainable disciples.

You may not feel like you have four years. I have felt that way. We have too many people. We have too little time. The work needs to get done. The people need to be discipled now, and we need people to be ready to disciple them. I get it, but I would argue that we do not have time not to take the time. Think about it from a different perspective. How many of us would turn over our multimillion-dollar business to a college graduate with no experience? Sure, they have an education, but they have no experience. Most of us would not hire a CEO for our successful company unless he had a proven record of personal success. We would demand far more than three years of experience. However, we so often hand over the most precious thing in the world (people) to leaders with little experience or proven success. How many would-be followers have fallen away or stalled out because their leaders were not capable of handling the challenges of leading? How many would-be followers have been abandoned by small group leaders who did not count the cost? How many would-be leaders have never matured because their leaders are not so mature? We so often provide less than disciple-making small groups and classes because we do not have seasoned disciples to lead. It takes time to make disciples who will replicate and make disciples. Disciple makers need to have been made disciples first. They need to have lived, survived, and thrived as disciples before they lead others. They need to be prepared, confident, and skilled.

Shortcutting the process of making sustainable disciples does not just affect would-be followers. It puts unprepared leaders at unnecessary risk. Paul warned his protégé Timothy of the dangers of early promotions:

> *A church leader must not be a new believer, because he might become proud, and the devil would cause him to fall. Also, people outside the church must speak well of him so that he will not be disgraced and fall into the devil's trap.*

> — 1 TIMOTHY 3:6–7

Paul's concern was the spiritual preparedness and experience of new leaders. I have witnessed (and sadly, participated in) the destruction of would-be great leaders who were pushed into leadership before they were spiritually ready. These leaders end up worn-out, burnt-out, and most often, washed out, leaving ministry and the church. Every seasoned spiritual leader has watched this happen.

The followers and the unprepared leaders suffer when we forget the goal of making disciples.

> *Making disciples introduces people to God, who loves and understands them, helps them understand who they are and what they can be, helps them apply God's transforming truths, and releases them as prepared, confident, and skilled to live their best life ever on earth.*

Discipleship is all about transformation, and there are no shortcuts for sustainable discipleship that results in transformation and replication. Great things take great amounts of energy, time, and investment. Even Jesus spent three years preparing the first disciples to make disciples. We have learned that the process should not take longer than four years. We have learned that the training in each phase should not exceed one year in duration.

Alike the shortcuts, every time we let a disciple take longer, the process breaks apart.

We believe the "take longer" breakup comes because discipleship should not take longer. When discipleship takes longer, the disciple is not exercising the discipline and dedication needed to consume the truths of God. The disciple is not experiencing God. Ultimately, it is not the extended time that breaks the process. It is the disciple not being a disciple that breaks the process. You cannot make a disciple out of a person who does not want to follow. The mantra here should be "four and no more."

We believe the "shortening" breakup comes because of a violation of a natural time frame for developing relationships. We have tried shortening the process because someone already knows the Bible or is experienced in ministry. In both cases, the process breaks. Discipleship is about relationship. Discipleship is about who the disciple is and is becoming. Discipleship is not about education. We have found that even experienced folks thrive and find a better life when they experience the process over four years.

Before you say, "We don't have four years," and put this book aside, let me ask you a few questions.

- How many years did you train for success in your job?
- How many years does it take to raise a child?
- How many years does it take to grow an investment?
- How quickly can you solve decades of years of relationship problems?
- How long does it take to turn a troubled organization around?
- How long does it take to reform a leader?

Cliché, perhaps, but nothing worth having comes quickly. Nothing worth having comes without great investment. There is no "lottery" for making disciples. Now let me ask you another more important question: Why don't you have four years?

The answer to that question usually reveals the more significant issues in our world and in our ministries. Do you need helpers and leaders right now? If so, you may not have been recruiting and training them for the last four years. Your ministry may be growing quickly, but you have to start somewhere. Our model results in great leaders. It does not produce them it—it results in them. We do not focus on raising up leaders. (That would be pretty self-centered.) We make disciples so that people have a great life. We get people to God because it benefits them. God calls and develops them into leaders—it happens.

Do you wonder if anyone will invest four years?

A recent Census Bureau poll indicated that 33.4 percent of the population graduates college.[1] Bureau of Labor Statistics show that more than 60 percent of all high school students enroll in college and 75 percent of all high school graduates are active in the workforce learning skills.[2] How many people over eighteen years old do you know? Multiply that by 75 percent and you will have a high estimate of the number of people who have or are investing more than four years into something worth their time. A low estimate is 30 percent of the people you know. How many families invest far more than four years in learning sports, dancing, fishing, or rock climbing? People will invest four years if the investment is valuable.

Discipleship is valuable. Humor me asking one more question: "Have you invested four or more years in a discipleship relationship?" If you have, you know the power of your testimony and the value of discipleship.[3] Discipleship done well is worth four years. Discipleship as a culture does great service to the people who are going to sit in the pews for four years anyway. We have seen the demand for discipleship increase exponentially in proportion to the number of people who are transformed by discipleship. John Maxwell calls this the Law of the Big Mo[4] (momentum). Like it or not, success begets success. You have to start somewhere.

I promise you, four years will pass quickly, and people will want more. I promise you, your heart will pound as you watch the transformations and hear their personal testimonies of how discipleship changed their lives. You will rejoice as you build deep relationships with the members of your church. There is one more promise I will make to you: you will have all the leaders you need within three generations. Mature disciples not only make new disciples, but they also surrender to God's bigger plan. He, then, calls these equipped followers to incredible success inside and outside the church.

But what do you do if you are just starting up, have no leaders or have a church that is blowing up with new people? You embrace the second part of this model, comprehensive discipleship.

10

DEPLOY COMPREHENSIVE DISCIPLESHIP

"We used to do many things for many reasons. Now we do one thing—make disciples—in many different ways."

O ur journey led us to the obvious: reaching people individually is the best way to lead people to a thriving life in Christ. Reaching people individually is the most effective way to make disciples that will, in turn, make disciples. However, all of us face particular challenges in reaching individuals.

- We lack disciples who can make disciples. This problem is prevalent in new churches or churches that begin to embrace a biblical model of discipleship.
- Our healthy disciples reach others for Christ in an exponential way. One healthy disciple may reach four or ten people who become Christians and need access to discipleship. The demand for discipleship

can quickly exceed the ability to provide it intimately.

- Healthy disciples are not made quickly, leaving us with a longer ramp-up time to meet the need.
- Exponential growth results in increased ministry needs. Ministry, running churches, and leading communities takes time. The more people you have, the more leaders you have, and the more ministry you do all decreases the time available to intimately disciple others.

Luke, the great Christian historian, recorded these same four challenges in his history of the beginning of the first church.

Those who believed what Peter said were baptized and added to the church that day—about 3,000 in all. All the believers devoted themselves to the apostles' teaching, and to fellowship, and to sharing in meals (including the Lord's Supper), and to prayer. A deep sense of awe came over them all, and the apostles performed many miraculous signs and wonders.

— ACTS 2:41–44

But as the believers [disciples] rapidly multiplied, there were rumblings of discontent. The Greek-speaking believers complained about the Hebrew-speaking believers, saying that their widows were being discriminated against in the daily distribution of food. So the Twelve called a meeting of all the believers. They said, "We apostles should spend our time teaching the word of God, not running a food program. And so, brothers, select seven men who are well respected and are full of the Spirit and wisdom. We will give them this responsibility. Then we apostles can spend our time in prayer and teaching the word."

— ACTS 6:1–4

Jesus had gone to heaven. The Spirit had fallen and lit people on fire. Their radical conversion transformed their lives. They got noticed. They shared the Good News with those who noticed. More people came to Christ—sometimes thousands at a time. The spiritual, leadership, and physical needs grew as the community of believers grew. There were a limited number of disciple makers, and those disciple makers were quickly being drawn from being prepared and available to lead others into ministry. The entire church would gather to hear from few leaders.

Their solution was to teach and make disciples of individuals, of emerging leaders, and of crowds. They made disciples, however and wherever they could. In the middle of the crunch, the apostles returned to making disciples and passed off much of the service of ministry to capable followers of Christ, who had quickly risen as respected and full of the Spirit.[1]

The Church grew as converts intentionally went out to the whole world. The Good News spread as Christians moved away from persecution to new homes. The leaders were faced with the same challenges every time the Good News went out to a new area, and masses came to Christ. The apostles traveled, doing their best to invest and disciple these new groups, but there were not enough prepared, capable, and skilled leaders. Crazy, wrong leaders with natural charisma and passion rose up intentionally and unintentionally teaching bad doctrine. These leaders led the masses away from God's truths. Division became the newest challenge to making disciples.

The apostles reacted by announcing who was trustworthy and denouncing those that were not true disciple makers. They wrote letters of theology, recorded Jesus's words that they had heard, and addressed the questions and needs of individual churches. They even wrote letters to specific leaders, training them from far off. The model was very Mosaic in nature. Jerusalem became the headquarters of seasoned elders who sent out evangelists and raised up more seasoned disciple makers.

They sent out trainees with the experienced. They provided truthful teaching and answers drawing people toward unity in Christ.

The number of prepared, confident, and skilled leaders grew over time and began to make disciples and lead the churches near them. Replication occurred, and now the work of making disciples was delegated. The apostles continued to travel, championing new church plants and discipling existing plants. They raised up capable men and women to make disciples in cities and towns. The masses were now dispersed, and faithful men and women were called to make disciples in smaller groups and with individuals. When a significant move of God resulted in mass conversions, the church mobilized workers to make disciples and raise up disciple makers.

The apostles used comprehensive discipleship to make disciples of masses and to make individual disciples. We do not know if the plan was God-given or an accidental success, but it worked. They simply made disciples the way that Jesus made disciples: comprehensively. It worked for Jesus, it worked for them, and it will work for you too.

Comprehensive discipleship is key to sustainable discipleship. It is your best friend when you start up discipleship or win a ton of people to Christ. A comprehensive discipleship plan fills the gaps as you make disciples who will then, naturally, make disciples. A comprehensive plan primes the pump, allowing new people to be discipled along the way toward a formal process.

The apostles and the early church leaders continued to use a comprehensive plan even when the church was not growing fast. They continued to disciple crowds, they continued to spread the word widely, they continued to disciple churches, and they continued to build leaders.

A comprehensive discipleship plan endures long after you have solved the problem of not having enough leaders to disciple others. It is the marketing funnel of your church. The single goal of the church is to make disciples, and that opportunity begins when someone walks into your church on their first Sunday. The opportunity to make disciples exists at every function. The opportunity exists in every meeting, on every team, at every retreat, and on every mission trip.

Individual discipleship may trump mass discipleship, but a comprehensive discipleship model will involve every type of opportunity. Comprehensive discipleship includes all of the opportunities that we have.

- Discipling large groups every Sunday morning (or whenever you meet)
- Discipling your leaders every time you meet
- Discipling through every event, mission trip, and big effort
- Discipling while you grow, build, and expand the Kingdom
- Discipling while you provide focused education
- Discipling individually

Discipleship helps people understand who they are and what they can be. Discipleship helps people apply God's transforming truths and releases them as prepared, confident, and skilled to live their best life ever on earth. Comprehensive discipleship leverages every opportunity to do these great things. It secretly pushes people to their best in every moment, without a program. Comprehensive discipleship adapts the principles, goals, and methods of individual discipleship to larger groups and different circumstances to continually focus on making disciples

It transforms Sunday-morning messages into useful, life-transforming moments as teachers focus on applying biblical truth to daily living, issues, and opportunities. Sunday-morning messages come alive when the goal becomes passionate transformation instead of well-orated education.

Each moment working with another leader is a moment of

discipleship. Open and graceful challenges for leaders to provide biblical backing for decisions and plans push each of us to follow God. Continuing education on "not hot" topics and deeper theology should be a part of every leadership meeting. Discipleship pushes each of us toward even more biblical leadership.

Every corporate event provides the opportunity for discipleship as we swap cheesy opening prayers for times of prayer over each individual and prayers that God will empower and transform us.[2] Interactions with leaders and followers of events provide endless opportunities to teach the "why" behind the "way" we are approaching this ministry event. In fact, events themselves will be transformed as we seek only to have life-transforming events. Life change for the participants and leaders becomes the goal for each trip, retreat, and outreach. Every moment is a discipling moment.

Comprehensive discipleship focuses the work of the church on making disciples. Comprehensive discipleship minimizes the distractions to discipleship by offloading ministry tasks to free up disciple makers to make disciples. A comprehensive plan will transform the "what we do" to reflect the "who we are"—disciple makers. It pushes us to shut down ministries and events that prevent our people from making and being made disciples. A comprehensive plan kills the busyness of doing for the beauty of being disciples. How many classes would be canceled if we chose only classes that would disciple the participants? How much more meaningful would our time together be if it focused on us thriving as followers? How much more transforming would our ministry be if discipleship was the primary goal?

A clear understanding of what discipleship was and how to make disciples allowed us[3] to leverage every opportunity and circumstance to use a comprehensive discipleship model intentionally. My teaching on Sunday morning changed. I regained my passion and returned to my roots as being a pusher of change. I did crazy things before they were popular. I wrote a series focused on transformation. I focused even more on application. I taught with the authority and humility of a transformed follower. I challenged people to adjust their lives to God. We pushed our leaders to be disciples and disciple others. I asked them point blank who they shared the Gospel with, if they were tithing, and if they were reading God's word. I realized that we could not lead people anywhere that we had not been. We could not model service without being servants. We could not cheer on transformation if we were not transformed. Comprehensive discipleship invaded our leadership structure and our culture. We decided that believers should live in unity, so we chose unanimity as the basis for our leadership decisions. We agreed that democracy had nothing to do with church and ditched meetings and voting for elders and a solid staff that worked together. And all along the way, we kept making individual disciples as the foundation of our comprehensive discipleship model.

Long before we embraced comprehensive discipleship, we did missions, education, small groups, retreats, outreach, events, and age-focused ministry. We did so much that we struggled with doing any of it excellently. We did so much that we struggled to raise up capable leaders and to have time to walk with them. It is so much easier now. We still do all those things, and we have time to train, to live with, and to raise up incredibly effective leaders and ministries. Each activity, each ministry, every trip is done under the umbrella of comprehensive discipleship. Each is part of our overall discipleship plan focused on the acquisition and application of God's truths. Each focuses on transforming us. Each event and activity are entry points to individual discipleship and exercises for current disciples, and all of them have a disciple-making focus. We used to do many things for many reasons; now we do one thing—make disciples—in many different ways. Discipleship is the foundation, the glue, and a biblical call to our culture and ministry.

Discipleship should invade our every opportunity with the people, but comprehensive discipleship is nothing without individual discipleship. Every method of making individual disciples can and should be applied comprehensively, but individual discipleship is the beginning and end of discipleship.

Jesus discipled individually. Yes, he taught the masses, but Jesus also discipled the small group and the individual.[4] The apostles taught the masses to follow God, but they returned to individual discipleship as soon as possible. The apostles taught local pastors to disciple others so that those people could disciple others. When the mass conversions settled down, things always came back to intimate discipleship along the way of life.

Comprehensive discipleship is a necessity. It is the natural result of a church focused on Jesus's primary call to us: make disciples. But comprehensive discipleship will always be founded on a clear understanding of making one individual disciple. There is a predictable pathway to sustainable discipleship. It takes time, but it is worth it. You are not alone on this journey. You are surrounded by virtual mentors and God's Spirit longing for every individual to find transformation and the best life ever.

You and I can make individual disciples. We can make it a priority. We can make time. We only need to be prepared, confident, and skilled.

11

LEVERAGE THE PREDICTABLE PATHWAY

"The pathway to maturity is predictable. We can and should disciple people differently along that pathway."

I had been making disciples for a while before Phil helped me put words on the process. People got saved, they learned, and they longed to get more involved. More involvement, coupled with applying God's truths, led to them wanting to lead others. They went "all in" following and serving God. Experience in leadership led them to a bigger picture of God's plan. These mature disciples became filled with a passion for changing the world and winning others to Christ. We simply inspired those who became followers to be followers. We drew them from topical studies on finances, relationships, and marriage to reading the Bible cover to cover. We challenged them to assimilate and apply whatever truths they found. We pushed them to adjust their daily lives to the truths they discovered. We fueled their transformation along the way. We made disciples, but we had no real understanding of a system. We just made disciples the best we could. We saw it happen, but if you asked me what was happening, you would get a wandering, long answer. It was so difficult to train anyone how to make disciples. You may be in the same place right now.

Phil's and my relationship grew out of a mission trip. I was a team leader. He was the camp director and leader of a network of churches. His passion for discipleship was undeniable and unstoppable. I did not ask him to disciple me. He discipled me by force. He discipled me with great love. He pushed me, cheered me on, and believed in me. He was rough, old-school, and hard at times, but he wanted me to succeed in my calling. He wanted me to disciple people well. He was so frustrated that I could not articulate my system. Standing high atop the steel structure of a conference center rising from the desert, Phil drilled me on how I was discipling others. He saw our incredible teams of followers and wanted to know what we were doing. He was also getting frustrated as I rambled on. Then came the moment God opened a window for me. Phil asked, "Have I ever told you about our seven levels of discipleship?" He lit up with passion and holy fire as he shared the seven levels that he used. Here are his seven levels:

- Repentance
- Illumination
- Service
- Leadership Preparation
- Consecration
- Leadership
- World Vision

Phil was onto something! I immediately had a word for each of those steps that our disciples just seemed to walk through. I grabbed a piece of steel and a Sharpie, and wrote them down. That piece of steel beam still sits on my office shelf. Phil's seven levels were the beginning of my ability to approach and communicate our process.

Naturally, people got saved (**repentance**), they learned (**illumination**), and they longed to get more involved (**service**). More involvement, coupled with applying God's truths, led to them wanting to lead others (**leadership preparation**). They went "all in" following and serving God (**consecration**). Experience in leadership (**leadership**) led them to a bigger picture of God's plan. These mature disciples became filled with a passion for changing the world and winning others to Christ (**world vision**).

The steps made sense. The steps were reflected in every successful follower of God throughout the Bible. Phil's words were the beginning of me seeing there was a predictable pathway to becoming a disciple.

I continued to study discipleship and try out every idea I found. I tested our "accidental" methods against every discipleship concept I could find. I eagerly looked at other discipleship models. Our team didn't find models focused on "being." We didn't find customizable processes for a broad audience. We wanted so much more than an education program. Again, I was at a loss for words to communicate how we made disciples and customized discipleship. Those we made disciples did things, but "doing" was not our goal. Our goal was who they became. If we could get them to "be" followers, the "doing" just resulted.

The do-do-do confusion was solved for me during a whiteboard session with our team. I was ranting about the do-do-do of the levels, and it dawned on me: "be" always precedes "do." I had been seeing that trend in my research for several projects. It fit here. It solved what seemed to be missing, and it filled in the gaps. Our model needed to identify who we were leading disciples to be. Then we could help them apply truths to do life and leadership. It was an epiphany. The result was fourteen steps—seven "be" and seven "do"—arranged into a pathway. (You can see the infographic in the back of the book.) Each of the fourteen steps occurs throughout biblical history in a predictable, natural sequence. Left undisturbed, the discipleship process will happen along this fourteen-step "be–do" path. The predictable path allows us to improve our disciple making.

"Where are you?" is the most potent question we ask people. We use this chart when consulting on church leadership. We use this chart when people begin discipleship. We use this chart when we are helping people over spiritual growth barriers. We always ask, "Where are you?" and almost every time, we get a "do" answer instead of a "be" answer. Humans are so "do" oriented.

We also find something interesting when we ask our second powerful question, "At what step are you serving? Like, where is what you are doing on the chart?" More often than not, people are in "over their heads," living out roles farther down the path than the "where they are." (And we probably put them there!)

Our experience continues to show the vast majority of people are serving beyond their preparation, confidence, and skill. No wonder so many great people experience frustration, burn-out, and unhealthy living. No wonder so many followers are cheated by not having fully prepared, confident, and skilled leaders. Everyone is set up for destruction. Remember Paul teaching Timothy this principle:

A church leader must not be a new believer, because he might become proud, and the devil would cause him to fall.

— 1 TIMOTHY 3:6

But pride is not the only thing that destroys would-be servants of God. Money, family, and many other things destroy immature followers. Why are so many people "doing" beyond where they are "being?" Sometimes it is their fault because they

- want to control,
- are compelled to lead,
- find identity in doing,

- are performance oriented,
- cannot sit—they have to get it done now—or
- do not know better.

Sometimes it is our fault as leaders because we

- use leadership, jobs, and teaching positions to get people involved;
- have not learned that "who a person is" is all that matters to God;
- recruit the unprepared because of people shortages; or
- are simply afraid to say, "No. You are not ready yet."

It is no wonder that people are serving beyond their capacity when only 25 percent of them are being made disciples. But leadership is also failing, with only one in five leaders currently discipling another person. There is a lack of disciples. Do the math. If your community has two hundred people, you have a potential pool of fifty prepared, confident, and skilled people to reach the world. The 20/80 rule[1] seems so logical now.

Worse still, doing before being is terrible for followers and leaders. I have participated in the destruction of would-be, incredible leaders. I hate it. I regret it. There was Lou,[2] who I could see was gifted to be a pastor. I pushed him and put him in the job before he was called and before he was ready. He fell under the pressure. He is a pastor now after years of recovery. There was Billy, who was an eager beaver ready to teach us all how to do evangelism. We needed help, but I did not stop long enough even to wonder how mature he was. I lost, he lost, and so did a bunch of our people. Suzy had all the qualifications and skills but had a huge character flaw. She crashed and burned, exploding in a ball of fire that the enemy used to consume a hundred or so people. All these disasters might have been avoided with the discipleship process. Lou could have grown into his capacity, Billy would not have hung around, and Suzy could have found hope and healing. I have participated in the mess. I have contributed to people not having their best life. I never want to do it again.

Sustainable discipleship allows us to fix this for followers. It allows us to solve this for the Kingdom. The fourteen steps reveal what is next for each person—at any time, anywhere, and in any church. The steps help us intentionally lead each follower to the next place of growth. The fourteen steps are universal and universally crucial to each of us taking that next step. The steps apply to the new believer and the seasoned disciple. Understanding the steps is critical. Understanding the steps reveals the importance of focusing on who a disciple is (be) versus their actions (do). Remember, "be" always comes before "do." Always.

Step One
Be Convicted

Agreeing with God is the first step to following God. We follow God because we become convicted that He is right and that His way of living is better than what we have. We follow when we are convinced.

God convicts us because He loves us. He convicts us to do things. He convicts us not to do things. He convicts us of things that are right. He convicts of things that are wrong. He convicts us of who we are and who we are becoming. At the beginning of our faith, God convicts that He is God and that we are far away. God convinces us that He loves us. He convinces us that we need Him. He convinces us that He has a plan for our lives. He convinces us to accept that plan. God convicts us. It is a "do" for God, but it is a "be" for us.

We become convicted when we hear and agree with God's conviction. Convicted is a "be" for us. Being convicted that we need to be disciples happens in three ways.

- I can be convinced that I need to become a Christian. That would be the beginning of discipleship for me.
- I can be convinced that I need to be made a disciple, that I need to follow him for my own good. That would signal a need for discipleship.
- I can be convinced that as a disciple, I need to be part of a community focused on discipleship as practice. That would be the beginning of me walking with other disciples along the way.

Discipleship always begins with being convicted, but healthy conviction comes only from God. It is not our job to convict, to convince, or to cajole people into discipleship. It never works. These people will quit. Our role is to create a culture that allows God to convict (a good thing) each person that he needs to be a disciple. How can we create that culture?

- We take part in the process and practice of discipleship. We model its effectiveness.
- We teach people God's truths in a relevant, applicable way. We can make truth useful and show them that discipleship works.
- We illustrate value by sharing our success and failure.
- We invite them to join us in our best life ever.

Discipleship always begins with some form of conviction. And being convinced leads to a change of direction.

Step Two
Repent

Repenting is the thing we do after becoming convicted. Repenting is our response to God convincing us that we need to follow Him. Repenting turns us from our way to God's way.

Repenting is my response to God convincing me there is a better way. Repenting is me adjusting my life to God's truth. Repentance is necessary for anyone wanting to follow God.

Repenting happens one decision at a time as we turn our focus toward God and apply His truths. It is a process—sometimes happening quickly and sometimes taking more time. New believers repent as they become followers of God. They accept his conviction and take action. They say to Him, "Not my way. Your way. Forgive me." New believers turn from what they were to find who they are designed to be. They follow God as they turn toward their new faith and their new identity in Christ.

Repentance is the next step for anyone wanting to be closer to God. The follower turns from how he has been following and turns to a different process or practice. She turns from devotion to learning. He turns from rote prayers to meaningful, honest conversations with God. She begins to consume God's words and apply them to her life. He follows mentors and leaders experienced in the art of following God.

Repentance is not only a response to God convicting us that we are wrong. God also convicts us of what is right, good, and profitable. Repentance is always a positive response. It is the appropriate response to being convinced of God's better way at the moment. We need to show people how excited we are about repenting and how excited they should be, every time we repent. Repentance turns us to God—every time. It is a healthy part of the process and practice of discipleship.

The journey of discipleship is endless. Opportunity for great living expands with each truth we learn. But without repentance, we will find ourselves parked along the road, going nowhere.

Step Three
Be Taught

Disciples long to know what to do and what not to do. Conviction leads to repentance. Repentance leads to success.

Success with God leads to wanting to know more. Disciples need to be taught God's truths so that they can be convinced and follow God to even more successes. Being taught is not learning on your own. Being taught focuses on someone leading you. Being taught is like a baby bird in a nest, mouth open wide, chirping for more food.

Convicted, repentant people are humble. They recognize their need, and they are open to teaching. They, naturally, want to be taught. They reach out for more truth. People who want to go deeper are no different. They need God's word. They need mentoring. They need teaching. They need more truth.

This is where well-meaning churches and leaders fail. We lead people to God, we call people to a deeper walk, but we fail to teach them. We fail to have the time, resources, and leaders to walk with them along the way. New disciples need to be led. It is unrealistic to expect them to learn on their own as they begin their journeys. Their new life is full of more great opportunities and promises than they know. They do not even know what they do not know. They feel a change that they do not understand. They need to learn the truth. They need to learn how to adjust and apply God's truths. New disciples need to be led.

New disciples flounder, struggle, and often stall if we fail to provide the truth. We need to provide teaching from present and virtual mentors. We need to help keep the lights on until they learn to learn. They need to be taught useful truths that can be immediately applied. We need to show them what salvation means and who they are in Christ. We need to open the doors to an abundant life with God.

Teaching infuses the promise and hope that build confidence in disciples' lives. Teaching disciples how to apply truth fuels transformation. Teaching is critical to making enlightened and prepared disciples.

Step Four
Be Enlightened

It may sound a bit mystical for mainline Christianity, but people become enlightened as they are taught the truth. Truth is a light shining in the dark. A new light comes on each time we are exposed to a new truth about who we are, what God's promises are, and how applied truth can launch us to an even better life. Hope increases and brings peace with it. Expanded understanding of God and our relationship begins to transform us. We begin to know how to pray, and the Spirit moves less hindered in our hearts.

Enlightenment comes with every truth that we consume. I become more and more enlightened along the way of discipleship. I become more and more aware of who I am, who God is, how this works, and how to live the best life ever. Enlightened is the "be" that adds fuel and passion to the beginning of our discipleship path.

Step Five
Be Called

Being enlightened naturally leads to being called. Being called is not just about doing some great work for God, His church, or other people. God's simple truths call us to spend more time with Him. God calls us to worship. He calls us to let go of the old way and to live the new way. He calls us to believe each new truth. He calls us to be available for others as His love for us begins to revolutionize how we love others. He calls us to help each other as our focus moves from ourselves to Him and to His people.

Calling is a "do" for God. Being called is a "be" for us. I am a called person with a purpose and a mission. Hearing, feeling, and sensing His calling to be like Him, to join Him, and to enjoy life in community will lead people to do. But being called is who they become. We do not have to invite them to do anything. God is more than capable to move deep in their hearts as they hear His call to be His disciples.

Healthy followers hear God's calling. It is a natural result of focusing on God and spending time in communion with Him. I love it when one of our team begins to move from new enlightenment to being called to do that next new thing. Watching God move his troops around, and watching Him call His kids to him is fantastic. Being called is something we are. Being aware that we are the "called" of God changes us forever, and being the called of God seems to always lead to doing things for God and others.

Step Six
Serve

Discipleship is about following God. Following God will transform people into the very image of Jesus. Jesus served. Maturing followers will want to help as God transforms them to "think more of others."

God's truths and Spirit call the follower to do simple, fun, great, and humble things that are good for them. Service is part of our intricate design. Transformed people begin to stand at the end of the line, hand out the silverware, clean up after events, welcome newcomers, change tires, and help around the house. Deeper understanding causes us to put others before ourselves. Experiencing God causes us to put God's objectives before our calendars. We feel good as we serve. We feel that we have a purpose. We feel worth. Ultimately, we are feeling what it feels like to be who we are: transformed followers of God.

Unfortunately, Christians often mistake serving (doing) for maturity. Serving is only one step along the way. Churches associate serving with being a part of the church. There is much (really, too much) to do in our churches. Churches drain people with the chores of being a community. Leaders equate attendance and involvement with success. Christian movements stress putting others before ourselves while neglecting the self-care required to serve others. Churches get people so busy that they do not have time to feed the very thing that empowers service. More Christians stall at this step along the predictable pathway than anywhere else. Doing is not supposed to be the end goal, and doing often stifles being.

Serving is not the source of our worth. Serving is not our purpose. Being a follower of God is the source, the starting point that allows us to serve. Balance is the key to healthy growth at this step. We need to remind them to rest. We need to remind them that God did not save us for church life or for the world. He saved us to have an intimate, transformed relationship with Him. He wants us to thrive.

Serving, however, is critically important in discipleship. Service always reveals unseen amounts of selfishness that we can surrender. Service causes us to apply God's truths for living with each other and following leaders. Service provides opportunity to apply God's truths to our weaknesses and our interpersonal interactions. Service raises questions about ourselves and others. Service leads us to new breaking points providing a launching pad for growth. Nursery, sweeping, and other chores are the paths to humility. Serving is part of growing in Christ. Serving offers more opportunities to learn about God and follow Him than any other "do" on the list. It will happen; the disciples will serve.

Step Seven
Learn

Being inspired by great new truths, experiencing a relationship with God, and seeing His creation a bit differently fuels the fire for more learning. Perhaps it is the law of momentum.

Perhaps knowing a little good causes us to want to know more good. Perhaps it is curiosity. But there comes the point where disciples want to learn more. This is a critical juncture in making disciples. If we want to make sustainable disciples, we need to begin to teach them to learn on their own.

Disciples reach a point where they do not want to be given fish; they want to fish on their own. Children do this on their journey to adulthood. We teach them. They learn. They do. But there comes the point when they want to do it on their own. The yearning for independence comes in the toddler stage, in the teenage age, and with great fury in the twenties. This yearning to independently learn to learn should not be impeded. It is a significant step. It is an important step. Parents should hope for this step. Children need to become independent to become adults. It is time for parents to let go a little.

Discipling someone is the same. Leaders should have a secret agenda to get people to a place where they have learned to learn on their own. Leaders want them to begin to get the food, cook the food, eat the food, and for sure, clean up their mess. Becoming independent by learning (do) on your own is the gateway to you being prepared (be). Sustainable discipleship starts this process at the beginning of year two.

Step Eight
Be Prepared

What does it mean to be prepared? Being prepared is about being prepared for what is next. Being prepared will look different for different disciples. It varies based on their specific opportunities and direction. But it means what it means: the disciple is ready for what is coming next.

Prepared is a state of being fueled by truth and transformation. What is coming next does not matter. The disciple has been taught, practiced faithfully, endured trials, heard God, and learned to learn. The disciple knows that God is his God. He knows that he is a follower. He is confident. He understands enough and has faced enough challenges to know that he can succeed. She is prepared, confident, and skilled enough to begin to make disciples of others.

Sustainable discipleship leverages a variety of "first opportunities" at this step. Disciples are given "one-off" teaching opportunities. They take on assistant leadership roles on mission trips. They get real-time feedback, challenges, and questions to broaden their preparation. They are being prepared to follow and serve God. And they are ready to go "all in."

Step Nine
Be Consecrated

Being consecrated is being set aside for God. It is not something that someone does to you. It is not something you do. It is not something that God does to you. Being consecrated in the discipleship process either happens or it does not.

There comes the point where disciples will walk away or will walk through a door from which they will never return. It is a bit mystical, but it is very real. It is like Neo in *The Matrix* movie. He reached a point where his eyes were opened. He had a choice to go back into the matrix, or he could go on the journey for the truth. His mentor said,

> *You take the blue pill—the story ends, you wake up in your bed and believe whatever you want to believe. You take the red pill— you stay in Wonderland, and I show you how deep the rabbit hole goes. Remember: all I'm offering is the truth.*[3]

Disciples may have a moment where they decide to go all in. They may also just become all in. Becoming consecrated happens.

The disciple is set aside for God, abandoned, never wanting to go back. Being consecrated is not a youthful or emotional thought. It is a seasoned, count-the-cost, "I am all in" thought. It is the fulfillment of Jesus's words in the life of a disciple: No one can be my disciples unless he takes up his cross and follows me.[4]

Going back, walking away, is not a thought anymore. The implications of being consecrated are huge. Being consecrated sets oneself aside for God and for anything that He wants. Consecrated followers are set aside to lead others. They are His. They will always be seen following. They will always be seen serving. They will always be seen learning.

Step Ten
Residency

Residency is a period of "doing" something with a safety net. Residents get continued wisdom and guidance from an experienced mentor. The first step in residency takes place in year three[5] as the disciple makes other disciples. These new leaders now do the work of discipling. They lead a group through discipleship one. They are responsible, but they still have their leaders as a constant resource. Residency adds confidence and skill to their disciple making.

Residency, in year four,[6] focuses on the disciples' specific calling—their passion. God has told followers to use their gifts, to be wise, and to do their part for those around them. He has told them to reach the world. He has told them to reconcile the world to Him. Residency in year four adds the skills to their preparation and confidence.

Disciples take a year off from making disciples and begin to lead, to teach, to do that thing of passion. They still have a safety training net. Leaders walk beside the disciple as he "does" the work. Leaders make sure disciples have experienced people around them. Leaders help guide them spiritually and call to mind all the disciples have learned

Residency offers incredible opportunities to hone down skills and spiritual gifts, and explore opportunities. Residency provides a safe environment before disciples lead on their own. Jesus did this as He sent out disciples to heal, to spread the good news, and to teach.

Step Eleven
Lead

Prepared, confident, and skilled disciples set off to lead solo. Mature disciples lead their families differently. They repair relationships and embrace friendships where "iron sharpens iron." They have been led to follow God. They are pursuing their best day ever by following God's design. They strive to follow God in every moment, decision, and thought. They are confident, prepared, skilled followers. You will not be able to stop them from leading.

They will long to lead. They will lead, formally and informally. They will be models, teachers, and mentors to everyone in every situation. They will lead in the boardroom, in the kitchen, and in the break room.

They will lead among the body of believers as well. Some may become teachers, elders, pastors, and ministry heads. Others may lead in service as they are the head of the hands and feet. Maturing leaders may lead beside or behind emerging leaders. But disciples will lead. Disciples need to lead. They are prepared, confident, and skilled models, teachers, and mentors.

Sustainable discipleship always passes the torch to the next generation and is willing to follow their lead.

Step Twelve
Be Servant Driven

The discipleship pathway does not end with leadership. Leadership is the fertile ground where we face indignation, pride, self-worth, frustrations, and our own barriers. Leading is where we learn to live well with those we lead.

Jesus's model was service because He was a servant. Everything about His mission was founded on self-sacrifice that led to service. He served us the Gospel. He served individuals. He served up His life so that we could return to God. He was a servant, so He served.

This is the mature "be" of the earlier "do" service. I become a servant. I serve God and I serve others because I am a servant. Personally, I believe this to be the pinnacle of individual spiritual maturity.

We embrace humility in leadership. Servants are comfortable in their brokenness. Servants are comfortable giving all the credit to God. Servants are comfortable following. Servants serve those they follow, "washing their feet" at the end of those long days. Servants live the power of empathy and gratitude in their life and leadership.

One of my favorite things is serving under leaders I have raised up. I may be their teacher, but when they are leading that mission trip, event, or effort, I serve under them. I serve them. I do not take the questions from other followers. I have their back. And I always learn when following and serving these new leaders. It is counterintuitive to how most ministries function, but it is beautiful.

Servants are comfortable just standing by God's door, listening and waiting. It is about making God a success. It is about God.

Step Thirteen
Be Kingdom Minded

Being Kingdom minded is the corporate version of servant minded. Disciples begin to see that Christianity is not about their individual church. It is about the Church overall. They become part of God's bigger picture. They see God's plan to save the world. They embrace God's desire to save the world. They embrace the truth that the Kingdom of God is already on earth, waiting to grow.

Kingdom-minded disciples are deployable troops for God. He can use them in communities, ministries, and the lives of other people. They are available for His service wherever He is working. Kingdom-minded disciples get excited when other disciples hear the call to go somewhere else. Kingdom-minded disciples hold everything with an open hand.

The transition from being a servant to being Kingdom minded is part of discipleship three. Leaders push servants to see the global need. Disciples begin to pray for the world around them. They yearn to reach the world for Christ, to plant churches, and to participate in the bigger work of God. They are open to whatever is best for the Kingdom of God.

Being Kingdom minded is the corporate version of servant minded. Disciples must become Kingdom minded to become complete. It is the corporate version of personal selflessness.

Step Fourteen
Send

Disciples who are (be) Kingdom minded send (do.) They send help. They send leaders. They send themselves. They send around the world. They send next door. They send across the city. Kingdom-minded followers do not ignore the service they do in their local world, but they realize that their world is part of a bigger picture.

Kingdom-minded disciples invest their time, talent, and treasures in things that build up the Kingdom of God on earth. They invest in things like creating a culture of discipleship and making disciples. Kingdom-minded disciples plant churches and do missions. They work wherever and whenever it benefits the Kingdom of God on earth.

The discipleship pathway is intuitive and predictable. Our awareness and understanding of the pathway allow us to leverage God's truths at each step. We do not need to get new believers to be residents. Instead, we push them to repent and learn. We push residents to apply what they know by asking questions rather than give the answer. We do not launch people into leadership training until they are consecrated. The discipleship pathway guides our work as we guide individuals through the formal process of discipleship.

But the pathway also guides our comprehensive discipleship plan. It helps us think intentionally as we craft messages, plan events, and fill up our schedule. The classic questions of "Whom are we teaching?" "What do they need?" and "Where are they at?" come alive as we include different audiences in our discipleship plan. We can craft series that address the needs of the crowd to repent or to become enlightened. Our church shamelessly uses short-term mission trips as part of our comprehensive discipleship plan. We have developed a mission matrix that divides team members into categories along the pathway. Knowing whom we are traveling with allows us to use each planning meeting to move disciples down the path. Leveraging the discipleship pathway is one of the essential elements of sustainable discipleship.

As for a formal discipleship process, the pathway joins a four-year plan and comprehensive discipleship, almost completing the foundation. There are just a few more blocks to put in place in the sustainable-discipleship foundation.

12

USE THE SEVEN CORE PRACTICES

"The only thing worse than not having a plan is not using a successful plan that you do have."

— ANONYMOUS

Seven basic, necessary practices lie at the core of sustainable discipleship. Each of these practices is another building block in the foundation of sustainable discipleship. The seven core practices are as critical as

- planning on four years,
- deploying a comprehensive discipleship plan, and
- leveraging the predictable pathway.

Willing?

Each practice is used throughout each phase, each year, of sustainable discipleship. The seven practices are essential to the success of formal discipleship process. Sustainable discipleship will flounder, fall, and eventually fail if you do not employ these practices.

✳ *Core Practice 1* ✳
Regular, Structured, Efficient Meetings

Humans are creatures of habit. Routines work well for us. Same-day, same-time, same-place meetings make life easy. Groups tend to fall apart if the days and times move around too much. Again, humans can schedule anything, but regular things become, well, regular.

Weekly meetings are ideal for disciplineships one and two. Every-other-week meetings have some success for one-on-one discipleship but, always, fail with larger groups. Reviewing two weeks of reading takes too long in groups and reduces the effectiveness of learning along the way. It is important to note here: our experience shows that disciples have a greater tendency to waver, procrastinate, and stall out in the every-other-week method.

Weekly meetings keep the learning manageable. There is a limit to how much information the human brain can process in one sitting. Once-a-week meetings also keep discipleship involved and intimate. You will be amazed at what you learn, what you pick up on, and how easy it is to stay in touch with the ones you lead when you meet once a week.

Having two weeks between meetings can actually be a benefit during discipleship three. Disciples are beginning to transition from the formal process of discipleship to a lifetime of practice. They work more independently as they actively lead others and serve in ministry. Meeting every other week can enhance their independent work and prepare them to stand on their own. However, even discipleship three should begin with weekly meetings as you lay the foundation of expectations and knit the group together.

Discipleship meetings are always structured. Weekly meetings should not be a chit-chat session. There is important work to do. There is truth to be discovered and applied. It is imperative that the Bible be placed higher in importance than outside reading. The Bible is the key resource and should be covered before any other resources. Sustainable discipleship utilizes the following agenda for meetings.

Life Update and Prayer (5 minutes)

- This is the time when you ask those questions like, "How was the week?" or follow up on previous questions, such as, "Did you make up with your spouse?" Imperatively, each person prays aloud and only for himself and what he needs. Here are a few tips:
- Keep the questions and answers quick.
- Listen for needs that need to be met outside the meeting.
- Listen and pray that God will inspire your Bible review time to reveal truths that apply in real time to the needs you hear. There is nothing better than God providing a miracle answer, unplanned from the text being reviewed. Look for it.
- Prayers are not about spouses, kids, aunts, or ministries.
- Keep it short.

Bible Reading Review (55 minutes)

- This is the time when you review the highlights from the previous week's Bible reading. When done in a group, you do it all at once. "Did anyone have anything in chapter 2?" The group will quickly find a rhythm that you do not have to manage. Use this time to push and hold accountable anyone who has not been reading well. Use the "Critical Thinking" method[1] to review the week's text.

- Cover their highlights, relate truths, and make connections.
- Adjust the reading schedule, if needed (customization).
- Point them to any big truths they may have missed.

Extra-Biblical Reading Review (30 minutes)

- This, like the Bible review, is done using the Critical Thinking method.
- Focus on application.
- Remember, "be" is the first application, not "do."
- Ask, "What do you do with it?"

Relational Chit-Chat (no more than 30 minutes)

The target duration for the formal part of the meeting is ninety minutes—no more, no less.[2] Experience has taught us that longer meetings are less profitable. Longer meetings have no greater results than a ninety-minute meeting. We have also found that meetings less than ninety minutes are "cheating" somewhere. Disciples may not be reading well, or leaders are tired. Somewhere, a shortcut is happening. The ultimate goal is ninety action-packed minutes, once a week. Every-other-week meetings will need more time.

Core Practice 2
Cover-to-Cover Bible Reading

Disciples read the entire Bible in each year of discipleship using a clear, weekly plan. They will read God's words four times along the way. What better can we do for people than to get them to consume all of His biblical truths, principles, and precepts? The Bible is the record of mankind's interaction with God from the beginning of time. The successes, failures, stumbles, repentance, faith, miracles, and lives recorded spark priceless thoughts and provide endless teaching opportunities.

Comparing creation with evolution and God's forgiveness with mankind's forgiveness introduces the opportunity to see the greatness of God. Wrestling with God's selection of really messed-up leaders opens the door to understanding God's value of brokenness. Watching God's interaction with men and women will deepen the disciples' understanding of God. Reading how Moses changed God's mind, how Saul fell from his throne, and how murderous Paul became a model Christian challenges the best of believers.

Reading cover to cover quietly models and teaches the best study method: inductive, exegetical study. Students begin to discover truths in their immediate context and, later, assimilate those truths cover to cover. Reading the complete Bible four times provides the disciples with endless truths to apply along the way. God's words become the fuel that His Spirit can use to transform the disciples' lives.

The method of Bible reading systematically changes each year, moving the disciple from an observer to a learner, to being apt to teach.[3] There is no replacement for this foundational block of sustainable discipleship.

Core Practice 3
Extra-Biblical Reading

Sustainable discipleship leverages extra-biblical literature to provide virtual mentors and to customize the discipleship process.

> *A wise man is full of strength, and a man of knowledge enhances his might, for by wise guidance you can wage your war, and in abundance of counselors there is victory.*

> — PROVERBS 24:5–6 (ESV)

The "sustainable-discipleship library" is broad. It includes fifty or so extra-biblical novels and doctrinal, creative, business, topical, theological, inspirational, and instructional books read throughout the three phases.[4] The library broadens the discipleship platform, bringing in new voices and virtual mentors. Each volume has been tested and integrated to achieve specific teaching purposes. *The Book of Mystical Chapters* by John Anthony McGuckin is only used in discipleship three. *Do Over* by Jon Acuff is used to customize discipleship in any phase. Other volumes are specific to the specific steps on the predictable pathway. For example, the "16 Key Topics in Christianity"[5] workbook is always covered in the first sixteen weeks of discipleship one. Some books speak to leadership for those in business or in discipleship three. *Six Thinking Hats* by Edward de Bono is used as a launching pad for how our regular meetings will work. We use *Good to Great* by James C. Collins, *Deep and Wide* by Andy Stanley, and *Breakout Churches* by Thom S. Rainer during the preparation and residency steps. *How to Pray* by R.A. Torrey and *The Search for Significance* by Robert S. McGee are essential during discipleship one. Novels such as *And the Shofar Blew* by Francine Rivers and *This Present Darkness* by Frank E. Peretti open up the topics of spiritual warfare, prayer, and the challenges of ministry and community. The list goes on and on, with each resource creating a needed push for the one being made a disciple.

The learning and discussions that come from the extra-biblical reading are incredible. Disciples apply truths, discern, and think differently as extra-biblical reading is tied to biblical truths already learned. Sustainable discipleship keeps people reading and pushes for timely, while realistic, completion deadlines. There are no breaks in outside reading.

The sustainable-discipleship library has been designed to support the discipleship process in very specific topical and theological ways. It is a strategic library focused on what will get disciples to the next step or meet their current needs. The library has been developed and tested reactively over many years, and it works. However, our experience helping others disciple in varying cultures, denominations, and journeys has shown that adapting the library is sometimes beneficial. There are times when additional books or replacement books work better.

Whether you use and modify our library or develop your own, keep your library manageable and strategic. It should only include resources that are necessary and, more importantly, timeless. It should not have repetitive volumes but unique resources that represent the best work on a topic or matter.

Core Practice 4
Mission Trips and Service Opportunities

Sustainable discipleship leverages mission trips and service projects to disciple people along the way. Mission trips and projects create unique stress and pressure points for participants who they may not usually face. Here are a few examples:

- Most people do not live, eat, or sleep with fifteen people. Living together on mission raises issues of modesty and character. Living together for introverts is a real push.
- Different cultures, food, schedules, and environments create opportunities for empathy, patience, and endurance.
- Exhaustion from long days tends to expose weaknesses otherwise left dormant.
- Doing the work of evangelism, teaching, or construction pushes people to learn new skills, take risks, and build confidence.
- Experiencing the challenges of poverty and death fosters brokenheartedness.
- The endless amount of need for ministry fosters world vision and Kingdom mindedness.

- Faith is required to do things that are different, greater, and beyond us. Learning to use power tools, being asked to create an agenda, and trying to meet endless needs requires faith and active prayer.

There is a unique power to "being in the trenches together." Leaders and followers experience life differently together. Relationships grow deep, and intimate discipleship blossoms.

Short-Term Mission Trips

Mission trips are a vital component in our disciple-making process. Mission trips require that people live and work together for an extended period out of their usual context. Mission trips provide an excellent opportunity to accelerate and enhance the discipleship process. There is something about being on the front lines, tired, happy, scared, excited, and desperate for God that bonds us and creates real opportunities for discipleship "along the way." We use *The Perfect Trip* discipleship-based, mission training program for our teams. It reinforces God's truths about teamwork, unity, the body of Christ, self-worth, prayer, and faith. The Perfect Trip focuses on who the participant is and will become as a result of the mission.

Sustainable discipleship relies on short-term mission trips. If that does not work for your context, replace it with something exhausting and challenging. Create opportunities requiring the sacrifice of time, talent, and money. Get them in the field, doing something unfamiliar, challenging, and meaningful. Create circumstances for intense growth over the course of several days.

Service Opportunities

Discipleship is done along the way. Special and regular service opportunities are an integral part of our model. Special service opportunities are one-offs. Regular service opportunities are day to day. These opportunities model, teach, and mentor disciples as they regularly serve others. Day-to-day service has its own unique challenges.

It is one thing to go on a challenging, fun mission trip; it is entirely a different thing to clean toilets every Sunday before guests arrive. It is one thing to go on one trip a year; it is another thing to serve regularly by sprucing up the place, taking care of children, or setting up for that next event. Our church let go of our janitorial service to create challenging service opportunities for disciples. We challenge the experienced to step aside and create service openings when we prepare for events and services.

Leaders serve alongside, looking for opportunities to cheer, encourage, and teach. You will be amazed at how much you can model and teach while you clean a bathroom. Leaders push, require, and recruit disciples to serve with them. Regular service confronts the challenges of endurance, dedication, pride, and family time. Life happens day to day. Discipleship does as well.

Walking and working together provides endless opportunities to ask questions, to challenge followers, to point out truth, and to share your story with those you lead. There is nothing more powerful than truths coming alive in the moment. There is nothing more powerful than being there in the moment to care for, guide, and walk with those you lead.

Core Practice 5
Critical Thinking

The Foundation for Critical Thinking defines critical thinking as

> *That mode of thinking — about any subject, content, or problem — in which the thinker improves the quality of his or her thinking by skillfully analyzing, assessing, and reconstructing it. Critical thinking is self-directed, self-disciplined, self-monitored, and self-corrective thinking.*[6]

The oldest documented method of critical thinking is the Socratic method. The Socratic method "is a form of cooperative argumentative dialogue between individuals, based on asking and answering questions to stimulate critical thinking and to draw out ideas and underlying presumptions."[7]

Critical thinking leads the disciple from being taught to being one who learns. It is essential to developing prepared, confident, and skilled followers of God. Critical thinking provides the opportunity for followers to learn, synthesize, and apply the truths of God.

Critical thinking also keeps the Bible in context. It underlies reliable, exegetical Bible study. Disciples learn to interrogate the words of God and see what those words have to say. Disciples question why God said what He said. Critical thinking gets behind the rules and looks for the principles and precepts that drive the rules.

Critical thinking pushes disciples to the point of application and develops a much deeper understanding of God's truths. We need to improve the overall quality of our thinking. We need to ask God our questions. We need to compare the words in one part of the Bible with the word in other parts.

Sustainable discipleship does not use classroom teaching. It asks and answers questions to help disciples grow their understanding and their ability to understand.

- Weekly Bible reading focuses on what the disciple "sees" as he reads. This approach forces him to read the Bible, expecting and looking for truth. In essence, the disciple is approaching the Bible with an initial question, "What does God have for me today?"
- During the review time, the leader asks, "So what did God show you? What did you find? What was awesome? What don't you understand? Let's go over your highlights."

- In response to an "aha" highlight, the leader may ask, "So how do you apply that?" and then, "How does that apply to others?"
- In response to an "I don't know" highlight, the leader might ask, "Where else have you seen that topic?"

The leader is guiding the disciple back to God's words and causing him to think critically. This teaches the disciple to learn on his own. Yes, there are times when you will need to give an answer. There are times when the well of knowledge is not deep enough yet for the disciple to make a needed connection. However, you should push the disciples to critical thinking because it causes them to integrate and remember all that the Spirit has taught them.

Critical thinking must be paired with a mindset of application to make sustainable disciples. Truth left unapplied is nothing but knowledge. Every moment that we make disciples is a moment to guide the application of God's words and truths. Sustainable discipleship constantly reinforces the truth that transformation comes by application. Disciple makers must stay focused on application, in the trenches, along the way, during reading reviews, and in every casual moment.

Use questions. Guide. Let them learn how to follow God.

 Core Practice 6
Teach What You Know to Be True

This was Jesus's command to us. "Teach what I have taught you," He said. There is no room for guessing or opinion in discipleships one and two. We should have no doubt about the truths that are consumed by those we lead. There should be no doubt when we are asked to help with a difficult passage. "I think" is a fine phrase for the one being taught, but "I think" does not work for the leader. You must teach what you know and teach only what you know.

I came out of a life of partying and, well, excess. Salvation, forgiveness, and love made me never want to be who I was. I associated drinking with my old life. My first church did too. I noticed something inconsistent on my first complete Bible read: everybody drank wine, everywhere, all the time. Heck, even Jesus made excellent wine. I asked a few leaders and got the classic answers: it was really grape juice; and it was the only safe beverage. I accepted those answers. I was young. I quietly became a nondrinker and less quietly judged those who drank. While studying in seminary, I realized that wine was wine in the Bible. (Everything fermented—they had no refrigeration!) I realized that no one banished wine. The Bible taught, "Do not drink too much," but that teaching was less forceful than the teaching on gluttony. Even Paul told Timothy to drink a little wine for his stomach. I softened but still abstained.

Then I got sick, and my doctor told me, "You need to have two small glasses of red wine, twice a day." Paul's words to Timothy rang in my head. I will never forget buying my first bottle. I kept looking up and down the aisle to make sure that no one I knew was around. I was nervous at the checkout counter every time. It was so stupid. I joke that Paul probably had to tell Timothy to drink a glass of wine because Timothy was just as worried as I was. I can see him standing in the market, facing the same uneasy feeling. I can see him looking for those, like me, who judged. The point is that I was put into bondage, led to judge, and had to struggle later because someone taught me what they thought instead of what the Bible said. They could have taught me the real truth instead of some truth they inherited by tradition. I could have handled it. I needed it. I would have learned the truth of balance, avoiding its dangers and not needing to drink alcohol. I would have focused more on freedom, balance, and wisdom. That, however, is not the end of the story—I became "them."

I taught people for years that tattoos were pretty much of the devil. The Bible said it. It was simple. I loved people, and I did not judge them, but I taught anti-tattoo theology and quietly questioned those marked-up people. God loved them. Why did they ignore His words? Then a tattooed lady asked me for a verse. I went to find it and found that what I thought was there was not so clear. It had been taken out of context by those who taught me! We were told not to mark ourselves in mourning like the pagans. The truth was about being different from those who have no hope in death. I had been failed again, but this time, I also made the error of not checking out what I was taught. I was teaching what I thought, not what I knew to be true.

The Berean Christians were praised for checking truths out. They did not assume or inherit.

And the people of Berea were more open-minded than those in Thessalonica, and they listened eagerly to Paul's message. They searched the Scriptures day after day to see if Paul and Silas were teaching the truth. As a result, many Jews believed, as did many of the prominent Greek women and men.

— ACTS 17:11–12

Dangerous, legalistic, judgmental, and life-wasting truths are passed on and taught because we teach what we think rather than what we know. We should teach what we know and can show.

Knowing and showing are the guarantee that you teach what you know. You should have a simple, irrefutable verse or verses that taught you what you teach. Avoid useless arguments about doctrine, tradition, and things we cannot solve. Be confident enough to say, "I do not know. I will look it up," or, "I have studied, and I just do not know. I may never know, and I cannot find anyone who can know and show." There are things we will never understand on this earth. Accepting that you will not (and perhaps should not) know everything reaches all the way back to Genesis chapter 3. Remember the serpent saying, "You can know. You should know. You need to know." It was a lie then. It is a lie now.

Teach what you know and what you can show. Teach what is useful and what is important to God. Do not use His words to make your point. Do not lead those you lead astray. Give them the best—teach what is useful and what you know to be true.

Core Practice 7
Push Them

Discipleship is not a spectator sport. It might be better described as a full-contact sport. Those who make disciples not only teach and guide, but they also push. Sustainable discipleship is a constant push to each of us. It is a push during the formal process. It is a push in our lifetime practice. Those who make disciples will have to push those they make as disciples. Peer disciples will push each other to grow, to apply, and to remain steadfast as followers of God. Discipleship pushes each of us to be all that we are designed to be.

In the early years, we tried to be gentle and accommodating. We wanted to disciple as many people as we could. We have also been timid and intimidated by strong personalities who did not want to change. We should have found someone else to disciple those people. Discipleship never works when the disciple leads the process.

You have to lead the process. You have to push them to read and stay on schedule. You have to push them into missions and service experiences beyond them. You have to push them when they make excuses or fail to apply truth. You have to push them to open up. You have to push them to embrace transformation. You push them like a coach, a trainer, and a friend. You push them so they can be closer to God and experience the incredible life that He has designed for them.

Disciple leaders need knowledge and confidence so that they can push when they need to push. Pushing is not bullying or badgering. Pushing does not exasperate people. Pushing is course correction done with great empathy and transparency. Pushing may require that you tell part of your story that illustrates success and failure. Pushing requires a balance between passion and compassion. But you must push because you want the best for them.

13

CUSTOMIZE THE PROCESS

"To such an extent does nature delight and abound in variety that among her trees there is not one plant to be found which is exactly like another."

— LEONARDO DA VINCI, *THOUGHTS ON ART AND LIFE*

C reation is full of variety. Humanity is no different. Humanity is full of varying personalities, talents, thought processes, and gifts. Some of humanity's variety comes from birth, through genetics and creation. Some of humanity's variety is inherited through environment, challenge, hurt, and upbringing. You will never create sustainable disciples without understanding and embracing God's variety. Jesus changed His approach when He discipled crowds, small groups, and individuals. He addressed people's challenges individually and leveraged those lessons for the groups that surrounded them. Jesus addressed the twelve followers differently than He did the larger groups. The apostles were a mixed bag of men, and Jesus interacted and led them differently along the way. He taught the group, but He discipled them intimately and individually. They were a group of individual followers. It seems so obvious, and yet it is counterintuitive to most discipleship methods.

I signed up for a popular, intensive prayer-and-discipleship program during one of the tougher seasons in my life. It began with a four-hour session designed to get to the root of the problems. The couple who led me were passionate and seemed to really love God, but the whole thing failed me. I arrived, and we began talking. They looked at their three-ring binders as they asked questions, pushed for honesty, and poked and prodded. It did not take long to realize that they were using a decision tree to try to get to the root of "the problem." It did not take much longer to realize that I did not fit into any of the program's three categories: addiction, sexual immorality, and daddy issues. It was brutal. They asked me why I was there. "I am here because I am broken, tired, and suffering persecution from my peers. I am open to anything that brings hope and healing." It was as if they did not hear me. They went back and asked if I had an issue with porn, if I had ever been abused, if I had ever had a homosexual experience, if I was using drugs or alcohol to cope, and if I had a good relationship with my dad. The male leader got so frustrated that he got somewhat abusive: "We cannot help you if you will not be honest and open up about these things!" They had me close my eyes, pray, and picture a wall blocking my path. "What is the first block that needs to go for you to be healed?" I had no idea. And back we went again to the program's three core men's issues. They finally gave up and told me that they could not help me. I agreed and got out of there.

This program has a big reputation for bringing hope and healing to people. I have no doubt that they have helped people with addiction, sexual, or daddy issues—but what about the people like me who do not fit their model? Almost every discipleship model or method has a standard target or set of teaching.

Leaders, most often, approach discipleship with a cookie-cutter approach. We package programs for mass distribution. We provide standard plans. Little of this reflects God's two irrefutable models of discipleship.

The goal of discipleship is to help individuals understand who they are and what they can be. Discipleship helps individuals apply God's transforming truths and releases them as prepared, confident, and skilled to live their best life.

One size does not fit all when it comes to life matters. We are in different places and in different situations. We come to discipleship with different physical and spiritual maturities. We learn differently. Some of us face significant learning challenges. Groups have exponential variety and challenges. Embracing variety, with all its challenges, is one of the keys to sustainable discipleship. I call it "customization." Sustainable discipleship customizes discipleship by

- following God as He transforms each disciple,
- reaching people according to their design and experience,
- adjusting to practical limitations of disciples, and
- using group discipleship.

Understanding, adjusting to, and leveraging variety brings exponential power and effectiveness to the disciple-making process.

Following God as He Transforms Each Disciple

God can make disciples without you. He is the one who makes disciples. He is the one who transforms. My life—and many other lives—is an example. Anyone who wants God and wants to follow God is a follower (disciple). Anyone can become prepared, confident, and skilled on their own. We are only the guides.[1] Both of the biblical models of discipleship

- call people to God,
- proactively (ahead of the need) pass on the truths of God,
- reactively (in the time of need) teach and illustrate how to apply God's truths, and
- remind people of the value of knowing God and living out their God-given design.

The idea here is that we will intuitively know what to teach (proactively and reactively) as we walk along the way. We will know the next step to call people to as we walk along the way. We will remind them and cheer them on relative to their current journey. In essence, we join God as physical guides, helping them with tips and tricks to find and follow God. We watch their journey and disciple in every moment. Henry Blackaby and Claude King taught me an incredible truth in their work, *Experiencing God*: "Watch to see where God is working and join Him."[2]

Sustainable discipleship observes God working in the disciple and joins him there. This method of discipleship customizes discipleship for each person as they encounter God. Sustainable discipleship leverages this natural customization as disciples read the Bible cover to cover, identifying the truths and questions that "stick out" as they read.[3] Disciples are asked to find things that surprise them and confuse them as they read God's word. Disciples are asked to uncover truths about God's character and connect those truths to other biblical truths. Disciples are asked to find truths that seem disconnected from the rest of the Bible. Each phase of discipleship has a different focus as disciples are asked to see different things. Each reading of the Bible brings a new set of observations as disciples experience God's word, challenging and transforming their lives. The

Holy Spirit prompts different truths for different disciples at different times. George Mueller addressed this decades ago when he wrote,

> *Whilst we are in the body, we need a change even in spiritual things; and this change the Lord has graciously provided in the great variety which is to be found in His word.*

— GEORGE MUELLER, *ANSWERS TO PRAYER*

The Spirit works differently in each follower. It is our job, as disciple makers, to stay out of God's way as he individually transforms individuals. It is our job to help individuals see the bigger picture and see the truths of God in their highlights. Some truths will be stored, and others immediately applied. Some truths will push big concepts, and others are one-time revelations. Disciples highlight what "sticks out" to them, allowing God to use His Spirit to raise topics, convict, and guide each disciple along the way. We only need to see where He is working in their lives and help them find Him there. We should rarely coach or coax them to find particular truths in the text. Instead, we should address what the Holy Spirit raises in the individual. We cheer on the "aha" moments and, perhaps, expand or correct the disciple's understanding of those moments. The process of making disciples becomes customized as we follow God, answering the disciple's questions that arise as he reads God's word. Joining God where he is working instead of teaching a standard curriculum extends to the disciple's extra-biblical reading. Joining God, where He is working, leverages learning moments while disciples do missions, serve others, and live day to day.

You have two critical roles in the natural customization of discipleship: allow the Holy Spirit to guide the disciple; and help the disciple understand, expand, and apply the truths that the Spirit raises in his life. We should follow God's leading as we lead the disciples to follow Him. Being aware of the natural process of customization brings the opportunity to plan for customization intentionally.

Reaching People According to Their Design and Experience

Each person is a unique creation. God did that. Each person has very different experiences. Life did that. Everyone has a different brain, personality, soul, and experience. Disciples have different histories, different talents, different gifts, and different futures. Some followers will be analytical, some touchy-feely, and some entrenched in traditions. Others will be big-picture thinkers, introverts, or dreamers. You will have to guide the analytical away from details that are certain to derail big God ideas. You will have to guide the more emotional to base their lives on the data of what God's word actually teaches. Dreamers will need to embrace the discipline of doing the work. The workers will need to be pushed to dream. Leading people requires that we understand how they think—who they are designed to be. This is the intentional method of discipleship that customizes discipleship to each person—who they are, where they are, and what they need.

Amber and I have an incredible life-and-ministry coach. We met Charity at Blessing Ministries during our premarital coaching. As Charity talked to Amber and got to know her, I began to hear that Amber did not feel understood or, often, heard. I thought we were great. Sure, we handled conflict differently. I wanted to talk, and she wanted me to stop talking. She thought quietly about problems that we faced. I impatiently (and apparently inconsiderately) waited. It was becoming apparent that this was a bigger problem for Amber than I knew. I was getting overwhelmed. Charity asked, "Doug, do you get introverts?" My blank face begged for hope. "Extroverts get their energy from interacting with others. They restore and refresh with interaction. Introverts are the exact opposite. They restore, renew, and refresh alone. Introverts need alone time. Extroverts process externally. Introverts process internally."

A light bulb went off in my brain: Amber and I were not the same, and we have never been the same. It clicked. One of the most confusing moments in our dating was me questioning her feelings for me because she wanted to be alone. The light was on! I had been seeing Amber through the eyes of an extrovert, where withdrawing meant that you did not want to be around someone. Who would want to be alone or away from someone they loved? Who wouldn't want to talk? An introvert—that is who. I needed to let Amber be who she was, and she me. This simple understanding brought new power to our team. I began to see her through new eyes—eyes that had a great appreciation for her strengths that balanced my exuberance. We adjusted. Amber tags along with my extrovert needs, and I learned to let her be alone and to give her time to process. Funny, I am so much more comfortable without people now.

I mention this example because it revolutionized how I make disciples. One of the first things I discover is whether the disciple is more introvert or extrovert. If they are introverts, I do not worry so much if they are quiet or doodling while we talk. If they are extroverts, I push them to breathe a bit. Introverts require a day or two to process a big push or challenge from God. Extroverts need to finish the process live. People are different. We need to disciple them differently.

Relating to people who have been hurt by others is another excellent example. You must build trust before pushing a wounded person too much. You have to be careful not to exasperate them. You have to give unconditional love and acceptance. You have to show them that you will not abandon them. You have to show them that you are on their team and want the best for them.

Relating to analytical introverts presents a big challenge. They tend to get sidetracked on details that will never transform them. These unique, powerful learners need to be pushed away from historical detail. They must be pushed to focus on finding God's character, His desire. You have to show them how to uncover truths that will transform how they think, decide, and live. The list goes on and on, but the truth does not change: we need to know whom we are leading and customize our approach to their lives. We need to embrace the strengths of their makeup while building up opposing strengths to make them well-rounded followers. We need to be considerate of their weaknesses and push them to move forward. Discipleship is a dance —each time with a different partner, on a different dance floor, to a different tune.

When done well, sustainable discipleship allows God to determine the tune for the dancers He created.

As we allow the Holy Spirit to customize discipleship naturally, we need to partner with God to intentionally customize discipleship. Our approach to each disciple should be Holy Spirit driven, wise, and specific to his life. The opportunities that we create for growth need to correlate with what God is doing in their lives. The resources that we get them to read (and when they read them) need to be consistent with where the disciple is and where they need to go next. The mission, service, and other opportunities need to relevant and appropriate.

Bailey was in one of my coed, larger groups. She had a few years of Bible college under her belt. She showed up with only one or two highlights ("ahas" or questions) of her Bible reading. She had also been hurt by churches. She was timid. I knew what was going on. She grew up in the church. She went to Bible college. She was not reading the Bible fresh. She was a trained Bible-study person. She had studied the facts. Sadly, she was missing many incredible life-transforming truths right in front of her. Bob was also in our group. He was raised a Christian. He had heard all the stories. He, too, was not reading fresh. He was not focusing on the task of finding truths that apply to his life today. Both of them were skimming the text, taking mental shortcuts because they had been exposed to it before. The problem got fixed, but I took a different approach for each of them. I did not push Bailey too hard. "Bailey, do you have any highlights in this chapter? No? Okay, let's see what other people have found." I was still building trust, and I eventually pushed her to do the work. I had one of our lady discipleship leaders there when I sat with her individually, explaining and pushing her to do the work. I lovingly stressed transformation as the goal. Bob was different. I pushed him in front of the group. He is an extrovert, confident, transparent, and open. "Bob, come on, you are not reading this fresh. How could you not have found one life-application truth? You've got this. Did you see how Moses got in God's face? What can you learn from that?" My "Bob" approach would have destroyed Bailey.

We need to know where each disciple is along the pathway and provide what is needed at that point. Even in groups, we need to dance with them individually and intimately. Our ability to connect with them, to hear the Spirit guide us, and to be good observers are our strengths. John Russell, former president of Harley-Davidson, said, "The more you engage with customers the clearer things become and the easier it is to determine what you should be doing."

Knowing who they are is one part of the equation. Understanding the pathway and having an individual, intentional plan to get them to the next step is our strategy. The formal assessment[4] and observing each disciple along the way will aid you in doing your job to lead each person to God. Identifying where the follower is on the predictable pathway identifies the starting point for their discipleship. Sally was always getting defensive when I would ask her to pray more specifically. She rolled her eyes when I asked her why she highlighted a particular passage. Her defensiveness came out as cranky challenges to my ability. Her insecurity drove her to challenge my pushes to others in the group. She would actually interrupt and say things like, "I do not think you are being fair to Sue. You have to understand her," or, "So you are saying that lying is okay? I disagree." After two weeks of this, I pushed back. "Sally, do you trust me?" The group got quiet. "It's okay if you don't, but you need to know that I actually have a plan. You need to know that I love you." The group stayed quiet. "I'm sorry," she started. I said, "No. Don't be sorry. It is okay. I am fine with you. If you could, just listen all the way through my comments and not assume that I am hurtful." Then I turned to the group: "We are all coming from different places. Some of you have been hurt by churches, pastors, and people. Some of you have had to fight to be heard. It is not like that here. We are all on this journey together. Our goal is to face the challenge of God's words individually. My job is to help each of you as individuals along the way." It turns out that Sally knew that she was terribly performance oriented. She was pushed as a young adult to be perfect. She was wounded by people. She resorted, like most of us, to controlling her environment. She needed to be reached individually and uniquely so that we could all continue to explore God's truths in the Bible. She needed to be pushed to the step of repentance.

The predictable pathway is biblical. You will find yourself developing standard approaches and solutions for common challenges. Sustainable discipleship is very practical, but discipleship requires customization. We must pray for God's insight, His words, and His help to guide individuals. Hearing from the Holy Spirit in the moment is critical to help the disciple identify and apply God's truths. Hearing from the Holy Spirit is the key to know when to push and when to avoid exasperating the one you make a disciple. Intentional customization is more complicated than a cookie-cutter approach to making disciples. It requires you to be prepared, confident, and skilled in God's word and in leading others. You have to be ready to react. You have to know your stuff. You have to be quick on your feet. You have to be listening to the Holy Spirit. You must customize your approach if you want to make sustainable disciples.

Adjusting to the Practical Limitations of Disciples

Some people have limitations. Life happens. We need to be willing to adjust our process. Nathanael is a dear friend, compadre, and part of my third generation of disciples. "What do I do with this?" his email opened. I sat back and read the note from one of the men in discipleship: "I am sorry, I don't want to quit. I just can't read. After my illness, this is the first time I have tried to read like this. It is killing me. The doctors are trying to find a medicine . . ."

Jack had suffered through five years of a traumatizing brain illness. The illness changed everything from his personality to his ability to process. He had risen above the challenge and was returning to ministry, but Jack had new limitations.

"I haven't faced this before," Nathanael said. "Any thoughts?"

"I wouldn't let him quit."

"How is he going to do it without the reading?"

"I have no clue. Never faced this in twenty years. But surely, Jesus would not turn him away. If we had a guy in a wheelchair, we would build a ramp. This sucks for him. We need to figure out what ramp to build."

Many disciples struggle with reading. They would have excelled in the old days, when everything was passed by oral tradition. We recommend Audible and YouVersion for those who struggle with reading. Some disciples struggle with attention deficit, language barriers, and poor study habits. We recommend tricks, translators, and great ideas to study a little at a time. This, however, was the first time that a physical disorder prevented reading.

"What if we let him just come and sit in? He wants to be a disciple. He just can't read without killing his brain. So let him keep coming, praying, and just let him interact. He will get what they get and get some things as he asks about their things."

"What is that going to do to the whole 'you only talk about your own stuff' in discipleship groups?" Nathanael asked.

It was a good question. One of the prime directives of sustainable discipleship is that people get discipled individually, even in groups. The leader can lead the entire group, but the individuals only ask and interact on their highlights. What I proposed was a serious violation of our usual group practices. Would Jack interacting on others' highlights derail the group? How would Nathanael guide the process? Would the group meander? Would it affect the individual discipleship of others?

"I guess the stuff he hears and what the Holy Spirit does in the moment will be his stuff. We will just have to deal with it and figure it out."

Jack returned to the group. Nathanael was honest with the group about the challenges. The group embraced Jack. Nathanael navigated the customization. It was not ideal, but it worked. You will face similar, very practical challenges when discipling people as individuals. Customize discipleship, pray, try things, and make discipleship available to everyone. No discipleship model should limit the ability of people to be made disciples.

Using Group Discipleship

Discipling Jack required that Nathanael customize the group. Customizing group discipleship is exponentially more difficult than individual customization. There are so many different personalities and pathways coming together. Would it have been easier to disciple Jack individually? Would every person benefit from the individuality and intimacy of one-on-one discipleship? Years of experience, trials, and errors have proven the exact opposite to be true. Sustainable disciples are made more effectively and efficiently in groups.

It sounds counterintuitive. So many people think the crown jewel to making disciples is to make them one-on-one. The parental model of discipleship in Deuteronomy seems to support this idea. I do not know who started it or when it started, but I inherited this model as well. One person making one disciple was the optimal method. It sounded great. It was definitely intimate and individual. It allows the maker to focus on one person. But if one-on-one is so great, why do most discipleship programs use groups? The answer is simple: making disciples one-on-one is inefficient because we do not have enough prepared, confident, and skilled disciple makers to pull it off.

Dallas Willard said, "We are coming into a time when many churches and Christians who are in leadership positions will be able to say, 'It's all about discipleship and transformation into Christlikeness.'"

If your dream is like Dallas's, you will face the inefficiency of one-on-one discipleship. You will need to figure out a way to disciple many people at the same time. You will need to disciple groups without losing the beauty of individual, intimate, along-the-way discipleship.

But even when we have the capacity to make disciples one-on-one, groups remain more effective. Why? Groups allow disciples to experience more of God's truths. Disciples get to "listen in" on someone else's individual discipleship. They experience others' "aha" moments and the coaching and teaching that goes along with those moments. They are part of a mini-body of Christ. Learning becomes exponential as the body of Christ functions the way it is supposed to function. Each individual brings something different to the table, making up a complete meal.

Our experience and research show that a group with one leader and three followers is optimal. A one-to-three ratio is the most effective and efficient way to make disciples. Disciples made this way are sturdier, more well rounded, and more challenged. They get more "bang" for every hour invested. Jesus did this. He leveraged individual discipleship for groups again and again. One of my favorite examples is the story of the paralytic. The paralytic's friends brought him to Jesus for healing. Healing was their perceived need for their friend, but Jesus has something different in mind. He skipped the friend's perceived need and met the real need of the paralytic.

Then they [the friends] lowered the sick man on his mat down into the crowd, right in front of Jesus. Seeing their faith, Jesus said to the man, "Young man, your sins are forgiven."

— LUKE 5:19–20

The crowd of religious leaders went crazy, saying, "Who does He think he is? That's blasphemy! Only God can forgive sins!" Then Jesus leveraged his individual disciple making for the crowd:

"Why do you question this in your hearts? Is it easier to say 'Your sins are forgiven,' or 'Stand up and walk'? So I will prove to you that the Son of Man has the authority on earth to forgive sins." Then Jesus turned to the paralyzed man and said, "Stand up, pick up your mat, and go home!"

— LUKE 5:22–24

Experiencing the benefits of individual discipleship as a group is powerful. Disciples learn the lessons of others. They learn to adjust to and embrace the variety of God's people. They learn from the variety found in groups. Larger groups are more difficult but doable. Mass groups work less well, but all groups produce better followers than the one-on-one model. Groups make many disciples simultaneously. The problem is that most group approaches become standardized processes or classes. How do you provide intimate, individual discipleship in a group? You customize the group.

Sustainable discipleship leverages the power of group discipleship by

- protecting individual discipleship,
- alternating group membership, and
- strategically designing groups.

Protecting Individual Discipleship

Sustainable discipleship protects intimate and individual discipleship by having group standards. Standardization to ensure natural and intentional customization? Yes. Some group standards protect and promote the need for us to make individual disciples. I remind groups again and again, "You are not in group discipleship. You are being discipled individually in a group. I am discipling each of you, individually. You are just getting the benefit of others' thoughts, comments, and discipleship truths." Focusing on the individual is critical even though disciples read the same Bible, read the same resources, and take part in the same outside events. Here are the standards that we use in groups:

- No cross talk. Each disciple discusses the highlights that he or she has from reading. Each disciple prays their prayers. Other disciples do not comment on, extend, or originate questions based on other disciples' highlights or prayers. "If you did not highlight this verse, you do not talk about it. But you can send me a note, text, or call me if you need to talk later." The focus is on each disciple's God-led journey.
- No outside conversations. Disciples do not discuss their highlights, questions, or challenges outside of discipleship. This is challenging for couples in discipleship. We encourage them to talk after discipleship and not before. This method keeps the questions and revelations fresh and untampered. The

disciples are not discipling each other. They are being led by one leader.

- Everyone shares every one of their highlights. One disciple may ask about a verse that several have highlighted. That disciple gets their answer. If others have highlighted that verse and need to share a different question or "aha," they share. If they have nothing new, they simply say, "I had that one too," and we move on.

Alternating Group Membership

4 or 20

Groups of four seem best, but surprisingly, groups of twenty are easier to lead than groups of ten. Groups with membership around ten have consistently provided the most problems; however, a group size around ten seems to be the most common need as discipleship starts up or reacts to fast church growth. Nathanael and I recently took on a group of ten disciples to test a few new ideas and continue to work out the kinks of this troublesome group size. Nathanael leads when I am not there. Tom is in the group. He recently closed an email question to Nathanael, writing, "I really need to write down to-dos immediately 'cause I have the memory of a gnat. Anyway, I enjoyed the discipleship time yesterday. You and Doug have two different styles when it comes to leading this, and I appreciate both of them."

Do you see it? Disciple makers are more effective when we embrace variety, but disciples also benefit from variety. Disciples need to hear and be led by a variety of leaders. We do our best to provide followers a different leader for each phase of discipleship.

Disciples also benefit when the membership of their groups is different during each phase of discipleship. Mixing up the groups exposes disciples to a broader range of truths along the pathway. Mixing up groups also increases the number of healthy discipleship relationships. These relationships will be valuable as disciples move from the process to the practice of discipleship.

Alternating leaders and members is a powerful method of discipleship. This method also provides discipleship leaders with the opportunity to strategically design discipleship groups.

Strategically Designing Groups

Sustainable discipleship designs groups that leverage variety for the benefit of each individual. We intentionally avoid homogenous groups and create groups that embrace the words of Proverbs 27:17:

As iron sharpens iron, so a friend sharpens a friend.

Everyone is an individual in group discipleship. Disciples are not responsible for (nor should they be) teaching, leading, or challenging each other. So why design a group that will self-sharpen? Disciples will interact outside of your group. They will travel together, serve together, and live life together. In those moments, they will either self-sharpen or dull each other. Variety sharpens variety. Seeing things differently allows us to cover each other. Seeing things differently pushes us. Bold champions quiet to speak. Quiet quiets loud. Patient encourages impatient. Confident shores up insecure. The body of Christ completes itself. Homogeneous groups tend to have the same bents, strengths, and weaknesses. Homogenous groups tend to be less challenging, less encouraging, and less fun.

Single people are exposed to incredible proactive truths as they do discipleship with married people. Older followers find inspiration and vigor in younger disciples. They also learn how to deal with the frustration of younger people. Young disciples observe wisdom from those who have survived and thrived a few more years than they. Business leaders watch and learn incredible truths as they listen in on workers' discipleship. You get the idea.

Designing groups that will self-sharpen is a matter of observation, prayer, and trust. Designing healthy, challenging discipleship-two groups is easier. You have had a year to assess, observe, and watch the followers. Designing discipleship-one groups is more about trusting God and doing your best. You have to trust the process. Let your confidence, skill, and preparation guide the disciples to intimacy, transparency, and trust. You have to be patient as the fruit grows on the tree. By the time you create a discipleship-three group, less design is necessary. These disciples have passed the consecration step on the predictable pathway—they are all in and durable. They know the benefits of being in a group. They are wide open to challenge. The pathway has pushed them to be in a much "closer" journey.

There are benefits to some homogeneity. It is helpful to have women disciple women and men disciple men.[5] I could quote a bunch of scripture here about men teaching men and women leading women, but it is not necessary. This method is just practical and intuitive when it comes to personal things. Men and women think and see the world differently. I can say things to guys that would offend the incredible women I know. Men need to be pushed differently than women.

I used to disciple women. I could never find women who were prepared, confident, skilled, and willing to disciple other women. My mentors pushed me. They challenged me. Quite frankly, they ticked me off. I felt offended. What were they thinking? I was not a creep. Did they not trust me? Mentors! Luckily, I found out they were right before it was too late. Many married women quickly latch onto a male leader, as he provides a version of godliness that they lack at home. Things got weird. I quietly stopped discipling women. There was a gap until I married a great lady who loves God and is a disciple-making machine herself. She has now replicated herself, and we have women leading women.

Humans are prone to temptation. Disaster can happen when opportunity and temptation collide. David fell in that collision.[6]

Avoiding temptation is a good reason for same-sex discipleship, but the better argument is that men understand men and speak the language of men. Women get women and speak the language of women. The Bible makes this point.[7] Same-sex discipleship is efficient. But what do you do when you do not have any women ready to lead other women? What if you have no men to lead men? How do you start the process? If you are married, I suggest that you work with your spouse as you improve your disciple-making process. If you have great men and women, or willing men and women, make your first discipleship group coed.

Coed groups also provide a wealth of iron-sharpening-iron moments. Coed groups offer incredible opportunities to learn and grow in our interactions with the opposite sex. We have seen women who have no trust in men come to understand that all men were not the "men" in their history. We have seen men finally realize that women take things differently. Moms have a different perspective than men.

We are careful to design balanced groups. You should never put one woman in a group of a bunch of men. If she is the only woman to be discipled, then you simply have to settle for one-on-one discipleship. You should avoid putting too many of those "Bible college" types in one group. Never create discipleship groups of only leaders. They will be cheated, as will the ones they lead. There is power in followers finding that their leaders are broken and learning too. Ensure variety. You can push with variety. You can lead people to increased truth through variety. Whatever you do, design your groups to be challenging. Create challenges. Create rubs. Intentionally let iron sharpen iron.

Conclusion

Understanding, adjusting to, and leveraging variety brings exponential power and effectiveness to the disciple-making process.

Embracing variety, with all its challenges, is one of the keys to sustainable discipleship. Discipleship is all about who someone is and is becoming. Discipleship is about the "be." Discipleship has to be customized along the way because customization is God's way of growing with us.

God is simultaneously all things to all men and intimate with each man. He is everywhere but very present in each of us. His truths are universal and always active, but He impresses and guides each individual very personally. Discipleship should mimic God's interaction with His followers. God interacts, trains, encourages, and lives with each of us individuals. When we come together, He refers to us as the "body of Christ" and combines us in a synergy of tremendous power, safety, and support.

Customization is essential, but customization should never become catering. Customizing is about effectively making disciples, but customization never adjusts truth. You adjust the process of disciples finding truth, but you never adjust truth. Discipleship is all about humans adjusting their lives to God's truths. God's truths apply in principle and precept to all of us.

Customization is about us joining God where He is working, and intentionally being intimate and relevant as we make disciples. Working with God while not derailing His work is critical work. Sustainable discipleship requires that we be prepared, confident, and skilled leaders. The next step is to make sure we are clear about our role as disciple makers.

14

UNDERSTAND YOUR ROLE

"God is and we are not God."

— ANONYMOUS

The end goal of discipleship is to make "fully devoted followers of God," not followers of men or me. You and I are not good enough to be followed. We might be teachers, models, or mentors, but we are not good enough to be followed. If people follow us, they will always be limited to us. Eric Russ puts it this way: "Discipleship is the relationship between a teacher (discipler) and student (disciple)."[1]

From the moment that a person begins to follow Christ, they are, by definition, a follower of God. From that first moment, and in every moment that they follow Him, God is the teacher, and they are the student.

The original Jewish law contained some 613 commandments. The religious leaders added 6,200 pages of commentary, interpretation, and explanation in the Talmud. The goal of the Talmud was not to make new law. The goal was to help Jewish followers know how to apply the original law. But what started out as a helpful explanation became a massive expansion of the law, with endless rules and regulations.

For example, the Talmud instructs that lighting a lamp is work and should not be done on the day of rest. The modern application of the Talmud commentary is as follows:

> *Lights which will be needed on Shabbat are turned on before Shabbat. Automatic timers may be used for lights and some appliances as long as they have been set before Shabbat. The refrigerator may be used, but again, we have to ensure that its use does not engender any of the forbidden Shabbat activities. Thus, the fridge light should be disconnected before Shabbat by unscrewing the bulb slightly and a freezer whose fan is activated when the door is opened may not be used.[2]*

Jesus addressed these expansions of God's law, saying,

> *"The teachers of the law and the Pharisees sit in Moses' seat. So you must be careful to do everything they tell you. But do not do what they do, for they do not practice what they preach. They tie up heavy, cumbersome loads and put them on other people's shoulders, but they themselves are not willing to lift a finger to move them."*
>
> — MATTHEW 23:2–4 (NIV)

Jesus constantly brought followers back to the simple original intent of the law. Here is an example of His challenge to religious Jews regarding one of their Sabbath rules:

> *"The Sabbath was made to meet the needs of people, and not people to meet the requirements of the Sabbath."*
>
> — MARK 2:27

What was He saying? He was saying the day of rest should be a benefit, not a burden. It was to be a blessing for the Jews and not a curse. God wanted his people to take and enjoy the needed rest for their bodies, souls, and minds. He wanted this for their good.

We make the error of those old religious leaders if we place ourselves between God (the teacher) and people (the students). We should explain God's ways to those who follow, but we must be cautious to teach them His ways and His heart, and to follow what He said.

Humans take two classic shortcuts when it comes to following God. The first shortcut is made by followers when they say, "Just tell me what to do." The second is made by well-meaning leaders when they answer that request. These, as shortcuts, bypass a more complete path. What is that path? God has created each person in His image, with the ability to learn, understand, apply, comprehend, and choose. His design is that people would have an interactive, intelligent relationship with Him. He has put His Spirit within each Christian to guide them in His ways. His path is a path of relationship that is alive and present in every moment. His path is a relationship of inspiration and conviction. He has given us the ability to synthesize His truths to make incredible choices.

When we simply tell people what to do, we deny His path, we reject the majesty of His creation, and we make them dependent on us. We also set ourselves up as priests and clergy—the modern-day version of the religious Jew. We put ourselves between God and His students. We interrupt the divine path of man's relationship with God.

We need to seek to create self-sustaining learners. Paul understood this goal and wrote,

There is much more we would like to say about this, but it is difficult to explain, especially since you are spiritually dull and don't seem to listen. You have been believers so long now that you

ought to be teaching others. Instead, you need someone to teach you again the basic things about God's word. You are like babies who need milk and cannot eat solid food. For someone who lives on milk is still an infant and doesn't know how to do what is right. Solid food is for those who are mature, who through training have the skill to recognize the difference between right and wrong.

— HEBREWS 5:11–14

Our immediate goal as we teach, lead, model, mentor, and disciple others is to get them off milk and onto solid food. We should help them become people able to learn, apply, and synthesize God's words into their daily lives, decisions, and disciplines.

Our role is to get His truths in others. Our role is to push them to apply those truths. Our role is to guide them to the true guides: His truth and His Spirit. I always reminded myself of the transforming truth of Micah 6:8, which instructs us to live humbly. I am not good enough to be followed, but God is good enough to be followed. I particularly love the loose paraphrase of Micah 6:8 from the Message (MSG):

But he's already made it plain how to live, what to do, what GOD is looking for in men and women. It's quite simple: Do what is fair and just to your neighbor, be compassionate and loyal in your love, And don't take yourself too seriously— take God seriously.

God is the teacher. The follower is the student. We need to guide while staying out of the way. That may be the most straightforward summary of our responsibility in making disciples. We need to lead them to the truth, let the Holy Spirit work on them, and stay out of the way. We need add only the words that need to be added. Our responsibility is to help three encounters happen:

- the encounter with the truths of God;
- the encounter with the Holy Spirit that brings those truths to life; and
- the encounter with God that results from following God.

What we know does not matter unless it applies to their journey. The focus should remain on the disciple's encounters with God and his truth. We add and clarify. We help correct the course when it strays into immaturity or education. Our responsibility is to watch, to listen to God, and to speak like Jesus.

> *"I don't speak on my own authority. The Father who sent me has commanded me what to say and how to say it. And I know his commands lead to eternal life; so I say whatever the Father tells me to say."*
>
> — JOHN 12:49–50

Your role will be different in different moments. You may use authority to push, exercise empathy to heal, be a cheerleader to make confident, or be a brother to carry them. Your responsibility is to guide while staying out of God's way.

Too many words can prevent the disciple from hearing God. Too few words can let them stray from the process that works. Cheerleading can be inappropriate if it creates dependence on the cheerleader. Paul told us,

> *Fathers, do not exasperate your children; instead, bring them up in the training and instruction of the Lord.*
>
> — EPHESIANS 6:4 (NIV)

Disciples may not be our children, but this instruction still applies. Too much pushing can exasperate the new follower and push them to anger, frustration, and giving up. Too little pushing can cause them to stall and not experience all that following God can bring to their lives. Our responsibility is to find the right balance.

You will need the right balance as you encounter four classic challenges.[3] The first three are named after the discipleship pathway step where each occurs typically. The fourth challenge derails and destroys more disciples than any other. It is our responsibility to help disciples avoid or conquer these four challenges.

- The "4b Challenge" as they become more and more enlightened.
- The "9a Challenge" as they move from being prepared to being set aside.
- The "10-11 Challenge" as they get busy leading.
- Money, family, and pride all along the way.

The 4b Challenge

Disciples may face this challenge as they get smarter about God in step four of the predictable pathway: "Be Enlightened." The 4b challenge is similar to the teenage years. You are leading, and disciples are getting more intelligent and aware. Suddenly, you hear, "Why do I have to do that?" This is the classic "I already know" or "know-it-all" challenge. The disciple is learning that he is loved by God and that his salvation is by grace and not works. She is learning about her freedoms in Christ. Then she hits the lesson about tithing. You ask, "Are you tithing?" She has two options: she can hear you caring, or she can feel like you are checking up on her. Even if she is tithing, defenses can rise if she forgets that you are in this for her good. You have been a teenager, right? You get this. Your role becomes a balance between empathy (we have all been here) and a bit of account-ability. You need to get the disciple to encounter God. The goal is to figure out why whatever is bothering them is bothering them and guide them to safety.

The 9a Challenge

The 9a challenge most often occurs at the tipping point between being prepared and being consecrated. Step nine on the predictable pathway, "Be Consecrated," is that point where disciples go "all in" as a follower. The 9a challenge is similar to what happens after a guy buys a wedding ring. It is like what happens when you get into those final interviews for the job opportunity of your life. Do you know that feeling? A great future is available, you are ready to jump in, but something inside you resists change or commitment. Perhaps you begin to calculate the risks. You think things like, "Wow! I love her, but my single life is over. I have to mean this one," or, "What if these guys fire me in a month? What if I do not do as well as they think I will do?" Disciples will be tempted to "get out of the fire" and abandon the discipleship process. It is our responsibility to slow them down and help them adjust. Our role becomes one of under-standing and encouragement.

The 10-11 Challenge

Residency and leading, steps ten and eleven along the path-way, bring the 10-11 challenge. This is a challenge of exhaustion and attacks from the enemy. Disciples rarely abandon disciple-ship at this point. They are all in. The benefits are incredible, they have turned that corner, and they love giving back to others. They are discipling people. They are leading. And they get tired. When you push them to take a Sabbath rest, they push back with, "I love this stuff." When you push them to say no, they push back with an incredible worldview of the lost needing to be found. It is our responsibility to teach delegation and pacing during this challenge. Disciples need to be reminded that the work of God is a marathon. They need to be pushed to have their own walk; after all, this is where all the fun started. As well, spiritual attacks increase in steps ten and eleven. Our common enemy knows that these people will make a difference if he does not disable them at this point. We need to help identify his attacks. Our role is to be their experienced mentor.

The 4b, 9a, and 10-11 challenges are normal, acceptable, and very real. It is our responsibility to get disciples successfully through these waters. We have been there in our following. We have survived. They can survive, but it takes a balance of empathy and pushing.

Money, Family and Pride

The "holy trinity of cooking" is a mixture of celery, bell peppers, and onions. It is the base for almost everything Cajun. The aroma and the flavor are incredible. Chef Paul Prudhomme popularized the term in the 1970s. If it is Cajun, you can be sure that it started with the "holy trinity." Guaranteed.

There is an unholy trinity that you can be sure to encounter as you make disciples. Its aroma reeks of death. Its aftertaste is caustic. The ingredients are money, family, and pride. You can be sure they are at the base of every discipleship failure. Any one of them can quickly derail the discipleship process. The enemy is all too aware of our weak points, and he does not want people getting closer to God. Bet on it. Count on it. You will face the mother of all challenges when someone you lead faces money, family, and pride. And your responsibility is to get them through it as a balanced guide.

Family is important. We need to affirm that truth. God is more important. We need to affirm that truth. Disciples drop everything to follow. It is true. We should not abandon our marriages for ministry. That is true as well. Jesus called the disciples to walk away from their homes and jobs. It is true. Can you see how balance is going to be needed when a new job is offered that will cause a disciple to stop discipleship? Can you see how balance is going to be needed when that husband (selfish dude, you know him) demands that his wife stop doing all that church stuff? Can you see how balance is going to be needed when that up-and-coming leader struggles with the pride of residency?

Your responsibility to guide while staying out of God's way never changes. Your method and role will change. In the beginning, you are a guide. Toward the end, your role will become one of launching. Between discipleship phases, your role is to move the disciple to the next place. Mark Dever writes,

> *Love allows us to end discipling relationships. We need a love that humbles us enough to recognize that what they need is not us, but God, and that God can use us for a while, and then use someone else.*[4]

Marshall Segal, a staff writer for desiringGod.org, adds these questions to the discussion.

- *Do I think of myself as savior or as one instrument among many in the Savior's hands?*
- *How do I think about my role in this particular person's life — as essential and irreplaceable, or as complementary and temporary?*
- *Am I willing to help move this person on to other disciplers when their needs or circumstances suggest it's time? To that end, it may be wise to establish a clear time frame up front (e.g. a month, a year, two years), so that neither person assumes the disciplining relationship is indefinite.*[5]

I co-led[6] one of the most dysfunctional discipleship groups. It was going nowhere. First, we had to help a guy who was better than us go back to discipling himself. Second, we could not get a routine schedule. Third, we were easy on the guys who were not making meetings or reading. Out of six disciples, only two were really hungry. At the same time, there was a young guy in a different group who was getting cheated by his leader's schedule and exhaustion.

It was time for a change. We prayed for wisdom. We paired the two inconsistent guys with my inconsistent co-leader and sent them off to try something more casual. I moved the young, hungry guy into our group and carried all three hungry guys to the end. The exhausted leader rested and is preparing to lead better next time. The inconsistent group fell apart. One of the three hungry guys started discipling the inconsistent group a year later. They thrived and succeeded. We are responsible for doing whatever is best for those in the discipleship process.

Our greatest responsibility as an intentional guide is to keep it all in context. We need to keep the disciple focused on exegetical Bible consumption. We need to keep the disciple challenged with topical outside reading. We need to keep the disciple in situations that stretch her beyond what she can do without God. We need to teach what we know and keep all of this in context. Sustainable discipleship is designed to help people draw closer to God, know His truths, apply those truths, and be transformed. We are responsible for keeping all of the "dos" in context with the "bes" of transformation. If the disciple be not transformed, all is lost.

Who You Should Be in Discipleship

Who should we be in the process of making disciples? Are we ready? Are we capable? Do we have any idea of what to do when it comes to disciple making? So many questions, but we really only need to answer the first question. "Be" always comes before "do." If we can figure out our role, who we are, in making disciples, the rest will come naturally.

Being a disciple maker is no different than being a disciple. God is the teacher, and you are the student. You have reached a point on the predictable pathway where you want to assume the responsibility to make disciples. God has led you to see the value of making disciples. He has made you prepared, confident, and skilled. He has led you to a place where you are turning from learning to teaching, from watching to modeling, or from being led to mentoring others.

I have a dear friend, Tim, whom I had the privilege to disciple. He was so frustrated the other day. He was trying to get a ministry partner to understand why their request was wrong. "There is so much wrong here," Tim continued, "but they will not listen. They do not get it. I can help them fix the problem, but they need to understand why it is a problem." He was so frustrated. I listened as he vented, and then I said, "You need to stop trying to teach people who don't want to be taught. Just help them get it done." His response? "I gave up all the other teaching points, but I couldn't help but push her on the culture of their organization. It is so easy to see."

If you knew Tim before, you would know that this is new. Tim used to keep his wisdom to himself. Now he cannot help wanting to teach people. He wants to show them a better way and to challenge them to be great so that they can do great. Tim has become a teacher. Discipleship transformed him from a spiritual consumer to a producer.

But the turning point causes each of us to ask, "Am I ready?" Tim's question came when we pushed him to start discipling others. He was not convinced, but he trusted us enough to begin training. We were not training him how to do discipleship. That would be easy—he just finished two years of the process. Tim was being pushed and trained on how to be a disciple maker. A light bulb went off for Tim as we defined the role, the character, and the life of a disciple maker. This is what Tim shared with the group and those of us who were preparing him:

> *When I graduated from med school, people would bring me their infants and hand them to me to fix them. People would come to me and trust me to help them with their medical needs. They asked my opinion and asked for direction. I thought they were crazy. I did not know anything. I just graduated. People would ask me, "How do you like being a doctor?" I would simply answer that I like it, but deep inside, I didn't feel like a doctor. Then one day, when all of this medical knowledge was falling out of my mouth, I realized that these people did not know what I knew. I actually knew things they did not know, and I was a doctor. I had spent all of my time growing and learning with others who learned what I learned. I saw myself just as a student among them. But I had grown, I had learned, I was a doctor in regard to other people. It just dawned on me that this process is the same. I can do this. I know things that others need to know. I have become a disciple. I am ready. I mean, I still have stuff to learn, but I can do this. I see what you see.*

Tim is a doctor. He is educated, practiced, and skilled, but at some point, Tim became a doctor. It is who he is. Tim is also a disciple maker. He has the character and life of a disciple maker. You and I need that character and those characteristics. Let's take a look at who a great disciple maker is.

Great Disciple Makers Are Spiritual

Our lives should be spiritual, fully devoted to living out God's perfect design for us. We should be consumed by God, always listening to the Spirit, and prepared with truth. We should know the voice of God and be able to get answers from God. We should be people who listen in every moment for God's wisdom before we speak, act, or decide.

Great disciple makers have an active, fresh, meaningful, enduring relationship with God. They are spiritual people, and spiritual "dos" weep out from their lives.

Great Disciple Makers Are Humble

We are smart to think we are not good enough. Just wait to see who those you disciple become. If you make disciples well, you will find yourself humbled by their excellence and, even more so, by their wisdom.

We need to take God very seriously. We need to teach what we know. We need to submit to His truths even when they are hard to grasp. We need to understand how privileged we are to be followers and to lead followers. If you have a problem with pride, please do not disciple anyone.

Great Disciple Makers Are Serious about Discipleship

> *"I tell you the truth, unless you turn from your sins and become like little children, you will never get into the Kingdom of Heaven. So anyone who becomes as humble as this little child is the greatest in the Kingdom of Heaven. And anyone who welcomes a little child like this on my behalf is welcoming me.* **But if you cause one of these little ones who trusts in me to fall into sin,** *it would be better for you to have a large millstone tied around your neck and be drowned in the depths of the sea."*
>
> — JESUS, IN MATTHEW 18:3–6

When people allow us the privilege of leading them to God (the teacher), we also become a teacher. We have earned their trust, and they will listen to what we have to say. They submit to us as we guide them to God's truths and ways. If we lead them astray, we are idiots. Disciple making is not a game. Disciple making is the spiritual reproduction plan that allows the world to have a deep relationship with Christ. If we mess this up, if we get in the way, if we become their god, then we ruin things.

We need to be conscious of God's truths and be committed to showing them to people. We need to be aware of the great privilege we have to give or take life from the followers of God.

Great Disciple Makers Are Prepared

We need to have consumed and understood every resource that we guide people to read, use, or try. We need to know His truths. We need to have mastered applying God's truths. We need to know how to keep God's word in context.

It's simple: we cannot teach what we do not know.

Great Disciple Makers Are Disciples

We cannot teach what we do not know, and sadly, we do not know what we do not know. The journey of discipleship is never over. I have three younger and three older men who continually pour wisdom into my life. I am accountable to them, and they are bold enough to push me. They teach me. They learn with me. They are invaluable.

We must be people who watch and who expect to learn. We must have intentional discipleship relationships with smart people invested in making disciples out of us.

Great Disciple Makers Are Bold

Disciple making is not for the weak, the self-conscious, the insecure, or the timid. Disciple making seems to stir up conflict. Disciple making requires that we push one another toward God, toward God's truths, and toward action. We need to be bold (with grace and kindness), pushing those we lead to consume His word. We need to push them to meet their goals and to be disciples.

We need to be proud of God's truths and not waver when those truths are challenged. We need not make excuses for His words but love others as they adjust to Him. We need to care so much for their lives that we will push.

Great Disciple Makers Are Enduring

We cannot quit on them. We cannot bail out. We cannot collapse under tests and trials. We cannot abandon those we disciple. We need to be enduring and have an enduring mindset.

An old Chinese proverb says, "The ox is slow, but the earth is always patient." We need to be resilient. We need to be patient people. We need to accept that discipleship is full of challenges. Discipleship challenges the one who makes disciples and those being made disciples.

Disciple makers reflect the disciple that they have become. Disciple makers have certain roles. Disciple makers have some clear responsibilities, but there are also a few things to avoid in the discipleship relationship.

What Your Discipleship Relationship Should Not Be

I hate teaching what you should not be, but I would be remiss in not sharing what we have learned along the way. There are roles that you should not assume, things you should not do, and one big thing you should not be.

Trust the experience of our failures here. Embrace the warnings of those we ignored. Learn from the research. Sustainable discipleship will fall apart if these things are part of your relationship with those you make disciples.

You Are Not Their Best Friend

I have a friend named Caleb. We are partners in the same

church community. Our friendship is more rooted and rewarding because Caleb has a ban on shop talk when we are together. He is fine with me leading the gang. He is fine with me teaching, directing, and leading the efforts of the staff. But when it comes to our relationship, he is genius at being my friend and separating the work of the ministry from our time. He does not ask me about the church. He does not pitch ideas or ask stuff about what we are doing. You may have guessed that I am the leader of our church but not when it comes to my friendship with Caleb.

Caleb held off doing discipleship for almost two years, waiting for a leader who was not me. Caleb did not want me to be his discipleship leader. He said he wanted to keep being my friend. He did not want me to be his one-on-one leader. He did not want me to play that formal teaching role in his life.

Caleb's story illustrates something significant about the positive, and potentially harmful, role that a disciple maker can play in the life of a disciple. You have to be a formal leader when it comes to discipleship. You have to take the authority to lead the disciple. You have to set, secure, and see to the path of formal discipleship. You are not the "best friend" of the one you lead. In the early stages of discipleship, and when the challenges come, you have to be a teacher and mentor. You have to be able to push (even to the point of breaking) the disciple to follow, to confront the words of God, and to apply those truths. Your role cannot be compromised by friendship. There is something bigger going on. You are trying to connect the disciple (student) with God (teacher) and push them to be a follower.

You Are Not Their Lord

Followers are supposed to follow God. Jesus is the Lord. We should never guide their decisions, approve their ideas, or in any way get into the pie of their life. We should lead them to God's truths and help them learn to apply those truths. If anyone is going to tell them what to do, God should.

Likewise, you are not their spirit. The Holy Spirit is supposed to convict and guide them. It is not your job to dig around, looking for things that disciples need to change. You can destroy a follower by forcing them to face things that God is not showing him. Lead disciples to God, and His Spirit can do what He needs to do. Stay out of the way.

And be careful, you are not their father either. The truths and rules of their lives come from their true Father: God. You are not their priest. You are not their rule maker. You are not the one to discipline them. They should not be striving for your approval in any manner. The very nature of someone being a disciple of God's is that God is the authority. God's truths are the truths to which the disciple is accountable. The disciple is accountable to God if they do not apply those truths.

I understand that God has ordained authority and spiritual accountability relationships among his people. There are many day-to-day accountability relationships among Christians, with leaders, and in ministry. Later in discipleship, the disciple will be taught to manage and live under these relationships. He will embrace those truths and be able to follow human leaders when God gives them authority, purpose, or position.

But the discipleship relationship is different. We are not the spiritual authorities to those we make disciples. We are just guides, teachers, mentors, and models. We need to do everything in our power to avoid being positional leaders giving directions that must be followed. We need to be careful not to get between the disciple and God. Our most significant push is to teach, model, and mentor the disciple to be entirely accountable to God for all of their learning and choices.

 You Are Not Their Therapist

There is a common perception that discipleship is a counseling relationship. Not true! People often start discipleship to address their problems. If that draws them to follow God, great, but we should immediately direct them to God for an answer. We can listen to issues along the way. It is a privilege to hear a question, guide them to God's answer, and then challenge them to give it a try. If discipleship uncovers deeper, trying issues, get them connected to an independent, qualified counselor and move on with teaching them God's truths.

The core of the discipleship relationship is that we guide disciples to a student-follower relationship with God. The goal is to get people connected to their teacher: God. That goal gets distorted when we begin to try to fix behavior. Christian maturity is very organic—get the disciple in God's ground, dump on tons of fertilizing truths, and he will grow as designed.

Even if you are a psychologist, you are not their psychologist. This is not therapy—it is discipleship. It is learning about God, His ways, and His incredible path to the best life ever. If they need a psychologist, help them find one and get back to teaching and guiding.

You Are Not Their Accountability Partner

The accountability-partner approach to discipleship is just as disastrous as the best-friend approach. Accountability groups for recovery, counseling, and particular reformations of the soul are extremely valuable, but they have no place in discipleship.

We embraced accountability groups as a form of discipleship in the early Promise Keepers movement. It always failed. It always focused on issues and not on discipleship. We abandoned all this and outsourced help for issues needing recovery, counseling, or reformation.

Discipleship is about becoming a follower of God. Discipleship is about learning God's truths and learning to follow them. There may be times when you ask, "How are you doing with this or that?" but the disciple maker should direct the disciple to be accountable to God.

This One Thing

We have one simple task: make followers of God. We introduce people to God, who loves and understands them, help them understand who they are and what they can be, help them apply God's transforming truths, and release them as prepared, confident, and skilled to live their best life ever on earth.

Lead those you make disciples to a lifetime practice of following God. Help them learn to learn. Help them rely on God. Mission agencies have long embraced the adage from *Mrs. Dymond* by Anne Isabella Thackeray Ritchie: "If you give a man a fish he is hungry again in an hour. If you teach him to catch a fish you do him a good turn."[7]

You can give anyone a fish. The greater gift is a rod, a hook, and teaching someone to fish. So what is the "fish versus fishing" of discipleship?

Teaching people discrete truths gives them a fish. (They will soon be back for another answer.) Helping them learn to learn and rely on God (just like you do) teaches them to fish. Challenge them to become independent hunter-gatherers, producers, and successors. Teach, push, and cheer them to follow Him by finding His ways, consuming them, and applying them to their lives.

Help them learn about God, the heroes of the faith, and the failures in the faith. Help them repeat the parts of history worth repeating while avoiding the rest. Show them God's ways are not limiting but actually set us free to be exactly who we were designed to be. Your goal is to help them follow Him wildly into their next best day ever.

How do you do that? How do you actually make disciples? The next three chapters will carry you through a step-by-step process for each phase. What a privilege it is to make disciples!

PART IV

THE STEP-BY-STEP GUIDE

15

LAUNCH YOUR DISCIPLESHIP-ONE GROUP

"Give me six hours to chop down a tree and I will spend the first four sharpening the axe."

— ABRAHAM LINCOLN

D o you remember me saying we "faked it until we made it?" I had no idea what I was doing. Your journey is different. Your discipleship process begins with a solid understanding of God's discipleship models. You have a simple definition. You have the secret sauce and know the components that must be present. You have the seven action items making up the foundation of your process. But even with all that, uncertainty may arise. Uncertainty is natural, but you need to fight it. People who ask you to make a disciple of them need direction, surety, and leadership. You need to prepare and, inside that preparation, you need to lead. You must not wander. You need to lead them. You need to take the lead. Do not say, "Well this is my first time," or, "I am new to this." Inspire confidence. Discipleship has worked for you, and it will work for them. Leading may be new, but you can do it, and you need to believe that you can.

Fight the pride that can quickly derail the process. You are not being tested or judged. Your self-worth is not on the line. In fact, this is not about you. Just lead disciples where you have gone. Take the first step with confidence.

If you have never had the privilege of discipleship, you will have to get your own Bible and mark it up. You may have more "I will look that up and get back to you" moments. But always remember, it is their experience that drives the process. You are not teaching what you read. You are helping them learn what they read.

The first cycle or two requires that you read, and reread, the Bible and extra-biblical books. You need to stay ahead of those you lead. Preparation takes time, but skill and knowledge will build into confidence and efficiency. Discipleship is the long game of Christianity.

This chapter is designed to give you a simple, step-by-step guide to launching your first discipleship-one group. It is written from the perspective of launching a group, but the steps are virtually the same for one-on-one discipleship. These steps are the twelve steps that we can guarantee. These are the steps we use every time we start a new discipleship group. This is how we do discipleship one.

Step One
Review the Model

If you are reading this book through for the first time, reviewing the model may feel redundant. You may even skim over this step as you read. But I encourage you to do this step, to review the model, when you prepare to launch your discipleship-one group. I know the underlying truths of discipleship. I know the steps. I get the concepts. I have led so many cycles of discipleship one.

But I always review the model before I launch a new group. It helps me focus on the pathway. Reviewing the model reminds me of what I am getting ready to do and the best way that God has shown us to do it.

> *Making disciples is entirely about who someone is and becomes. It is not about what they do or how they do it. Doing is the natural result of being.*

The goal of discipleship is to teach those who want to follow and, while teaching, show the why and value of God's truths. We need to show them who they can "be" and how that can change their world. We need to show them, along the way, who they already "be." Discipleship is about the transformation of people, not the education or conformation of people.

Following God, being made a disciple, and being a disciple are entirely about being transformed inside. Following God allows people to embrace the best way to live so that they can thrive. Jesus said,

> *"My purpose is to give them a rich and satisfying life."*
>
> — JOHN 10:10

There are four foundational components to making sustainable disciples:

- The fuel for transformation are God's words.
- The process is intentional.
- The definition must be simple to keep us focused.
- The focus is on individuals.

Sustainable discipleship adds the preparation, confidence, and skill to be what we already are: followers of God.

The Fuel Is God's Words

There is no replacement for consuming God's words. His words bring life. His words complete us, prepare us, and inspire us to follow. His words show us His character, our design, and communicate the value of thriving with God. The greatest gift you will give disciples is to guide them through the Bible three times.

Every extra-biblical work should be tied to His truths and principles. Disciples should discover the connections, expansions, and applications of God's truths as they read the extra-biblical books. You have the privilege of revealing the connections disciples miss. The extra-biblical authors become virtual mentors applying the words of God in specific situations. We must always remember that the Holy Spirit uses God's truths to transform people.

The Process Is Intentional

Everything of value happens with intent. Effective and comprehensive discipleship requires intentionality.

Just like being comes before doing, a discipleship plan should precede discipleship.

The biblical models illustrate the need for and the methods of proactive and reactive discipleship. Discipleship should invade our every thought, interaction, and plan. Sustainable disciples are made along the way as we

- call people to surrender,
- ask tough questions,
- create relevant challenges,
- put people in residency, and
- release people.

Discipleship takes time. It is the long game of Christianity. You need a plan. You need to be intentional. You need to be comprehensive. Your goal is saying, "We used to do many things for many reasons. Now we do one thing—make disciples—in many different ways."

The process leverages the predictable pathway. You push people to the next great step, the next great place, in their relationship with God. You teach critical thinking and teach people to learn to learn on their own. And you do all of this with intent.

The Definition Must Be Simple

Sustainable discipleship uses a simple definition. Disciples are followers of God. Discipleship is making disciples.

Making disciples introduces people to God, who loves and understands them, helps them understand who they are and what they can be, helps them apply God's transforming truths, and releases them as prepared, confident, and skilled to live their best life ever on earth.

Discipleship prepares people to do it on their own. It is a practical, community effort for everyone. It is interactive and easy. Discipleship is natural, and we should not make it difficult.

The Focus Is Individuals

Sustainable disciple making focuses on individuals. It is an intimate, leader-to-follower process—even in a group. God naturally customizes an individual's discipleship, and we should join God where he is working in each disciple's life. We should customize discipleship according to each person's design, challenges, and practical limitations.

Step Two
Establish the Objectives

Discipleships one, two, and three each have specific objectives to guide and move people down the predictable pathway to independently following God. Each phase has a particular tone. Disciples will face certain dangers. The way the disciples read the Bible is different for each phase.

Discipleship one is a twelve-month process guiding disciples through the first six steps along the pathway:

- Be Convicted
- Repent
- Be Taught
- Be Enlightened
- Be Called
- Serve

The Focus of Discipleship One

Discipleship one begins with conviction and focuses on teaching God's truths to the disciple. The constant challenge is for the disciple to apply those truths. You walk alongside the disciple as he joins you getting involved with other Christians and serving. The disciple adjusts to reading, homework, and self-discipline during this phase.

The Tone of Discipleship One

The tone of discipleship one is one of building discipline. In discipleship one, you are firm while being loving and encouraging. Firm means that there is little room for variation. Firm means that reading is expected to be done. Firm means that disciples should show up on time. Firm means that disciples participate in the service and projects that are good for their following. Following takes personal discipline and routine. Discipleship one should quietly build that discipline and routine.

The Followers of Discipleship One

Discipleship one will have the broadest spectrum of followers of the three phases. If you are launching sustainable discipleship as a new process, you will want all of your future disciple makers to go through the process. That means you are likely to have some excellent scholars and teachers in discipleship one. You will have disciples who are blank slates. If your church is older, you might have people who think they know it all. You need to set the expectation that there is something for everyone to learn. You need to view all of them in the same light—they are new disciples. Great scholars and teachers love the process. They are looking for a new angle to reach people and to grow themselves. They will be trying to figure out your tricks. New people are open books. Leading them is easy. They would dress like a dinosaur if they thought it would fix their lives. Know-it-all people will be your greatest challenge. They will likely struggle with submission, trust, and control. They are likely to question everything as you lead them. You need to work with them to prevent them from derailing the group. Your goal is to keep control and guide the wide variety of disciples as new disciples.

The Bible Reading Focus of Discipleship One

Disciples use a standard plan to read the Bible cover to cover. The fifty-week plan calls for Bible reading each day. There are no days off. Disciples are pushed to read daily instead of cramming it all in the day before their meeting. We ask disciples to choose a Bible translation that they understand and use a Bible they are willing to highlight or mark up.

Disciples in this phase are asked to highlight the following things as they read:

- Baffling things. Things that do not seem to make sense.
- Amazing things. Things that are super cool and touched the disciple as he read. We call these "aha" verses.
- Questions. Anything that is a simple question. Like, did God make all the animals on that day?

Typical Bible study is not the goal of discipleship one. The goal is to allow the Spirit of God to raise specific truths and ideas as the disciple reads the Bible. We want them to discover God's word, to find the "aha" moments, to see a miraculous God, to discover His character, to ask those beginning questions. The current value of a shekel has little value to us following God. Noticing that there are two accounts of creation is valuable. Learning the difference between chronological and conceptual historical records empowers the disciple's ability to understand God's word. Tracing the genealogy from Adam to Jesus has no particular value. Seeing that Rahab, a prostitute, is in the lineage reveals God's accepting, redemptive, and loving character. Looking for "aha" moments and troubling items is the secret sauce to finding truths that can be applied to our lives and choices. We do not reveal this secret sauce. We just let the process work. And it does work.

We strongly suggest that disciples not take notes, use the internet, or do research in year one. Not "studying" will challenge the bookworms, the Bible-study geeks, and the analytical, but we discourage studying. We encourage disciples to simply let God's words wash over them. We push disciples to pick out what stands out. We stress prayer and teach them that the Holy Spirit is more than capable to bring to mind what each of them needs to learn. We do not get sidetracked on non-applicable truths. We do not reveal truths that they have not high-lighted.

Extra-Biblical Reading and Work for Discipleship One

Disciples complete the Discipleship Discussion Manual Volume 1, "16 Key Topics in Christianity," in weeks two through seventeen.

Outside reading in the remaining thirty-three weeks focuses on self-worth (identity in Christ), inspirational reading, and books modeling discipleship, grace, prayer, and forgiveness. We often add custom reading for those who struggle with stress or schedules. Your goal is to get a good foundation under disciples so that they can grow and thrive. Disciples should read at least six extra-biblical books during discipleship one.

We require disciples to read the following books during discipleship one:

- *The Tender Commandments* (Ronald D. Mehl)
- *In His Steps* (Charles Sheldon)
- *Improving Your Serve* (Charles R. Swindoll)
- *How to Pray* (Reuben A. Torrey)

The sustainable library categorizes the following books as additional resources for discipleship one:

- *The Search for Significance* (Robert S. McGee)
- *Fresh Wind, Fresh Fire* (Dean Merrill and Jim Cymbala)
- *This Present Darkness* (Frank E. Peretti)
- *The Shack* (William P. Young)
- *Ruthless Trust* (Brennan Manning)
- *The Pursuit of Holiness* (Jerry Bridges)

The library also has topical books appropriate for any phase, to address specific needs or to push the group forward. A few examples are *Do Over* by John Acuff, *Scary Close* by Donald Miller, and *The Best Yes* by Lysa TerKeurst. *Do Over* is excellent for people faced with life change. *Scary Close* focuses on intimacy and being real. *The Best Yes* is entirely about learning to say no and stay on track. If you choose to build your own library, make sure the books focus on the tone, the plan, and typical challenges faced in the first six steps of discipleship one.

Your entire discipleship-one group should read the same books at the same time. Pick wisely, trust God, and watch the truth unfold.

The Dangers of Discipleship One

The unholy trinity of money, family, and pride can quickly derail the discipleship process. Point these dangers out as soon as you see them. Save everyone time, and save the disciple from the enemy.

The 4b challenge may arise as disciples learn more. If you hear or sense disciples thinking, "Why do I have to do that?" they may be headed toward difficulties in following. This challenge is discussed thoroughly in Chapter 14. Your role in this challenge is a balance between empathy (we have all been here) and accountability. Your goal is to figure out why whatever is bothering them is bothering them and guide them to safety.

Mission Trips and Service Opportunities for Discipleship One

You should push each disciple to join you for one weeklong mission trip. There are bonding, power, and teaching opportunities on extended trips. Do not miss this opportunity. You should also require service at special church events. You should require one area of regular service within the first sixteen weeks. Disciples should serve, not teach or lead during discipleship one.

Step Three
Develop Your Plan

It is time to figure out the practicals and launch discipleship. You need to decide when you are going to start and when you will meet. You need to pick a great place to meet. You need to figure out childcare. But before you create your specific plan, count the cost. Asking people to give up a year of their lives to be discipled is a big ask. You need to be committed. Discipleship one has to be a priority. You may have to limit your travel to be there weekly. You may have to drop activities to make sure you have time to prepare. Starting something is always more time-consuming than doing it the fourth time. Count the cost, and plan well.

Making Time

If this is your first time leading discipleship one, you will have to read everything that the disciples read. You will need at least forty-five minutes of uninterrupted time a day to read and prepare. You need two hours a week to lead the discipleship meeting. You also need a few hours outside of the meeting to answer emails and texts, and have coffee with those you lead. You need to make time for service events, mission trips, and regular service. These are the times where you lead along the way and teach in the moment. It sounds like a lot of time. It is, but making disciples and practicing your discipleship is worth every minute. Plan your time one step at a time.

1. At what time, each day, will you read and prepare?
2. What day and time can you hold a regularly scheduled discipleship-one meeting?
3. What months are you available to go on a mission trip or an extended service event?
4. Does your church have a mission trip or extended

service event that you can plug your group into? If not, you may have to do a little research.

5. What regular service are you currently doing?
6. What other service opportunities are there—at that time—that your group can join you in? You may need to change your regular service to be around those you lead.

Pick Your Launch Date

Picking a launch date requires a bit of thought. Our church typically launches new discipleship groups in late January. There is something about starting in the New Year that feels good. Winter is slower, the holidays are over, and summer is five months away. The meeting schedule is rarely interrupted by vacations and activities. Summer is a difficult time to start a group. It is always tricky to get everyone's schedule to line up. Add in a few vacations and summer activities, and it can become impossible to find a standard meeting day. Launching in fall creates conflicts with the start of school, football, and holidays.

Every group will experience a week off due to the holidays. Every group will have the occasional member gone to see family. But weeks off and people being gone will derail your group at its beginning.

You also need to think long term. Your group will end, and the disciples will want to begin discipleship two. Three years from now, you will be trying to carry out all three phases of discipleship. It is best to have a comprehensive plan for launching all groups at the same time.

This gets difficult if you are super excited to get going with discipleship. Do you have to wait until January? No. You just need to have a plan that looks forward and is sensitive to how you will start your future groups.

When will you launch your group?

Pick Your Meeting Day and Time

Picking your standard meeting day and time is actually picking two or three times that will work for you. If you are launching several discipleship groups, you have the flexibility to plug followers into several different times. If you are the sole leader launching two groups, you will definitely need a few options and need to be flexible.

Nathanael led a group with traveling businessmen. Their schedules were crazy and often overlapped. The group ended up picking the next meeting at each week's meeting. It was not ideal for Nathanael and the other home-based men, but the value of discipleship was worth the customization. It required sacrifice, but it worked. Meeting on the same day and at the same time is easier. People are creatures of habit. Regular meetings are easy and predictable, and always work best.

What are your best days to meet?
What are your best times to meet on those days?
Are you willing to be flexible?

Pick Your Meeting Place

Realtors preach, "Location, location, location," as the most important thing in selling a property. Sustainable disciple makers preach the same for effective and efficient discipleship. Where you meet is critical. We have had terrible experiences meeting in homes. There were too many distractions. Phones rang. Doorbells rang. And, well, kids are kids. Coffee shops present challenges as well. Feeling rushed to free up a table or trying to hear over the noise are only the beginning. How real can I be in a coffee shop? Can I get frustrated? Can I cry? Church classrooms are terrible. Clinical spaces scream education and set a stage for the Sunday school mentality. Our best experiences have been in what we call "third-party" locations. Third-party locations are comfortable, relaxed, quiet locations that are not owned by anyone in the group. Places with comfortable, flexible seating are optimal. Many people love to sit on the floor. Third-party spaces are neutral ground. Third-party spaces have little to distract leaders or followers. Several leaders use my living room–styled office. I have used a creative shared meeting room with comfortable furniture and whiteboards. Whatever the space, make it comfortable and relaxed.

What three spaces can you access for your meeting?

Is the space quiet or, at least, not disrupting?

Is the space comfortable?

Will you feel rushed?

Does it have a whiteboard?

Pick the Books You Need to Read

Your first discipleship-one group will be more efficient and informative if you stay ahead of those you make disciples. If you have never read the Bible cover to cover, you may want to hold your launch until you do. Cover to cover for discipleship one requires reading the Bible front to the back. A proficient reader can read the entire Bible in about seventy-two hours. My usual reading schedule allows me to read the Bible in eight weeks. If you read the Bible as you lead people, you should still be several weeks ahead of those you lead. This allows the Holy Spirit time for God's truths to steep in your heart. It also allows you time to do a bit of work to be able to answer simple questions. Regardless of how you consume the Bible, we suggest that you highlight your discipleship-one verses the first time you read it for discipleship.

You will also want to be ahead of the disciples in extra-biblical resources. Make sure you complete the "16 Key Topics in Christianity" (fill in every blank!) before you have your first discipleship-one meeting. This text gives you a good feel for the pathway and the growth that you expect in the first six months of discipleship. We ask our leaders to be at least one book ahead of the reading plan they have for the disciples.

> How many times have you read the Bible cover to cover?
> Will you reread it before starting discipleship?
> Have you highlighted the Bible using the discipleship-one reading focus?
> Have you completed the "16 Key Topics in Christianity"?
> Have you reviewed the recommended list of books?
> What are the first two books that you will require disciples to read?

Set Up Your Standard Meeting Agenda

We use the standard agenda discussed in the "Seven Core Practices" chapter. Regular, structured, efficient meetings are critical to the success of sustainable discipleship. You need to determine the length and standard agenda for your meetings. I use the following agenda for discipleship one.

- Life Update and Prayer (5 minutes)
- Bible Reading Review (55 minutes)
- Extra-Biblical Reading Review (30 minutes)

How long will your standard meeting be?
What is your agenda?

Step Four
Set the Requirements for Discipleship

There are requirements for discipleship. Jesus revealed the biblical "requirements" for being his disciples as he taught various people. There are also practical requirements for discipleship. Jesus's requirements are His. The requirements He taught reflect God's truths and eternal realities. His requirements are statements about what it means to follow. His requirements are real and still true.

- Love God more than anyone else.
- Deny yourself, and take up your cross.
- Forsake all that you have.
- Count the cost.

Jesus's message to a large crowd illustrates that believing does not always result in following. It was a strong message—very strong. Greg Laurie writes about this in his web article "The Requirements of Discipleship":

> Jesus saw a large crowd gathering. He knew that these people believed and accepted His message in principle. Prior to this point, Jesus had shown how the message of the gospel was for everyone. He had exposed the Pharisees as the religious hypocrites that they were. As a result, He had become enormously popular. Now He wanted to weed out those who were following Him for the wrong reasons. Some wanted to be dazzled by Jesus' miracles, while others came looking for a free meal. A few even hoped that He would overthrow Rome and establish God's kingdom. So Jesus turned to the multitude and preached a sermon that deliberately thinned out the ranks. . . . Why would Jesus say such things to all those people who followed Him? It seems that He is intentionally trying to get rid of them. In a sense, He is trying to get rid of at least some of them.[1]

What did Jesus say? He taught we must count the cost of following Him. He taught that we must give up everything. He even taught that we must "hate everyone else" and "hate even our own lives." These comparative lessons made a serious point: following Him was about more than getting a selfish fix.

Following him could cost families, livelihood, and much more. He wants us to know the cost as we decide to follow. The message is true and relevant to this day. Here it is:

> *A large crowd was following Jesus. He turned around and said to them, "If you want to be my disciple, you must, by comparison, hate everyone else—your father and mother, wife and children, brothers and sisters—yes, even your own life. Otherwise, you cannot be my disciple. And if you do not carry your own cross and follow me, you cannot be my disciple. But don't begin until you count the cost. For who would begin construction of a building without first calculating the cost to see if there is enough money to finish it? Otherwise, you might complete only the foundation before running out of money, and then everyone would laugh at you. They would say, 'There's the person who started that building and couldn't afford to finish it!' Or what king would go to war against another king without first sitting down with his counselors to discuss whether his army of 10,000 could defeat the 20,000 soldiers marching against him? And if he can't, he will send a delegation to discuss terms of peace while the enemy is still far away. So you cannot become my disciple without giving up everything you own."*

> — LUKE 14:25–33

It is interesting that Jesus never taught this difficult message before that day. He did not tell his first followers these requirements. He simply said, "Follow me." We have no record of Him telling the seventy-or-so dedicated disciples these requirements. Could it be that Jesus spoke what needed to be spoken to that crowd on that day? Could it be that people grow to the point of self-abandonment as they follow? That seems to be the case with Jesus and his followers. Jesus taught along the way as they grew. We do not see him telling the followers before they followed that they could not leave the work to go to funerals. However, there was a day when he said that to one disciple:

> *Another of his disciples said, "Lord, first let me return home and bury my father." But Jesus told him, "Follow me now. Let the spiritually dead bury their own dead."*
>
> — MATTHEW 8:21–22

We should be wise and consider that Jesus spoke to His disciples as individuals. He intended to teach, to push, and to call them to follow ever more increasingly. Jesus's statements about what it took to be His disciple are valid today, but these statements may not be appropriate hurdles for every beginning disciple. The new believer may not even be able to comprehend the choices like these. Perhaps a passionate follower does not need to hear that he must put God before his family until that challenge rises in his life. Perhaps each step toward maturity requires increasing abandonment. Words and commitments are nothing until tested. We can say to someone, "You have to choose God over your family. Are you ready to do that?" But their answer is almost irrelevant until the test comes. Would you or I tell a man to leave his wife because she did not want him to follow God? Paul did not when he was asked that exact question.[2]

The words recorded in Luke were more relevant to the crowd caught up in the moment than to the twelve who walked away to follow Him. We should be careful about putting too many barriers in the way of those who want to follow. How many leaders who teach, "You must forsake everything to be a disciple," have emptied their bank accounts and left their families? The Pharisees made this mistake, and Jesus criticized them for it:

For they don't practice what they teach. They crush people with
unbearable religious demands and never lift a finger to ease the
burden.

— MATTHEW 23:3–4

It might be better to accept people where they are and teach
them along the way. There might come a day for the hard words
Luke recorded—there might not. They might learn and accept
Jesus's requirements along the way—just like the Twelve.

Following means absolute commitment, but none of us who
lead others can say that we have truly made those commitments
until we are tested. Mature disciples have counted the cost and
are ready to choose God above all. Immature disciples may have
to grow to that point.

There are three basic requirements to begin and sustain a
formal discipleship process. These need to be shared as you
recruit people for discipleship.[3]

- They need to be able to make the weekly meetings.
- They need to make time to read.
- They will be reading the Bible cover to cover.

Other requirements arise as the disciples begin to learn and
are challenged to apply God's truths. I share these as these
requirements, as challenges arise in disciples' lives. Once one of
these issues comes up, it becomes a requirement. You need to be
willing to terminate formal discipleship if the disciples do not
meet the requirement. It sounds tough. It is tough, but it is not
mean.

Stuart was super eager for discipleship. Stuart struggled with
money. Food stamps were part of his budget. I knew him. I
knew that, within the first six weeks, we would be learning about
money and tithing. I was pretty sure that Stuart was going to
implode. "Stuart. We are friends. I love you. In fact, I love you

enough to tell you something tough. I do not walk through the formal process of discipleship unless people are attending, tithing, and serving. It just never works out. I have found that if people are not attending, they aren't hungry. I have learned that if people aren't tithing, they haven't surrendered their stuff to God. I have learned that if people aren't serving, they aren't ready for the formal process. Are you tithing? Have you worked that out in your life?" Stuart meandered through an explanation. "Stuart, I am fine with you. I love you. I am happy to help you grow. There are a thousand ways to do discipleship, but the formal process is intense. I can guarantee you that it will work, but I can also guarantee it won't work for you unless you are attending, tithing, and serving. It just happens. Instead of starting something that will not finish, let's do something else."

Sustainable discipleship needs to be accessible to everyone. We need to disciple comprehensively. We also need to know the limitations of formal discipleship. Stuart got it. It was tough, but he accepted the answer. I made sure to intentionally check up on him and hang out with him over the next few months. I needed him to know it was okay not to be ready for the formal process. I needed him to take the off-ramp without disconnecting from the church.

Stuart's example illustrates addressing the requirement when it arises. I knew Stuart. I knew his challenges. I knew this was an issue. So we had a "let the dead bury their dead" moment. I do not know the lives of other disciples. I may not realize that materialism is a big deal until we grow to those lessons. When I teach about tithing,[4] I go around the room and ask, "Are you tithing?" I know it is bold, but it builds intimacy and transparency. It allows openness and coaching that benefits everyone in the group. If a group member is not giving, I reteach the requirement to attend, tithe, and serve. I remind everyone that three things will derail discipleship: money, family, and pride. The conversation and the requirement become an issue when they are an issue. You must be willing to create an off-ramp if disciples fail to apply truth. You need to love them enough not to waste their time—not to waste the group's time. You need to love them enough to create a push.

In the end, Stuart was thankful for the push. He faced his demon. We helped outside the formal process. We cheered him on and fueled his challenge. Stuart grew. A few years later, Stuart entered the formal process and finished like a hungry warrior.

Terminating discipleship does not mean ending relationships. Formal discipleship is not mandatory to be in a church. Formal discipleship is not the only way. Not everyone is ready for a formal process. We intentionally create off-ramps during the recruiting process to allow the interested but not ready to graciously back out.

You should not be hasty, but you must be willing and ready to terminate (or never begin) discipleship. Much like Jesus, there are times you will need to thin the crowd. Do it with grace and love. Create other opportunities for them to grow. Never give up on discipling people.

Always cover the basic requirements as you recruit. Here are four other requirements that we use when making sustainable disciples. You should share these as appropriate throughout the process.

There Is No Learning without Submission

Disciples need to have a teachable heart. They need to approach the process to learn and grow. They need to be willing to follow the plan. They need to submit to the plan and find its value. This challenge seems to occur around step two (repent) or during the 4b challenge.

Jose was a somewhat self-assured follower on staff who said to his discipleship group, "I see no value in you discipling me. You have nothing to offer that I do not know." Jose's statement was made in reply to my question, "Do you want to do discipleship?" The entire group could sense something was wrong. There

was an elephant in the room every week as Jose refused to interact, gave surface answers, and remained disconnected from the
group. My question was the beginning of my building an off-
ramp. Greg, a seasoned follower in discipleship, built another
portion of the ramp. "So, Jose, my son is in your youth group.
And you are telling me that he should be in discipleship, but you
aren't willing to be in discipleship?" The tense but gracious
conversation continued until Jose determined that he should not
be in the group. We prayed with him and loved him, and he left.
The group excelled in transparency and intimacy in the weeks
following his departure. Every group member intentionally hung
out with, texted, and stayed connected to Jose. Over the next
few years, Jose got over himself, left his teaching position, and
focused on his walk. Jose remains one of my best prayer partners
and comrades in the faith.

He could not see that his pride was pushing him out of
discipleship. It was tough, but I built an off-ramp for Jose's best,
the best for the group, and the best for the Kingdom.

Do you remember Sally's story? She was having trouble
following because of trust and control issues. She was experienced in church. She had led Bible studies. After weeks of
passive-aggressive conflict in front of the group, I asked, "Sally,
do you trust me?" The group got quiet. "It's okay if you don't,
but you need to know that I actually have a plan. You need to
know that I love you." I was building an off-ramp that I hoped
we would not need. The group stayed quiet as she said, "I'm
sorry." I immediately closed the off-ramp, saying, "No. Don't be
sorry. It is okay. I am fine with you. If you could, just listen all
the way through my comments and not assume that I am hurtful." Sally knew that she was terribly performance oriented. She
only needed to be pushed to the step of repentance. Sally began
to excel in discipleship as she trusted me and followed. We have
a great relationship today.

The formal process of discipleship will not work if disciples
are not teachable.

Attending, Serving, and Tithing Are Essential

Our experience has resulted in us asking a few challenging questions throughout discipleship one. One is an upfront deal breaker, one breaks the deal quickly, and one breaks the deal within the first sixteen weeks. We share these short-term and midterm requirements during the assessment process. We share them with hope:

- You must be attending regularly before we begin discipleship.
- You must be serving somewhere in the first six weeks.
- You must be tithing within the first four months.

We are not trying to build attendance, fill jobs, or raise money. We are trying to address the beginnings of commitment. If you are not growing inside a body of believers, you are missing out on a critical part of your faith and practice.

Michael had struggled with attending church and being a part of church stuff during discipleship one. I had pushed Nathanael, his leader, to think about building an off-ramp. Nathanael listened to my counsel but pushed back, saying that he felt like it was not time. He worked with Michael, and Michael finished discipleship one with inconsistent church attendance. As discipleship-two groups launched in the next year, I noticed that Michael's name was missing. "I noticed Michael is not enrolled in a discipleship-two group. What's up with that?" I asked. I loved Nathanael's response: "I told him that he should take off a year and focus on being involved with the church, the body, and connected to other Christians. I am not sure he will get discipleship two without it." Nathanael built an off-ramp. Michael took it even though it was not his desire. Not surprisingly, the off-ramp taught Michael. He consistently attended church, signed up for mission trips, attended service projects, and is excited about life and future discipleship. We are too.

Disciples will never be healthy without the community. If they will not serve, they will not follow. It is just what it is. Jesus said our hearts are where our treasures are. If you will not give, you will never make it over the threshold of surrender and thankfulness. These three areas indicate quite quickly how serious someone is about following God. We want people to follow, and we want them to experience the fullness of a great relationship. We also want to invest our time wisely, where it will yield fruit.

We have never seen fruit when people do not attend, serve, and give.

We Do Not Chase

We do not chase absent disciples. There is a little coaxing and coaching, and then we just allow them to walk away. We do it with love. We meet with them and remind them of our friendship. We remind them that formal discipleship is not for everyone all the time. We remind them that it is not the only way. We provide a graceful off-ramp.

Disciples have to read, have to make meetings and be involved regularly in the life and service of the church.

We Do Not Do Lying

There is no discipleship without transparency and honesty. There is no basis for a discipleship relationship without honesty. Being dishonest about life or assignments are deal breakers.

"Did everyone do the work in the 16 Key Topics book?" I asked my group. One guy said he was behind. Everyone else said, "Yes." I thanked him for his truthfulness. I shared, again, how truth and trust were essential for any discipleship to work. If we are not truthful with each other, it is unlikely we will be truthful with God and ourselves. Morgan stuttered a bit and interrupted me, "Uh. I said yes, but really, I think I am one behind. Did you say we were supposed to be done with chapter five?" Was she being honest now? It felt like she was still hedging instead of just saying, "I lied." I decided it was not worth pursuing and said, "Thanks, Morgan. Everyone, remember you are safe here. The truth is incredible. Thanks for correcting yourself, Morgan."

It takes time to build trust. People have been punished for being honest. People have been rejected for the truth. People have been pushed for not performing the way someone wanted them to perform. Lying comes in many forms. You need to be discerning as you model, teach, and push honesty. You also need to be ready to create an off-ramp if dishonesty derails the process of formal discipleship. The model will not work with lying because following God will not work with lying.

You may wish to add or subtract from these requirements as you gain experience. Your nation's or society's culture may necessitate changes to the requirements of formal discipleship. Be careful as you make requirements. Do not make discipleship impossible or too hard. Do not adjust the requirements for individuals. Requirements should be the same for the group—for anyone being discipled. Avoid legalism, and make sure that your requirements are biblically based.

Step Five
Recruit Your First Members

The first step in making disciples is finding someone who wants to follow God. Finding someone takes on two forms:

- Evangelism
- Recalling Christians

Bill is my friend and avid disciple maker. He also has the gift of evangelism. He reminds me of my older friend and mentor, Bob Canuette, who now lives in heaven. Bob simply and efficiently evangelized every moment of his life. I can still hear him at lunch. (I admit, I blushed a few times at first.)

"What would you like to drink?" a waitress asked.

"Sweet tea," Bob replied. "Do you know why I want sweet tea?"

"Uh, no, uh, you like it?"

"I do like it, but do you know why sweet tea is like Jesus?"

"Uh . . ."

"Once you get the sugar in the tea, you just can't get it out. Jesus is like that. He comes into your life and sweetens it. Then no one can get that sugar out."

I can still hear him. He leveraged his age to speak to everyone like a well-loved child. Bill is the same but younger. He cannot be stopped. His actions and words are a constant, gentle, caring invitation to come to know God through Christ. He is continually recruiting disciples through evangelism. There is no way around it, evangelism is part of the disciple-making process. It is one of the essential invitations to become a follower of Christ.

We also need to invite Christians who are not actively following God. Only one in four Christians has had anyone significantly invest in them becoming an active follower.[5] That means 75 percent of churchgoing Christians could be living a less-than life. Only two in ten people have read the entire Bible.[6] Christians have become disciples of Christ in choice but not always in application. These would-be, all-in followers are not bad people. Most of them simply have not been invited to learn and apply God's truths. They were called to salvation, and it is time for us to call (or recall) them to get all that God intends for them.

The best call to discipleship is your story of transformation and living a full life.[7] Your story coupled with the life-changing truths of God are the two most powerful tools to invite others to a life of discipleship.

The best call is intentional. We need to be intentional about reaching those who do not know how much God loves them. We need to be intentional to recall every Christian who is not actively following. We need to intentionally, consistently call from our pulpits, over lunch, and with people we meet along the way.

The best call is prepared. Invitations should have a follow-up or "what's next" plan. Getting people saved is great, but God called us to make complete disciples. The greatest challenge to evangelistic campaigns is the follow-up. We make tremendous strides leading people to Christ, yet we so often fail to feed these new babies. We leave them malnourished, and they never receive the end of their faith. We need to invest in people as if they were our responsibility—because they are our responsibility.

Discipling necessarily involves initiating. It's not passive.[8]

You need to initiate the process and the lifetime practice of discipleship. You need to invite people to a life that will transform them. You need to invite them to a solution.

Not Everyone Will Choose to Follow

Everyone will not become a follower. Jesus said that the road to hell is wide and the road to life is narrow.[9] The book of Revelation tells us there will be many who never replace themselves as gods with the one true God. In one of life's greatest tragedies, evangelistic and recall invitations will go unanswered, rejected, and ignored.

Stay encouraged. Your success is not based on how many followers you make. God wants every human being to know Him, to choose Him, and to find forgiveness. You should want the same thing. God wants every human to follow Him into an incredible life. You should be dying to give people this same opportunity.

However, you are not responsible if they do not choose to follow. It is no more your responsibility than it is God's responsibility. People are free to choose to follow God or not follow God. He is not responsible for their choice, and if He is not responsible, you are not responsible either.

The great commission makes us accountable to "make disciples."

> "Go therefore and make disciples of all the nations, baptizing them in the name of the Father and the Son and the Holy Spirit, teaching them to observe all that I commanded you; and lo, I am with you always, even to the end of the age."
>
> — Jesus, in Matthew 28:19–20 (NASB)

We are responsible to invite. We are accountable to teach them God's truths if they answer. We are accountable to push them to stand on their own and become our peers. We are not accountable for their answer.

Everyone Is Not Ready Now

Paul said, regarding evangelism,

> After all, who is Apollos? Who is Paul? We are only God's servants through whom you believed the Good News. Each of us did the work the Lord gave us. I planted the seed in your hearts, and Apollos watered it, but it was God who made it grow. It's not important who does the planting, or who does the watering. What's important is that God makes the seed grow. The one who plants and the one who waters work together with the same purpose. And both will be rewarded for their own hard work. For we are both God's workers. And you are God's field.
>
> — 1 Corinthians 3:5–9

The seed of evangelism grows in each person at different rates. The harvest sometimes requires more watering and "God growing time." The same is true for the recall invitation. Some of your invitations will be answered with "Not now" or "I am not ready" or "I don't have time." It is okay. Breathe. Everyone is not ready now.

The invitee did not reject you, so let the seed set. Water it from time to time. Let it be watered by watching the success of disciples. Let it be watered by invitations that come in other ways. Let it be watered by your church's culture of discipleship. Always be ready to harvest. Never fear to check the crop again, but be careful not to push too hard.

If you push someone into discipleship, one of the unholy trinity will undoubtedly push them out. Do you remember Jose's story? Jose was that somewhat self-assured follower on staff. He was awesome. We loved him and his heart. He loved God and lived for God, but he never became part of our culture. He had to do it his way. He questioned everything. We finally pushed hard enough that he felt he "had" to do discipleship. It ended terribly, as he told the group that he did not need them to disciple him. He believed he was "complete." At age twenty-four, he said, "I see no value in you discipling me. You have nothing to offer that I do not know." We pushed him into discipleship, and pride pushed him out. I wonder if he will be in the same place at thirty-four. I doubt it.

Sam had seen it all. Sam did not like reading. Sam had been a Christian since he was walking. Invitation after invitation to discipleship went quietly unanswered. Sam never signed up for discipleship—well, until one day when Sam realized that he was being kind of a punk. (Those are his words.) Years later now, Sam is finishing the process and champions discipleship for others. He has also learned to wait for people like him to accept the invitation!

God and life have a way of getting us to the point where we

are open to being made better disciples. Be patient. Put them on a waiting list and watch the crop grow.

How Do You Find the Right People?

Discipleship training materials often quote Paul's words to Timothy:

> *Now teach these truths to other trustworthy people who will be able to pass them on to others.*

— 2 TIMOTHY 2:2

Paul's words need to be kept in context. Paul is teaching Timothy how to select and train elders and leaders. Paul is not talking about a discipleship process. Paul did not turn away people who would listen. God has already selected the pool of invitees: everybody. Paul actually teaches Timothy this regarding making disciples:

> *Pray this way for kings and all who are in authority so that we can live peaceful and quiet lives marked by godliness and dignity. This is good and pleases God our Savior, who wants everyone to be saved and to understand the truth. For, there is one God and one Mediator who can reconcile God and humanity— the man Christ Jesus. He gave his life to purchase freedom for everyone.*

— 1 TIMOTHY 2:2–6

You do not have to find the right people. You simply need to recruit. Whoever answers God's call and becomes a Christian is more than worthy to be made a disciple. The qualification is simple. If they want to follow, help make them disciples.

How Many People Do I Disciple?

Some may not be ready, some may reject, but many will answer God's call through your invitation. What do you do when you get more yeses than you think you can handle? Jesus's followers grew and shrunk in number. Sometimes he had eleven, and other times he had hundreds. But he never turned anyone away. In the context of making disciples, Jesus told us to go to the whole world. Thousands were added daily in the early church. There is no limit to the number of people I will disciple. There should be no limit for you either. Our methods may need to adapt, but the biblical model for discipleship works for any number of people. We might have to recruit help, we might be tired for a few years, but there is no limit to how many people we can disciple.

Invite them. Trust God. Dream big.

Step Six
Assess Your First Members

Here they come! Your invitees are showing up. You responsibly invited them, but do you have a responsible plan for what to do with them? The next step is to figure out whom you might be discipling and make sure they are ready to get started. Internally, we use this planning step to begin our assessment of candidates. Externally, we use this information meeting to explain discipleship and answer any questions.

The internal goal is to discover what they think they need and where they are in their journey. The assessment is the first step toward customizing discipleship to each unique individual.

We use a six-step model in this group assessment.

1. Listen. This is a great time to see if the person is a Christian. This is a great time to understand why they responded to your invitation.
2. Explain, in easy words, what discipleship is, how it happens, and what the benefits of discipleship are. We tell our stories.
3. Answer their questions.
4. Hook, sell, and dream.
5. Call each person to action.
6. Plot, scheme, and determine a start date.

There are three outcomes of the assessment:

- The person is not a Christian, and we lead them to Christ;
- The person is not ready for formal discipleship, so we lead them to opportunities to continue to grow with other believers in a less formal discipleship context; or
- The person is ready for a formal process and excited, and we start.

If the person is not a Christian and we get the privilege of "harvesting" him. Then we lay out a simple plan for regular discipleship and get going. New believers do not need an in-depth explanation. They are fresh, in love, and ready to do more. Little do they know that we are going to focus on them "being" more.

If the person is not ready for discipleship, we practice affirmation. There are plenty of great people who are not ready to take part in formal discipleship. We are empathetic. We always create a graceful, group-wide off-ramp. No one has to do formal discipleship to do discipleship. Our goal shifts to strengthening the relationship that we have begun. We schedule a lunch or coffee and focus on being brothers or sisters in

Christ. We foster their desire for connection. Formal discipleship is not a deal breaker when you live in a culture of discipleship. Formal discipleship is only one avenue among many roads.

If the person is ready and excited, we call them to action and gather some basic information. We determine their best days and times to meet. We decide whether or not they will need childcare. This information helps us finish the group meeting plan.

In our experience, sixty to ninety minutes is plenty of time to share the gospel, get deep on what they need, and set a plan. Too much time may cause you to say too much. You do not need to tell them every single thing about discipleship. You need to focus on their stories. You need only communicate the big picture of the discipleship-one process. Do not rush. Even if someone is clearly not ready, do not squander the opportunity to sow the seeds of discipleship. Enjoy the time, and spread grace.

Group assessments with more than thirty candidates require a highly inspirational, energetic leader to encourage interaction and intimacy. There will be little discovery without interaction. It is difficult to do an intimate assessment in such a large setting, but it can be done.

Do not bring this book, a cheat sheet, a notepad, or a chart. Do not take notes, type things in your phone, or even use your phone. Gordon Ramsay says, "No color, no flavor," when it comes to cooking. We say, "No casual, no conversation," when it comes to assessments. Here is a little more detail on how we execute each step.

1. Listen

Listening always comes first. After a few minutes of chit-chat, ask the obvious, "So what can I tell you about discipleship? Are you excited?" This will lead to the obvious conversation for the day. Be clear in your answers. If you confuse, you lose. Be thoughtful, and let them speak. Here is the internal plan for the listening step:

- Ask, "What can I tell you about discipleship?"
- Ask, "Why are you interested?"
- Ask, "What do you need?"
- Expand their answers to that question, and listen to understand. Ask them about their answers. Affirm them.
- Ask, "What do you love? What do you like? What makes you thrive?"
- Ask, "Where do you spend your time?"
- Ask, "Are you a Christian?"

There are three internal goals in the listen step:

1. Identify which of the fourteen steps the person is on (without showing them a chart). Do this by listening to what his life is like, how she is spiritually, and what makes him tick. This is internal and intuitive.
2. Identify where they are operating in the fourteen steps. Are they serving as a leader? Are they teaching? Are they just studying?
3. Compare and contrast where they are with where they are operating to understand how discipleship can best help them.

If they are not a Christian, focus on salvation. For the recall invitation, the compare-and-contrast step is one of my favorite moments in the assessment. I am amazed at how many people who have never studied the basics are teaching. Again and again, I discover leaders leading without leadership training, mentors, or coaches. I am amazed when I find qualified people doing nothing. As I am comparing and contrasting, I check my observations with a different round of the same questions:

- Ask, "Are you happy?"
- Ask, "Are you fulfilled?"
- Ask, "Are you thriving?"
- Ask, "What would you not do if you could not do it?"
- Ask, "Who are the people around you?"

The listening step is so critical to beginning a discipleship relationship. Make sure you are praying while you listen so that you can hear the Spirit guide you to your next question. You will be amazed again and again as God directs the conversation to a helpful place.

2. Explain

Explain what discipleship is in easy, simple, clear terms. Tell them your success story. Tell them the benefits. Tell them some of your favorite truths that you learned. Expose the pathway to them.

Be careful not to go too deep in this step. There is no need to tell them how hard it will be at times, that the enemy will put a target on their back, or that it is going to take four years. Do not exasperate them. They came to hear about something they are interested in. Keep it at that level.

Be responsible in this step. Share the basic requirements for beginning and continuing in a formal discipleship relationship:

- They need to be able to make the weekly meetings.
- They need to make time to read.
- They will be reading the Bible cover to cover.
- They will need to pick a regular place of service in the church.

It is only responsible to make sure that they know what to expect.

3. Answer

Ask them if they have questions, and answer them succinctly. If they do not have questions, do not go trolling. Just assume that you and God have done a great job, and move on to step four.

4. Hook, Sell, and Dream

Now is the time to close the deal. The hook helps them identify the immediate value of the discipleship process for them. Take the pathway-of-discipleship infographic and ask them, "Where do you think you are at on this path?" Walk them to an answer. If their answer conflicts with your understanding, ask leading questions so that both of you understand and figure out where they are on their path. Here are a few ideas on leading questions:

- He answers that he is enlightened, but you are not so sure. Ask him a few of the "16 Key Topics in Christianity" and see if he can give clear answers. Be gentle, and guide him to question his perception if he does not have the basic answers.
- She answers that she is consecrated, but you are not sure. Ask her about the situations where she has walked away. Explore the things that make you question her answer.
- He answers that he is called, but he has no clear passion. Explain that a call usually results in a passion. Explore this idea.
- She says she is being taught, but you think she is already learning to learn on her own. Ask her about the difference between being taught and learning on her own. Ask her about self-confidence. Explore her answers.

Remember, it is their path, not your path. Help them focus their answer on who they are (be) rather than what they are doing. Finally, circle the answer.

Now ask, "Where do you think you are living, operating, or serving on this path?" You may have to explain this concept a little. Our experience has shown that most people are operating either below or far beyond where they are on the path. This conversation provides an excellent opportunity for you to hook them. If they are frustrated, hungry, and worn, show them how they are serving beyond where they have been prepared. If they have not had a great mentor in residency or have been abandoned in a leadership role, show them how great it could be to have a mentor or two. Use the hook moment to illustrate how the biblical maturity process should work. Show them how it can bless them and how incredible it is. Then move to sell.

The sell is simple. What could life be like if you could get to that next place in your Christian maturity? What if we could help you get what you want in life? What if you could become bulletproof? What if you get back to the basics? What if you could resolve that frustration? What if you could have an even better life? Show them how they can have a great life, doing great things. The sell is a great time to impress the importance and value of "being" before "doing."

Dream is the development of a bird's-eye view of the discipleship process for their future. Hook and sell are more about immediate and perceived problem-solving. Dream is selling the future value of discipleship for their lives and for the Kingdom of God. Dream is all about the future.

> *"The Kingdom of Heaven is like a mustard seed planted in a field. It is the smallest of all seeds, but it becomes the largest of garden plants; it grows into a tree, and birds come and make nests in its branches."*
>
> — JESUS, IN MATTHEW 13:31–32

Feel free to use Jesus's illustration about the future value of discipleship and the worth of the long-term investment.

Value is the key to hook, sell, and dream. People make decisions based on perceived value. People invest in what has value for them. The immature may be more focused on the value for them and their lives. That is okay. That is what the unknowing do. There is plenty of time in discipleships two and three to get them Kingdom minded. You know that discipleship has great value. Share that while you hook, sell, and dream.

5. Call to Action

Do they want to be part of a formal discipleship process? You may ask it more casually, "Do you want to be discipled?" The value of a call to action cannot be stressed enough. Ninety-percent of Christians surveyed said that discipleship was never offered to them.[10] Offer it. Call them to action.

If they say yes, move to step seven. If they say no, keep having coffee, stress that there are many ways and times to walk, ask them about their kids, and set a time to hang out again. Give them an easy, gracious exit point from the discipleship discussion. There is more to life than formal discipleship. Suggest a book or two. Enjoy the time with them.

6. Plot and Scheme

Plotting and scheming is first an external process and then an internal process. The external process is simple:

- Work out a meeting schedule with the group, using the available times you determined earlier.
- Pick a meeting time and location.
- Swap contact information.
- Tell them you will provide a Bible reading plan.

Internal scheming is a bit more intuitive. You may want to reach out to your mentor or your discipleship boss to get more perspective as you scheme. Experience is valuable in the scheming process. Internal scheming is done after the assessment and gets you listening to God about the best process for each person. Internal schemes answer questions like these:

- Which immediate, felt needs can be met?
- Which outside reading might be appropriate?
- What are the dangers (too talkative, engineering mindset, argumentative, self-conscious, etc.) of the discipleship relationship?
- What do you need to be praying for?
- Do they need outside resources, like counseling?

The assessment is a great opportunity to get to know another person in the body of Christ. It is a tremendous ministry opportunity. Done well, it sets people up for immediate or future success. Even if the invitee declines discipleship, the assessment is a great inspiration and teaching moment. Leverage the time for the Kingdom. Plant a seed. Water a seed. Maybe even harvest one.

Step Seven
Your First Meeting

The first meeting sets the tone and expectations for every meeting afterward. You should have a well-planned agenda for this first meeting and keep to it. You should cheer the disciples on as you set expectations and assign work. Structure and consistency are important in discipleship one and build a foundation for future phases. I use the following outline for my first meeting:

Open with Individual Prayers (15 minutes)

The standard agenda for sustainable discipleship opens with a time of focused prayer. Disciples are asked to pray one thing that they need in the moment. We tell them, "This prayer time is not for your aunt, your mother, or even what your spouse needs. Pray for one thing that you need right now." It may sound simple, but you will be surprised when you see how difficult it is for disciples to ask for one specific thing. Disciples open up with standard lines like, "Father, I want to thank you for this time," or, "God, I praise you for everything that I have." Some of these openers are genuinely prayed, and others are a bit rote prayers. Either way, after two or three, I interrupt the group and say,

"Hey guys. Sorry to interrupt, but God knows you are thankful for this time. This is a time to ask for one specific thing that you want. Can you see God in heaven saying, 'Stop with the disclaimers. Just tell me what you need.' I am glad you are thankful, but are you praying a standard prayer. When you talk to your wife, do you say, 'Honey, I am thankful for our marriage. I am thankful for today. I am thankful that you married me. Can you pass the salt?' Prayer is a conversation. Prayer is you talking genuinely to God."

Interrupting may sound intrusive, risky, and disruptive. It works for me. It sets the tone. You may want to wait and have this talk after everyone finishes, but you will have to teach them focus.

I also regularly interrupt this time to refocus the process and guide disciples to ask for one specific thing they need. When a disciple prays, "God, I need direction. I need to know what to do," I am prone to interrupt and ask,

"What is it that you need direction for? Do you need to know how to get there? Do you need to know what He would do? What is it that you really need? Are you confused? How can he help? Let's try it again."

When a disciple prays, "God I am struggling with finances and need help," I interrupt and say,

"What is it that you need? Do you need fifty dollars? Do you need to stop spending? What could God do right now that would really help you? Do you need to tell Him that you do not know what to ask for? What can God do for you right now?"

I interrupt. I disrupt. It allows me to teach disciples how to be raw and real, and talk to God about what they really need in the moment. It allows me to teach them to be aware and realistic. If God walked in the room and asked you what you needed right then, would you be ready? Would you know the number-one thing that you needed help with? Would you know the one thing to ask? This weekly prayer time is about ruthless, risky honesty in front of God and in front of the body of Christ. It gets disciples praying and carrying each other's burdens. You may not be bold enough to interrupt graciously. Be yourself, but make sure that you leverage this short time to achieve honesty and transparency. Use the time to help people identify their current needs.

Six Thinking Hats (15 minutes)

I use the *Six Thinking Hats* framework developed by Edward de Bono each time I begin a new group. I created a simple handout with six colored hats and each with its title. I share the idea that great teams communicate in different ways at different moments. I share this as the positive that it is. Here is a quick outline I use:

1. Identify the hats and share de Bono's premise.
2. I cover the red hat. Most of us use the red hat a lot when we encounter new things. We say things like, "I think," and, "I feel." Talking about what we are thinking and feeling in discipleship is entirely acceptable. Sharing how we feel when we read a

particular verse is good. Checking what we think about a truth is great. But we need to be clear that we are using the red hat, and we need to be seeking the data that the white hat provides.

3. I cover the white hat. The white hat in discipleship is what we know, what is true, and what should be applied to our lives. Data, truth, is what we want to build our lives on. We need to know when we are sharing white-hat truths.

4. I cover the black hat. Critical thinking is a big part of understanding, processing, and applying truth. We should never fear questions, critiques, and the "other side of the coin." Critical thinking is the pathway from being taught to learning on our own.

5. I cover the green hat. Green-hat thinking is the rollout of white-hat data and black-hat thinking. We need to dream and think about how truths are relevant to our lives. We need to be creative as we figure out how to apply God's truths to our lives.

6. I cover the blue hat. The leader wears the blue hat. The leader guides discipleship. The disciples are not discipling each other. They are not leading each other. They cannot be allowed to take the blue hat. You are prepared, confident, and skilled to guide the disciples. It is your job. Let them know.

The Group Relationship (15 minutes)

I launch from the blue-hat discussion to a simple explanation that although there is a group, each person is in an individual relationship with me. Each person is being individually discipled in a group. Each person benefits from hearing others' comments, but each of them only discusses their comments.

I share my contact information for questions outside of the group. I remind them that they are not to work together outside of class. I lead married couples to understand that they are not married while in the group. They are individuals. You may benefit from reviewing the section on designing groups in the chapter on customization.

I also share the basics of a healthy discipleship relationship to include the things that discipleship is not:

- It is not an accountability group.
- It is not a therapy group.
- It is not a class.

Leader Q and A (20 minutes)

Even when I am more familiar with groups, I make time to ask, "What do you want to know about me?" It is fun and, although it seems so basic, begins to build intimacy and a relationship. This valuable time begins to build transparency and trust with people you do not know. There is nothing more powerful than your story, and this Q and A is a great disruptor. Be ready with a few feeder questions. People are not used to interviewing you. Disciples may not know what to do with this kind of personal sharing. Have a few questions ready, like, "Do you know how I proposed?" "Do you know what my favorite thing in the world is?" or, "Do you know my deepest secret?" People learn to open up when we open up. Let the Spirit lead your answers, and begin to bond with your disciples.

The Reason for Discipleship (30 minutes)

I go around the room and ask, "Why are you in discipleship?" I make no comments while I listen. For the ideal group of three disciples, I just listen. I can keep track of their answers. For larger groups, I use my whiteboard or a flip-chart pad. I always get the classic answers:

- I want to get closer to God.
- I want to learn how to make better decisions.
- I want to understand my Bible more.
- I want to know what God wants me to do.
- I want to deal with my bitterness.

These are all great things to want from God, but none of them is a good reason to be in discipleship. I push, asking, "What do you mean 'get closer to God'?" I ask what it means to make better decisions. Does the disciple make bad decisions? What will he do when he understands more of the Bible? How will that fix things? I affirm that these are all great things to want from God, and then I say something like,

"What if you asked your wife why she wanted to be married to you and she said, 'To get closer to you. To make better decisions. To understand life more. To figure out what to do with my life and to solve my problems'? You might begin to wonder if your marriage was a good decision. It is the same with the most common answers to the question, 'Why do you want to be in discipleship?' They might be okay things to want from God, but they aren't reasons to be in discipleship. So much of our Christian lives is about consumption. What happens when you get this answer, this thing that you want from God? Is discipleship over? We should want to be followers because we love Him. Because He amazes us. Because we want to get to know Him better. Because we want to follow. Just like a human relationship, we want to be with God because we are head over heels in love. Sure, God will give direction, provide answers, and help. He is God. Just like you will help your spouse be better. But if your girlfriend only wants to be your girlfriend for what she gets from the relationship, how terrible is that? You want her to want to be in a real relationship. You want your best friend to be your best friend because he likes you, because he appreciates who you are. You want him to want to get to know you. It is the same with God."

The best reason to follow God is that He is incredible. His ways bring glory to Him. His ways work for us. Being like Him and learning from Him is the crown jewel of love. We should want to follow Him because He is worth following. I use this time to quietly teach what discipleship is all about. I teach that discipleship is a relationship, a journey, a walk to wherever it leads. Discipleship exposes me to incredible truths that transform me. It is about being what I already claim to be: a follower. Just like the opening prayer time, this short section sets the tone for what discipleship will be. I do my best to use this time wisely. I help correct, set, and expand healthy expectations. I affirm that they will most likely get what they need along the way. I also share that what they think they need may change as they learn more about God.

Money, Family, and Pride (10 minutes)

I transition from how incredible discipleship can be to a few quick warnings. I share stories from the Bible and life that reveal the battles arising whenever we step out to follow God. I teach how the enemy puts a target on each of us when we begin to make a difference. I share the unholy trinity that will derail discipleship: money, family, and pride. I do not discuss the 4b, 9a, or 10-11 challenges. These challenges will be shared if, and as, each becomes relevant. My goal is to warn them of potential challenges and put them on guard against the enemy. I want them to be self-aware and prepared to face battle. I also share stories of the many who succeed.

Practical Information (15 minutes)

I wrap up with some practical information. I share the standard meeting schedule. For the ideal group of one leader and three disciples, this is what we use:

1. Life Update and Prayer (5 minutes)
2. Bible Reading Review (55 minutes)
3. Extra-Biblical Review (30 minutes)
4. Relational Chit-Chat (after the formal meeting, no more than 30 minutes)

For the group of ten, we use:

1. Life Update and Prayer (10 minutes)
2. Bible Reading Review (65 minutes)
3. Extra-Biblical Review (40 minutes)
4. Relational Chit-Chat (after the formal meeting, no more than 30 minutes)

You need to provide the following materials:

- A forty-seven-week Bible reading plan. This allows for two breaks and compensates for the first meeting. Discipleship is a fifty-week event. To keep starting times consistent, you need to finish in fifty weeks. There is no reading for the first meeting, so we reduce the reading plan by one week. We also allow for two weeks off from reading, reducing the plan by two more weeks, for a total reading time of forty-seven weeks. In the first few months, your group will be more efficient in covering their highlights. We have found that the first five books of the Bible take much longer than all other books. You may need to call a week off from Bible reading to get caught up with the review.
- The "16 Key Topics in Christianity" workbook.
- The next three months of service opportunities.
- A list of mission trip/project opportunities.
- A meeting schedule, or at least the "weeks off" schedule for the year.

You may choose to use my first meeting agenda. You may develop an agenda that works better for you. Whatever you do, make sure that you set the proper tone and expectations for those you are going to make disciples. I encourage you to speak little about why you are doing what you are doing. Just do it, and let the results be experienced. The first meeting is the vision-casting meeting. Use it well.

Step Eight
Get the First Quarter Right

The second through the twelfth meetings are critical for a successful discipleship-one phase. And a successful discipleship-one phase is crucial to discipleship two. These meetings will cement the expectations, reading discipline, and standard meeting agenda.

Your goal in discipleship one is to expose disciples to God's truths that will cause them to be convicted, be enlightened, and be called to follow. The work is all about repenting, following, learning, and serving. Your role is a guide. You are not a classroom teacher. The disciples have to read, they have to attend the meetings, and they have to take part. If they do not engage, they will not be made disciples. They will not learn to be what they have already become: followers.

You shared the expectations in the first meeting. You will cement those expectations over the next eleven weeks. You will push them to focus their opening prayers. You will push them to be honest that they can find thirty minutes a day for God. Developing a habit of exposing ourselves to God each day is counterintuitive to our busy lifestyles. Making the time and repenting will be the simplest but greatest challenges in the first quarter. The expectations should not be shared as your expecta-tions. The expectations should not even be shared as God's expectations. You need to get the disciple to own the expectations. For example, take Roger, a businessman who was struggling with the discipline to read and prepare. "Roger, are you telling me that you did not watch football, read a paper, or do anything other than work, eat, and sleep every day of last week? Really? Let's be honest. You can make thirty minutes. How many hours did you study to get your business degree? Do you think that learning about God and how to live an incredible life will take any less time?" You will have to push disciples to accept the expectations and embrace them for their own good.

Making time to read is the most challenging expectation at the start of discipleship. But it is not the only challenging expectation. People will face challenges when they share and risk being transparent. They will face challenges when they read the Bible with the phase-one focus. People will struggle to let go of their analytical mindsets. They will struggle as you push them to think on their own. The adjustments during the first quarter are greater than any other time along the pathway. Choosing to follow requires a lot of personal change and discipline.

Be diligent in following the standard agenda in the first quarter. Keep the prayers short, do the Bible first, and finish it in time. Push them to be efficient. Push them to stay on track. Push them to focus on things that apply. Teach but be careful not to take too much of the time. You need to leave time to cover the "16 Key Topics of Christianity" well. These basic principles are important.

You will find that it takes much longer to cover the first five books of the Bible than any other books. How God created and who God created us to be are big topics in Genesis. The corruption of mankind is a pivotal topic raising many questions. The fact that God uses such imperfect leaders is at once hopeful and confusing. Addressing the failures of Abraham, the shortcomings of Aaron, and the life of Joseph will raise topics of deception, and God changing his mind. The laws that God established for his nation of people are hard to process. It is difficult to accept His best desires for His followers and apply those to our lives. It will be hard to get through all the highlights of "aha" and troublesome moments. Hot topics like cheating, homosexuality, and what constitutes murder will sidetrack disciples. They are prone to lose the focus, wanting to solve the world's problems instead of finding and applying His truth to their lives. We say again and again, "If it does not apply to you, accept it and move on." Discipleship one is not a theology class. It is not a Bible study. It is not a time for a disciple to decide anything for anyone other than himself. Discipleship one is a time to be exposed to and apply God's transforming truths to our lives. It allows us to learn the character of God and design of man. Leverage the challenges of the first quarter to cement the expectations and disciplines of individual discipleship.

Disciples face the expectations of attending, serving, and tithing during the first quarter. Disciples need to be attending church and discipleship meetings. Within the first six weeks, disciples should identify a weekly service opportunity involving them in the lives of others. It is vital that you model weekly service too. If there are not enough service opportunities, create opportunities. It is essential that disciples serve regularly.

Adjusting budgets and lifestyles to facilitate tithing is a big first-quarter challenge. Teaching about tithing might be a big challenge for you too. Teaching about money can be uncomfortable. It can be uncomfortable to ask, "Are you tithing?" But being able to talk openly about money and finances brings transparency and honesty. Money, family, and pride derail disciples. Tithing, attending, and serving are part of God's antidote to these dangers. Materialism fades in the face of thankfulness. Relationships deepen in community. Service fights pride as nothing else can. You need to create off-ramps if disciples cannot tackle attendance, service, and tithing.

You also need to challenge disciples to complete the first step of making disciples: evangelism. My friend Bill asks his group, "Who did you share your story with this week? How did it go?" He makes extra time to push this principle. He works diligently to get disciples to embrace the responsibility of sharing their new life story. Regardless of your approach, disciples grow when they share their story. Sharing their stories offers life to others and is part of following God's plan. Evangelism is the beginning of disciples making disciples.

The first quarter sets the stage for discipleship one. It also sets the stage for the other phases of discipleship. As the first few years of a child's life set the tone for his entire life, the first quarter is critical to the whole sustainable-discipleship process. It is much easier to start well than to try to change later.

Step Nine
Plan That Trip

Service projects and mission trips have been great tools in our discipleship process. Service and travel supercharge discipleship. Both require self-sacrifice of vacations, time, and money. These events also immerse disciples in challenges that provide many opportunities to apply the truths they are learning. Service projects and mission trips can be used intentionally to make disciples.

Check your calendar. Find opportunities. Share the options. Sign up for a trip and take your disciples on an adventure. Push them to sacrifice a week of vacation. Push them to do something greater than them. Walk with them through the uncomfortable. Prepare them. Stand beside them. Get to know them.

Step Ten
Your Twenty-Sixth Meeting

Discipleship one is very different from the other phases. The steps along the pathway of disciplehips two and three are much more ordered and discrete. The phase-two step of learning to learn leads naturally to being prepared. Being prepared leads naturally to the point of being consecrated. Discipleship one is messier. You should have noticed that a lot is going on at the same time. Disciples are repenting again and again as they are taught new truths. Disciples become enlightened as they learn, as they are convicted and while they serve. Conviction seems to happen throughout the process. There are moments when it looks like the disciples are standing on all six steps at the same time.

The halfway point of discipleship one is a great time to refresh the process. It is a great time to provide an overview of what is going on in discipleship one. It is a great time to recast the vision, tone, and focus of the phase. It is also a great time to reassess the individuals and the group. The halfway point may signal the need for some specific books on specific topics to move your group down the path. I use the following questions to launch a refreshing conversation:

- What are the three things that kill discipleship?
- Have you experienced any of the three so far?
- How did you resolve any challenges with the unholy trinity?
- Why are you in discipleship?
- What was your answer at the beginning?
- Has your life, your practice of following God, changed?
- What is the focus of Bible reading?
- Why do we use that method of Bible reading?

I always run a short reassessment of the group, asking things like this:

- Are you tithing?
- How is your weekly service going?
- How many service projects have you participated in?

The halfway point is also a great time to check up on your plan. Look back at the sustainable-discipleship model, and review the objectives. Walk through your original plan. Are you still on course? Will those you make disciples be ready for discipleship two? Are you still focused on transformation and "being" before "doing"? Take a look at where you are headed, and plan the next few books that the disciples will read.

Your group should have completed the "16 Key Topics in Christianity" and at least two other extra-biblical books. You should have completed a mission trip with the disciples or have one coming up soon. The disciples should be serving in basic capacities in the ministry of the body of Christ.

You are over the startup challenges. Regular meetings and methods have become routine, and leaders tend to lose the magic. Followers are doing what they are supposed to do. There are fewer challenges. It can be easy to forget why we are doing what we are doing. It can be easy to lose the vision to routine. The halfway point of discipleship one is your opportunity to refresh, retune, and ready the group for a successful second half of phase one.

Step Eleven
Your Thirty-Ninth Meeting

The final quarter of discipleship one has arrived. The cycles through conviction and repentance should have become easier. Disciples have become masters at making quick adjustments to God's truths. They should be more proficient at reading the Bible and allowing the Holy Spirit to guide their highlights and meditations. The ideas of educational and performance-oriented Bible study should lie far in the past. The push to focus on applicable truths should be a natural and intuitive process.

Your goal is to finish well and lay the groundwork for the next phase. You want the disciples to have an exciting, productive discipleship two. You want to hand off well-prepared disciples to the next leader. The third quarter is the time to prepare them for what is coming. So far, you have been championing the "aha" moments. You have been providing course correction as disciples explore God's truths. You have been teaching them to keep truths in context. You have been teaching along the way and helping the disciples become enlightened. You have pointed out applications along the way. You have brought to mind truths they have learned and pushed them to adjust their lives to those truths. You have pushed them to serve and live beyond their immediate capacity.

You have been giving them fish.

Discipleship two will shift the focus from being taught to learning to learn on their own. Disciples will learn to fish as they make direct connections from a truth they highlight to other verses where the same truth is taught. The third quarter is a great time to quietly begin to get the disciples ready for this new train of thought.

Bible reading will transition from the Old to the New Testament in this final quarter. Your first leverage point to prepare disciples to connect direct truths is that the disciples have consumed most of the Bible at this point. They know many truths, just waiting to be connected. Your second leverage point is that the New Testament continually references the Old Testament. Writer after writer makes direct connections from a new truth to truths handed down through generations. Your third leverage point is that the New Testament is easier to understand and digest. Most of the truths are taught simply, and the writers are prone to explain them well. Long-term Christians are also more familiar with the New Testament. They have grown up with the stories. They have heard the Gospel. It is easier to connect what we readily understand.

These three leverage points allow you to begin to scatter in questions. For example, when the disciple reads Peter's words,

As the scriptures say, "I am placing a cornerstone in Jerusalem, chosen for great honor, and anyone who trusts in him will never be disgraced."

— 1 PETER 2:6

you can ask, "Does anyone's Bible have a footnote telling you what Peter is quoting?" If they have a New Living Translation, the cross-reference is included in the Bible text. Other translations might use footnotes. You might have to read ahead and plan one or two connections a week. The direct connection for the verse above is Isaiah 28:16. Have the disciples stop, look it up, and then just move on. I encourage you not to connect every truth to another truth. Periodically point out a verse that can be connected easily. Ask the disciples if they see or know the connection. If they do not, help them connect it. Model the behavior critical to learning to learn: we should be asking ourselves, "Does this connect anywhere?" every time we notice something in the Bible. You do not have to give the secret away. Do not explain the behavior in detail. Simply model the behavior illustrating that the Bible teaches most truths again and again.

Your goal is to build toward the discipleship-two focus and skills. Your work is not to finish that work. Your work is to lay a foundation that the disciple will find familiar as discipleship two begins.

Step Twelve
Getting Ready for the Transition

Each new cycle of sustainable discipleship needs a solid, practical plan. The final quarter signals the time to begin preparing for the next cycle of discipleship. How do you prepare for that next cycle?

Preparing for your first transition is easier. You will move disciples from discipleship one to discipleship two, and hopefully, you will begin another discipleship-one cycle. If you are still flying solo at your church, this is about all that one person can handle.

Preparing for your tenth transition is more complicated. Disciples will be moving between multiple phases of discipleship. You will be recruiting for discipleship one. You will be looking for disciples who got "stuck" between phases. You will have more groups and a larger pool of leaders from which to select group leaders. We have a discipleship pipeline leader who prayerfully works to guide this process. He talks with potential leaders, assessing their readiness. He reviews the current disciples. He also thinks about things like meeting locations, meeting times, and launch dates. Our pipeline leader is a matchmaker combined with an event coordinator. You may have to do this on your own.

We use a simple set of questions to help us prepare for the beginning of each new cycle and to transition disciples from phase to phase effectively. Here is a bird's-eye view of how we plan:

1. We plan the launch date for the next cycle. We finish a cycle in about fifty weeks, allowing ourselves two weeks before we begin the next cycle. Typically, we start toward the end of January each year.

2. We start talking about discipleship at community gatherings at the beginning of the fourth quarter of the current cycle. We begin to announce the launch date in the eleventh month. (For us, that is late October.) We start taking names for discipleship one in the twelfth month.

3. We identify and talk to disciples "stuck" between phases in the eleventh month of the current cycles.

We assess their desire and readiness to move to the next step.

4. We calculate how many current disciples will be moving to their next phase. We prepare our estimate of overall enrollment in the eleventh month.

5. We quantify our available leaders for each phase of the new cycle. We give attention to who needs a break, who has been on a break, and what phase each leader has last led. Our goal is to mix up groups, leaders, and the phases that each leader leads.

6. We plan our discipleship-three groups. Our preference is a mixed-gender group of six to nine disciples. Disciples in this phase are efficient, prepared, confident, and skilled at processing truth. A larger group multiplies the preparation of leaders. It also increases exposure to different perspectives. We have found benefit in men and women participating together. Our second choice is a group ratio of 1:3. Our third choice is one-on-one discipleship in this phase. Smaller groups are always single-gender groups. We remove the disciples in this phase from the discipleship leader pool, as they need to focus on the finishing residency and adding skills to their calling.

7. We plan our discipleship-two groups. Our preference is a single-gender group of three disciples. Both years of this phase require much more time with each disciple. We do our best to only use this group size for discipleship two.

8. We quantify the number of people expressing interest in discipleship one. We plan those groups preferring single-gender groups of three disciples. If we need to use larger groups, we give serious consideration to mixed-gender groups. We have noticed that mixed-gender groups tend to be more

efficient and stay on track. We assign new leaders in the second year of discipleship two before we assign existing, available leaders.

9. We talk with current leaders about the disciples in their groups to get a feel for how much we need to mix groups up. We listen carefully to their feedback and work on the final group design for all phases. This fun meeting reminds me of football draft day, with all leaders and directors present.

10. We provide a "How to Lead Discipleship One" seminar for the new leaders of this phase.

11. We offer a "How to Lead Discipleships Two and Three" workshop for any new leaders of these phases.

12. We host a launch lunch meeting with all leaders, reviewing the model, casting vision, and spending an extended time in prayer.

13. We release the leaders to prepare their discipleship group plans. Our pipeline director provides support and accountability.

If you are entering your second or third cycle, the process may be much easier and annotated. But the fourth quarter is the time to plan for an effective and efficient launch of the next cycle.

16

CONTINUE LEADING DISCIPLES IN DISCIPLESHIP TWO

When you have confidence, you can have a lot of fun. And when you have fun, you can do amazing things.

— Joe Namath

Discipleship two is much different than discipleship one. The focus is different. The reading is different. The goals are different. Disciples transition from being taught to learning to learn. Discipleship two adds confidence and skill to the preparation of discipleship one. Not only is the focus of discipleship two different than one, but those you lead are also different.

Disciples coming to discipleship two have invested a year of their lives in becoming more prepared followers. They know more truth. They have seen God's truths work. They have failed, fallen, and learned how to get back up. They have seen God's promises honored as they apply his truths. They are much more durable and steady. These disciples understand the requirements and have counted the cost. They have shown themselves committed to following God more closely. You may need to remind them of the basics, but your more significant work is to help them begin to connect truths throughout the Bible.

Discipleship one was a simple exploration of the Bible. Cover to cover, the disciples merely observed and highlighted their "aha" and troublesome verses. They have been exposed to the entirety of the Bible, and the Holy Spirit has much truth with which to work. They have seen topics and truths in many different passages and contexts. As they begin discipleship two, the Holy Spirit will begin to bring to mind all they have been taught.[1] Your task is to help fuel connections and show them the power of connecting truths throughout the Bible.

The disciples are ready to take a deeper dive into extra-biblical resources that stretch their understanding of who they are in Christ and what salvation is all about. The focus of discipleship two is different. The disciples are different. And you are different too.

You are prepared. You are confident. You have experienced God's transforming power through the process. You have seen Him transform others. You know how the process works. You trust it. You have invested a year or two of your life in being made and walking with those being made disciples. You are confident in your ability to follow God. You are confident in the power of adjusting to God's truths. And you are confident that you can pass this on to others. You are confident that everyone can experience the full life that you have found.

If this is your first time leading discipleship two, you are going to have to reread the Bible and extra-biblical books. You will need to give attention to the focus and tone of discipleship two. You will need to know the method of Bible reading and the dangers inherent in discipleship two. If you have completed several cycles, you will be more confident in the material. You might simply review the works and methods.

This chapter is designed to give you a simple step-by-step guide to launching your first discipleship-two effort. It is written from the perspective of group discipleship, but the steps are virtually the same for one-on-one discipleship. This is how we do discipleship two.

Step One
Review the Model

We are in our fifth generation of making disciples. We are also a smaller church. There are times when I have not led discipleship for a year as I lead others to make disciples. If it has been a while since I launched a group, I take a few minutes to read "Review the Model" in the "Launch Your Discipleship-One Group" chapter. I also review the process and my role.

The three phases of discipleship are distinct in purpose and process. We need to be careful to embrace those distinctions in each phase and not take people too far forward or backward on the pathway.

- Discipleship one teaches. It challenges. It exposes. The leader follows the Spirit's work in the individual lives. Disciples are taught.
- Discipleship two causes disciples to learn how to learn. It teaches them to think, to pray, to hear from God, and to connect truths. It exposes them to deeper truths, moving them from milk to meat.
- Discipleship three teaches disciples to synthesize truth. It causes disciples to expand each truth they encounter. It pushes them to milk every applicable drop out of the initial truth and its connections. It focuses on making disciples who think about following in every moment.

Your role also changes as you begin discipleship two. You are no longer the teaching guide of discipleship one. You are the learning guide. You push disciples to connect direct truths to answer their questions. You give hints toward unseen connections. You might ask, "Have you thought about how everyone is saved the same way in both the Old and New Testaments?" as you point the disciple toward the truth that salvation has always been by faith. You say things like, "Great observation that salvation is for all men. Was it that way in the Old Testament?" as you point them toward the truth that any person could become part of the nation of Israel by choice and faith. You demonstrate the process of connecting. You grow disciples to become people who make the connections themselves. You teach the principles of inductive, exegetical study. You teach them how to study in context. The goal is to shift them from merely consuming truth to becoming those who produce.

Sustainable discipleship relies on the specific focuses of each phase and achieving those goals in each phase. This moves the disciple to the residency step of the discipleship pathway.

Step Two
Establish the Objectives

Discipleship two is a two-year process guiding disciples through the next four steps along the pathway:

- Learn
- Be Prepared
- Be Consecrated
- Do Residency

The first year of discipleship two is completed in weekly meetings using the standard agenda. In the second year, disciples are making disciples, leading discipleship one with your guidance.

The Focus of Discipleship Two

Discipleship two begins somewhere between the "dos" of serve and learn. This phase is focused on helping the disciple learn to learn on their own and be prepared to live well and serve God. Discipleship two almost always ends with the disciple becoming consecrated, abandoned to following God, and all in.

Discipleship two focuses on disciples making connections throughout God's word. It pushes disciples to figure out and make the applications of truth. The disciple moves from consumer to producer during this phase. The disciple begins to take on servant-leader roles, working with more senior leaders to carry out regular and special projects.

Teaching disciples to make disciples happens along the way and more directly at the end of the first year. The goal of the disciples making disciples needs to be presented quietly and casually from the first day of discipleship two. The comprehensive "how to" make disciples is taught in the final months of the first year. The focus of year two is you supporting, guiding, and leading disciples who are making disciples.

The Tone of Discipleship Two

The tone of discipleship two is one of growing independence from the disciple maker and one of preparation. Discipleship two allows a bit more flexibility on meeting schedule, with an increasing focus on getting the disciple into challenging situations that push them to apply stored truths.

The Followers of Discipleship Two

The followers in discipleship two are more focused and eager. Disciples will have learned to embrace their variety as an advantage without letting their uniqueness derail the discipleship process. They will better understand the overall design of humans and have figured out how their specific talents, skills, and personal makeup interact with God. They will not struggle as much with submission because they have seen the value of following others and God. The concept of trust will not be difficult, but you will still need to build trust with new disciples. It will be easier for you to keep control and lead. You may face some challenges as you push each follower to become a learner.

The Bible Reading Focus of Discipleship Two

Disciples use a standard plan to read the Bible cover to cover, daily. There are no days off. Disciples are pushed to read daily instead of cramming it all in the day before their meeting. Disciples are encouraged to use the Bible containing their highlights from discipleship one. Using the same Bible

- allows them to see which challenges or questions remain,
- reminds them of their previous answers, and
- intuitively focuses the reader on the passages that did not "catch" their attention in the first pass.

There are cases when it might be better for the disciples to use a new Bible. We often encourage new believers and those who struggle reading to choose an easy-to-read Bible for discipleship one. These disciples will benefit by stepping up to a more literal Bible translation. If disciples use a new Bible, we encourage them to transfer their highlights.

The first year of discipleship two asks the disciple to find new truths that he can embrace and answer. This year is all about moving from being taught to learning on your own. We ask the disciples to highlight the following things each week:

- New questions they notice. We ask them to try to answer those questions using only their Bible and what they have learned so far.
- Connections between a truth they discovered and other truths that they have learned. Here are a few examples:
- God used the elder leadership model in both the Old and New Testaments;
- the fact that Rahab was blessed for lying;
- the connections between New Testament quotes of Old Testament verses; and
- Jesus was present during creation in both the Old Testament and John's account that all things were created by Jesus.
- New "aha" verses that inspire or catch the attention.

We strongly suggest that they do not take notes, use the internet, do research, or use a study Bible. The objective is to fertilize exegetical, inductive study. Disciples should be encouraged to rely on God and on His Spirit "to bring all things they have learned to mind." Disciples use biblical text as they understand and learn. Disciples should be taught to see what the Bible has to say about the Bible. Disciples are also guided to "avoid foolish discussions"[2] and to let the Spirit of God guide their answers.

In year two, the disciples will read along with those they lead. They will not highlight new verses. They will be addressing the truths of those they lead rather than identify new truths.

Extra-Biblical Reading and Work for Discipleship Two

Disciples complete the Discipleship Discussion Manual Volume 2, "16 Key Virtues in Christianity," in the first sixteen weeks concurrent with other extra-biblical reading. The disciples are ready for this push. We select "lighter, shorter" books for the disciples to read while they work concurrently through the manual.

Disciples complete the "How to Study the Bible 101" course within the first seven months. This course increases the potential of disciples learning to learn. It "puts legs" on the big picture of the Bible. It covers topics like how we got our Bible, how the Bible was translated, broad biblical concepts, and beginning study methods. We provide this course as a weekend seminar to all discipleship-two groups.

In the remaining thirty-four weeks, reading focuses on biblical doctrine, leadership, deepening prayer, Christian living, and service. Disciples should read at least ten extra-biblical books during this phase.

We require disciples to read the following books in year one of discipleship two:

- *Mere Christianity* (C.S. Lewis)
- *Birthright* (David C. Needham)
- *This Present Darkness* (Frank E. Peretti)
- *And the Shofar Blew* (Francine Rivers)
- *Ruthless Trust* (Brennan Manning)
- *Well-Intentioned Dragons* (Marshall Shelley)
- *This We Believe* (John N. Akers)
- *Six Thinking Hats* (Edward de Bono)
- *Reflective Life* (Ken Gire)
- *Sit, Walk, Stand* (Watchman Nee)
- *The Way of a Pilgrim*
- *Sustainable Discipleship*

The sustainable library categorizes the following books as additional resources for the first year of discipleship two:

- *The Search for Significance* (Robert S. McGee)
- *Fresh Power* (Jim Cymbala)

- *Fresh Wind, Fresh Fire* (Dean Merrill and Jim Cymbala)
- *Piercing the Darkness* (Frank E. Peretti)
- *The Pursuit of Holiness* (Jerry Bridges)
- *Improving Your Serve* (Charles R. Swindoll)
- *Good to Great* (James C. Collins)
- *21 Irrefutable Laws of Leadership* (John C. Maxwell)

There is no break in the outside reading. Disciples should be pushed to read as many extra-biblical works as possible.

The library also has topical books appropriate for any phase, to address specific needs or to push the group forward. If you choose to build your own library, make sure the books focus on the tone, the plan, and typical challenges faced in the four steps along the pathway of discipleship two. The group should read the same books at the same time. Pick wisely, trust God, and watch the truth unfold.

Disciples do not read new resources during the second year as they are leading others through appropriate discipleship-one resources.

Making Disciples in Discipleship Two

We encourage everyone in discipleship two to take a year to lead discipleship one before they begin discipleship three. Those who spend a year making disciples thrive in discipleship three. The results are so compelling that we now make our discipleship two a two-year process.

Disciples get to give to others what they are receiving. Discipleship one drew them closer, made them free, and built confidence through application and experience. They learned to learn in the first year of discipleship two. They understand the value of being a follower of Christ. Passion and value form the launching pad for you to call them to disciple others.

The call begins quietly in the first year of discipleship two.

We set the goal that disciples will disciple someone when they finish year one. The call builds toward the middle of year one, with a discussion of who they know that might enjoy discipleship. The call continues as they pray for three specific people. In the last third of discipleship two, we begin to "reveal" the secret sauce, the model, and the "how-tos" of leading a disciple. Comments like, "Do you see what we are doing here and why?" and, "When you are leading someone, you will need to push them a bit," increase toward the end of year one. We begin light, "along the way" training for how to make disciples.

By the end of the first year of this phase,

- they will have a concrete recruiting list,
- they will have read this book, and
- they will take part in the "How to Make Disciples" seminar.

You will walk alongside them as they lead discipleship one in their second year of discipleship two.

There are times when a disciple will begin discipleship three without first making disciples. Life is challenging. There are times when a disciple is not ready or able to make disciples in year two of discipleship two. There are times when we create an off-ramp allowing followers to take a year off. We leave ourselves free to customize discipleship, but we desire that disciples lead disciples before beginning discipleship three.

The Dangers of Discipleship Two

The unholy trinity of money, family, and pride can quickly derail the discipleship process. Point out these dangers as soon as you see them. Save everyone time, and save the disciple from the enemy.

Disciples may face the 9a challenge as they move from being prepared to being set aside. Disciples will be tempted to "get out of the fire" and abandon the discipleship process. This challenge is discussed thoroughly in Chapter 14. It is our responsibility to slow them down and help them adjust. Our role becomes one of understanding and encouragement.

Emerging leaders can get cocky. One of our great leaders refers to this as "his punk phase." It happens. Preparation, skill, and mostly, their confidence can turn into pride. Emerging leaders struggle to submit. They often talk too much and counter their leaders publicly. You may watch them make decisions out of sequence. Address this head-on. Be frank and understanding. Many emerging leaders never make it past this danger and leave the process to start new things that they control. Love them though this danger. Share your stories. We have all been there. We have all done this.

Mission Trips and Service Opportunities for Discipleship Two

You should push each disciple to join you for one weeklong mission trip. We have already discussed the bonding, power, and opportunity to teach along the way during extended trips. Do not miss this opportunity with those you make disciples. You should require service at special church events and one area of regular service beginning within the first sixteen weeks. These opportunities should be junior leadership roles.

Step Three
Develop Your Plan

Developing a practical plan is critical. Discipleship two is the only phase that has a two-year duration. Year one is accomplished in weekly meetings. Ideally, year two has those you lead discipling others in a discipleship-one group. This step will help you develop a plan for year one of discipleship two. Your year-two plan is to provide checkups and support to the disciples as they lead others. Remember, discipleship without a plan will always fail. Count the cost, and plan well.

Making Time

If this is your first time leading discipleship two, you will have to read everything that the disciples read. You will need at least forty-five minutes of uninterrupted time a day to read and prepare. You will need two hours a week for the regular meeting. You will need a few hours outside of the meeting to answer emails and texts, and have coffee with those you lead. You need to make time for service events, mission trips, and regular service at your church. These are the times where you lead along the way and teach in the moment.

If your church is new at discipleship, you may still be developing leaders. You might be the guy or gal who is leading a new discipleship process. You might have to lead another discipleship-one group while you start this discipleship-two group. It happens. No one wants to derail or slow down the process. Make sure that you plan your time well. Do not overextend yourself. Plan your time one step at a time.

1. At what time, each day, will you read and prepare?
2. What day and time can you hold a regularly scheduled discipleship-two meeting?
3. Do you need to lead another discipleship group simultaneously with this group?
4. If so, what day and time can you hold that group meeting?
5. What months are you available to go on a mission trip or an extended service event?
6. Does your church have a mission trip or extended service event that you can plug your group into? If not, you may have to do a little research.
7. What regular service are you currently doing?

8. What other service opportunities are there—at that time—that your group can join you in?

Pick Your Launch Date

This is not your first rodeo! It should be at least your second. If your church has established a standard plan, your launch date might be just a week or so after the completion of discipleship one. If you do not have a standard plan, I encourage you not to wait too long between discipleships one and two. The first part of discipleship two can be completed in fifty weeks. Work to keep the launch dates of various phases consistent.

You may want to refer to "Pick Your Launch Date" in the previous chapter.

When will you launch your group?

Pick Your Meeting Day and Time

Picking your standard meeting day and time is actually picking two or three times that will work for you. If you are launching several discipleship groups with several leaders, you have the flexibility to plug followers into several different times. If you are the sole leader launching two groups, you will definitely need a few options and need to be flexible.

Meeting on the same day and at the same time is easier. People are creatures of habit. Standard meetings are easy and predictable, and always work best.

What are your best days to meet?
What are your best times to meet on those days?
Are you willing to be flexible?

Pick Your Meeting Place

What three spaces can you access for your meeting?
Is the space quiet or, at least, not disrupting?
Is the space comfortable?
Will you feel rushed?
Does it have a whiteboard?

Pick the Books You Need to Read

Your first discipleship-two group will be more efficient and informative if you stay ahead of those you make disciples. If you are only on your second or third read of the Bible, it is probably a good idea to read it through again. Remember, by the time a disciple makes it through discipleship, he will have read the Bible four times. Stay ahead. Stay fresh.

Be ahead of the disciples in extra-biblical resources too. Make sure you complete the "16 Key Virtues in Christianity" (fill in every blank!) before you have your first discipleship-two meeting. This text gives you a good feel for the pathway and the growth that you expect in the first six months of discipleship two.

How many times have you read the Bible cover to cover?
Will you reread it before starting discipleship?
Have you highlighted the Bible using the discipleship-two reading focus?
Will you highlight it before beginning?
Have you completed the "16 Key Virtues in Christianity"?
Have you reviewed the recommended list of books for discipleship two?
What are the first two books that you will require disciples to read?

Set Up Your Standard Meeting Agenda

We use the standard agenda discussed in the "Seven Core Practices" chapter. Regular, structured, efficient meetings are critical to the success of sustainable discipleship. You need to determine the length and standard agenda for your meetings. I use the following agenda for discipleship two.

- Life Update and Prayer (5 minutes)
- Bible Reading Review (55 minutes)
- Extra-Biblical Reading Review (30 minutes)

How long will your standard meeting be?
What is your agenda?

Step Four
Set the Requirements for Discipleship

The section "The Step-by-Step Guide" detailed the concepts behind the requirements for discipleship. Here is the summary of Jesus's requirements:

- Love God more than anyone else.
- Deny yourself, and take up your cross.
- Forsake all that you have.
- Count the cost.

We have three basic requirements to begin and sustain a formal discipleship process. You may want to review these with your new discipleship-two group.

- They need to be able to make weekly meetings.
- They need to make time to read.
- They will be reading the Bible cover to cover.

These are the additional requirements of successful discipleship:

- There is no learning without submission.
- Attending, serving, and tithing are essential.
- We do not chase.
- We do not do lying.

Again, you may wish to add or subtract from these requirements as you gain experience making disciples. Your nation's or society's culture may necessitate changes to the requirements of formal discipleship. Be careful as you make requirements. Do not make discipleship impossible or too hard. Do not adjust the requirements for individuals. Requirements should be the same for the group—for anyone being discipled. Avoid legalism, and make sure that your requirements are biblically based.

Step Five
Recruit Your First Members

If this is your first discipleship-two group, you may not need to recruit. You will be inheriting followers who recently completed discipleship one. If your process has grown or you have been discipling for a few years, you might actually do a bit of recruiting.

Life happens. Schedules come and go. Babies get born. There are times when people completing discipleship one will need to take a year off. Kim was pregnant as she finished her phase of discipleship. She was doing great. She was excited. But she was concerned about the time investment and group schedule with the baby coming. It made sense. I agreed with her. She was going to miss quite a bit of the group time. We both decided she needed a year off and came up with a personal growth plan of reading and involvement for the next year.

Delays between discipleships one and two also happen strategically. Do you remember Michael's story? Michael was struggling with attending and being a part of the community. Nathanael created an off-ramp and encouraged Michael to take a year off and spend time becoming an active part of the body of Christ. A year later, Michael was recruited to be part of discipleship two.

Review the list of people moving through sustainable discipleship. Check in on those in between phases. Talk to other leaders, and see if it is time to get them going on the next phase.

After you have determined your group members, here are the next steps:

1. Pick a day and time for your regular meetings.
2. Pick a place.
3. Pick your launch date.
4. Set a forty-seven-week Bible reading plan.
5. Distribute the information above. Get them reading, and share what you want them to highlight. The initial meeting will be much like a regular meeting, with time to review a week's worth of Bible reading.

I communicate all of this information in a short, inspiring email. I include a pitch that sets the tone and the focus of discipleship two. You may choose to meet with them over coffee or use another method. Disciples entering this phase know the plan. They simply need information.

Step Six
Assess Your Group Members

If this is your church's first discipleship-two group, you may be leading the same people you led in discipleship one. There will be little need to assess them. You know them. They know you.

You are in a groove. Discipleship two will pick up where each disciple is on the pathway. Your planning will be simple.

Leading the same group is easier, but it is not optimal. Hopefully, your church's process has grown, and you are strategically mixing up leaders, phases, and followers. Developing a responsible plan begins by determining where disciples left off. Your planning continues by getting to know them.

Discipleship-two group assessment is less formal than the assessment for discipleship one. There is no introductory meeting. There is no pitch. You should determine where the disciples left off in discipleship one before the first meeting. Talking to the disciples' previous leader is your greatest asset in this assessment. Disciples are still growing. They are not aware of the entire process or the concepts of sustainable discipleship. They might believe they are further along or further behind where they actually are on the pathway. Their discipleship-one leader can quickly get you up to speed.

Group assessment begins intentionally but casually in the first meeting. It continues throughout the first few meetings, with pointed questions. Observing the disciples in action is your greatest asset. The main goal of group assessment is to get to know the disciples. Your goal is to understand God's design of, the talents of, the personality of, and the gifts of each disciple.

The assessment is a tremendous ministry opportunity. Done well, it sets people up for immediate and future success. Leverage the time for the Kingdom. Plant seeds. Water the crop, and prepare them for the next step.

Step Seven
Your First Meeting

The first meeting of discipleship two is an extended regular meeting. The disciples will pray and review the Bible reading for the week. The extra-biblical time will be used to refresh a few discipleship group concepts. The extended time of this meeting will allow the disciples to get to know you.

The agenda should be well planned, and you should keep to the agenda. I use the following outline for my first meeting:

Open with Individual Prayers (5 minutes)

Disciples will be familiar with praying for one thing that they need in the moment. You may need to interrupt them or remind them at the end, "This prayer time is not for your aunt, your mother, or even what your spouse needs. Just pray for one thing that you need." You may need to rattle the cage a bit or remind them of the purpose of this prayer time.

Review of Discipleship Group Concepts (15 minutes)

I open every discipleship-two group with a quick review of how the discipleship group works. I am cautious not to overdo this review. I trust that the disciples are familiar with the concepts. I am only reminding them of the goals, responsibilities, and methods. Here is a quick outline of my review points:

1. I review the *Six Thinking Hats* method. I remind people that we are looking for data, truth. I set them free to have red-hat moments, and I champion the idea of black-hat, critical-thinking interactions. Discipleship two leverages critical thinking to connect truths. I remind them that I wear the blue hat.
2. I remind them that each of them is in an individual discipleship relationship with me. Each person is being individually discipled in a group. Each person benefits from hearing others' comments, but each of them only discusses their highlights and comments.
3. I transition to a reminder of what derails

discipleship. I remind them that the enemy puts a target on each of us when we begin to make a difference. I ask, "What three things derail discipleship?"

4. I close this item by reviewing the requirements of discipleship. I remind them that submission, attendance, service, and tithing are required to remain in the formal process. I remind them of the importance of honesty. I go around the room and let people share their service areas and how they are doing, and I ask, "Are you tithing?"

The Focus and Tone of Discipleship Two (10 minutes)

Disciples in the second phase are beginning to get the plan. I share the focus, objectives, and tone up front. I use the predictable pathway chart to show them that they are somewhere between the "dos" of serve and learn. I show them where they have come from and reveal the big goal for each phase:

- Phase one focuses on repentance and teaching.
- Phase two focuses on learning to learn and connecting truths.
- Phase three focuses on synthesizing truths, leading, and teaching.

I remind them that we are still not using outside resources. Our goal is to allow the Holy Spirit to connect the truths of the Bible cover to cover. It will increasingly be their job to figure out and make applications of the truth. I share that they should become producers in discipleship two. I share that we will begin to help them understand the process and reveal a few secrets.

I pitch the idea that they should make disciples in year two if they want to get the most out of the process. I pitch this in passing, trying to avoid overwhelming them. They do not need to worry about whether they will be able to make disciples. They need to focus on the immediate step of learning to learn.

Getting to Know Each Other (30 minutes)

This section of the meeting achieves two purposes: it allows the disciples to get to know me; and it begins my group assessment of the disciples. I do not share my secret agenda to assess them. I simply ask, "What do you want to know about me?" This time begins to build intimacy and relationship. It increases transparency and trust. This question-and-answer time provides the opportunity for me to ask them the questions that they ask me. It allows me to transition to getting to know each disciple. "My favorite color is black. I love the dark. What is your favorite color?" I respond. "My deepest hurt was a breakup. I never expected it. It sucked to get rejected. Have you ever been dumped? How did you handle it?" I transition their questions back to them. The back-and-forth movement between my story and their stories allows me to begin to sense who they are. Let the Spirit lead your questions and your answers. Use this time to bond with the disciples and to secretly assess them.

Reviewing the Bible (50 minutes)

We review each disciple's highlights. Disciples should have highlighted the following:

- New questions they noticed. They should have tried to answer these using only their Bible and the truth they know.
- Connections between a truth they noticed and other truths that they have learned.
- New "aha" verses that inspired them or caught their attention.

You have more experience. You know your culture and environment. You may develop an agenda that works better for you. Whatever you do, make sure that you pray together, review the Bible, and remind them of the requirements. Make sure that you set the proper tone and expectations. Again, I encourage you to speak little about why you are doing what you are doing. Just do it, and let the results be experienced.

Step Eight
Get the First Quarter Right

The first quarter sets the tone and disciplines for discipleship two. Discipleship two transitions disciples from being taught to learning to learn. Disciples increase in preparation and confidence as they connect truths from their weekly reading to other truths that they learned in discipleship one. Experiencing your brain and the Holy Spirit connecting stories and truths is empowering. Connecting truths gives the disciples a more comprehensive understanding of God's truths.

Of course, you need to stress the basic disciplines of reading daily rather than catch up. Teach them the value of being present with God daily and exposing themselves to His truth every day. Disciples do not read because they have to read. Disciples read to feed. The truths of God are transforming and challenging. His truths provide the necessary nutrition for growth. The Spirit uses God's truths to provide conviction and direction.

I use the first quarter to supercharge doctrinal understanding. I focus extra-biblical reading on what we believe about God, faith, and our design. The first quarter is the time to launch and almost finish the "16 Key Virtues in Christianity." I pair this workbook with four foundational books in the first quarter:

- *This We Believe*
- *Birthright*

- *Sit, Walk, Stand*
- *Well-Intentioned Dragons*

I have found that these books, combined with the first six or seven books of the Bible, provides fertile soil for the disciple to connect truths. You may choose different books, a different order of books, or a different library. But I encourage you to keep this quarter focused on advanced truths about Christianity and serving God.

I transition out of the first quarter with disciples reading *This Present Darkness*. This novel provides their first look into the unseen and the spiritual. It also provides a balance to the rather educational feel of the first four extra-biblical books. The first-quarter goals are to

- reinforce the basic truths of Christianity,
- expose them to the exegetical truths that they will find during Bible reading, and
- expose them to works that practically apply what they are learning.

You are guiding disciples to learn on their own. You are guiding them toward being more prepared. The consumption and connection of God's truths will make them prepared for every good work.

You should push the discipline of disciples connecting every highlight to similar truths. Provide hints, guidance, and help when they are stumped, but push them to learn how to directly connect one truth to another instance of the same truth. The Socratic method causes learning by asking questions. It will be your greatest asset in discipleship two. Ask that first question, "Where else in the Bible is this truth taught?" If the disciple does not recall an immediate connection, guide them. Ask, "How does that truth connect with the truth in . . ." "What is the concept of the verse you highlighted?" is another powerful starting point for connection.

You need to guide them away from indirect connections and expansions of truth. Affirm their ability to see the indirect, but remind them that the first year of discipleship two is about making direct connections. Establish this discipline for the success of the first year of this phase. Stress exegetical observation and inductive study of the Bible.

The first quarter of discipleship two is all about the hard work of connecting truths forward and backward through the Bible. It is about the hard work of laying a solid foundation of truth about God and the design of man. Discipleship two achieves its full potential when disciples learn to learn.

Do not forget to challenge the disciples to be sharing their story with new people each week. Be bold and ask the question, "Whom did you share your story with this week?" Evangelism is a challenge for people. Help the disciples see that it needs to be intentional, and help add preparation to their efforts.

Step Nine
Plan That Trip

Service projects and mission trips provide you the opportunity to model the real-time application of God's truths. Both require self-sacrifice of vacations, time, and money. These events also immerse disciples in challenges that provide many opportunities to apply the truths they are learning. Service projects and mission trips can be used intentionally to make disciples.

Check your calendar. Find opportunities. Share the options. Sign up for a trip and take your disciples on an adventure. Push them to sacrifice a week of vacation. Push them to do something greater than them. Walk with them through the uncomfortable. Prepare them. Stand beside them. Get to know them.

Step Ten
Your Second and Third Quarters

You established a foundation for learning during the first quarter. You focused on the method of learning to learn. You exposed the disciples to a large volume of truth about Christianity and God. You opened the door to the deeper realities of spiritual warfare and the unseen. The second quarter expands and begins to build on that foundation.

The biblical reading follows the same path of revealing "aha" moments and addressing troublesome verses. Connecting truths discovered to other directly related truths reinforces inductive Bible study. The disciples will become more and more adept and wise. Their wealth of knowledge will continue to increase. You may notice a tendency for them to become somewhat scholarly and interested in more detail. Keep them focused on truths that apply to their lives. Challenge them to focus on things that are transformational and not merely educational.

You should have the disciples complete the "How to Study the Bible 101" or a similar course at the beginning of the second quarter. "How to Study the Bible 101" covers four key topics.

- How we got the Bible that we read today.
- A brief survey of the books of the Bible.
- Basic interpretation guidelines powered by Spruell.
- The inductive method of study.

We offer this in a one- or two-day seminar and invite others from the church. I use the following extra-biblical resources in the second quarter:

- *The Way of a Pilgrim*, Part One
- *Piercing the Darkness*
- *Six Thinking Hats*
- *Improving Your Serve*

My goal is to deepen the understanding of our design and our daily spiritual lives as followers of God. *The Way of a Pilgrim* introduces a more mystical type of prayer, expanding on Torrey's very practical *How to Pray* from discipleship one. *Piercing the Darkness* continues the idea of spiritual warfare and mankind that began with its prequel in the first quarter. The other books are practical applications of how we learn and how we live.

The deeper dive into truths about Christianity begins with *Mere Christianity* by Lewis in the third quarter. I add several books that focus on soul care and leadership skills. You need to be mindful that you are moving through the step of being prepared to being set apart. Pick works that add to their preparation and set them up for being consecrated. Here is a list of the books that I add to biblical reading in the third quarter:

- *Mere Christianity*
- *Reflective Life*
- *Fresh Wind, Fresh Fire*
- *The Pursuit of Holiness*
- *And the Shofar Blew*

And the Shofar Blew is an incredible work by Francine Rivers, following the lives of a community and exposing the challenges of ministry, holiness, and consecration. It is the last book that I have disciples read in the third quarter. If the disciples have read *Fresh Wind, Fresh Fire*, I substitute *Fresh Power*. I use optional books from the sustainable-discipleship library to fill the gaps. You may choose different books, but I encourage you to keep focused on biblical preparation, soul care, and consecration.

The fourth quarter sees the disciples moving toward leadership in the community. In the second and third quarters, you prepare disciples to abandon themselves to God's work, to take the first steps of making disciples, and to begin residency.

Step Eleven
Getting Them Ready to Lead in the Fourth Quarter

The fourth quarter completes the first year of discipleship two. It culminates with a call for disciples to make disciples during the second year of this phase. However, the fourth quarter is not about preparing them to lead in discipleship.

The fourth quarter focuses on moving disciples from being consecrated to doing residency. The "doing" of residency and disciples making disciples will come naturally if you stay focused on the "bes" of discipleship two: disciples being prepared and being consecrated. You can leverage your guidance of Bible reading to illustrate the truths of consecration and holiness. The extra-biblical reading should support the call to consecration and residency as well. These are the books that I typically use in the fourth quarter:

- *Ruthless Trust*
- *The 21 Irrefutable Laws of Leadership*
- *Good to Great*
- *The Top Ten Mistakes Leaders Make* (Hans Finzel)

Ruthless Trust focuses on soul care and being sold out to God. The other three works focus on great leadership. My wife often uses *The Best Yes* by TerKeurst in this quarter. Disciples need to know how to sustain themselves as they begin to serve others in ministry. Disciples need to know what makes great leaders as they enter residency. Residency is about practicing leadership from the second chair. If the disciples have not read *Well-Intentioned Dragons*, you should have them read it during this quarter. Prepare these disciples to avoid the 9a challenge of emerging leadership. Include the example of Rehoboam's juvenile leadership blunders. Make sure that disciples tie leadership truths to biblical truths. Work in a discussion of 1 Peter 5:5–6 during extra-biblical reading:

In the same way, you who are younger must accept the authority of the elders. And all of you, dress yourselves in humility as you relate to one another, for "God opposes the proud but gives grace to the humble." So humble yourselves under the mighty power of God, and at the right time he will lift you up in honor.

Serving and leading others is the natural outflow of a sustainable disciple's life. Leading is not who they are. Leading is a natural "do" for disciples who "be" prepared and consecrated. Leading is just another step down the predictable pathway. We need to prepare them for leadership, but we need to remember that it is a "do." We need to add leadership preparation to these consecrated followers. We need to let that preparation become skill through residency. We need to make sure that they are ready to make disciples. But we need always to remember that we make disciples so that they can thrive in their personal walk with God. Discipleship is not about making leaders, but it will make leaders. Discipleship is not about building up the church, but it will build up the church. A community full of mature believers will be a mature community. The fourth quarter is a great time to refocus disciples on the purpose of their discipleship. It is a great time to remind them that the journey is entirely about their personal relationship with God. Stress it. Repeat it. Live it during the fourth quarter.

I am often asked, "So you are saying that everyone will lead? Everyone will make disciples?" I always answer no and then follow immediately with, "Let me ask you a question. Will everyone become a Christian?" The simple answer is no. The more profound question is, "Should everyone become a Christian?" The answer has to be yes. Then I ask, "So should every disciple lead?" The following silence begs the question, "If everyone leads, who will follow?" It seems logical. Not everyone can lead. There are simply not enough leadership positions. If everyone leads, who will follow? The truth, however, is that most everyone leads someone. People may not see themselves as leaders, but they are leading. Parents lead children. Supervisors lead workers. Teachers lead students. Volunteers lead other volunteers. Few people lead no one, but disciples will always lead someone. Why? Because disciples are following God, who told them to lead others by making disciples. Every Christian will not make disciples, but every disciple will make disciples. He tells us to make disciples. It is impossible to follow God without answering His call to follow Him. Leading people to follow Him is his direction. How can anyone be a follower of God without adjusting to the truth that He told us to make disciples? How can anyone be transformed and not offer the lifesaving transformation to others? How can anyone see the greatness of God and not be broken by the desperate condition of most of the world? Being a disciple should result in us wanting to make disciples. Experiencing success should create a passion in us for others to succeed. Having a full relationship with God should create a longing for others to have the same. So no, not everyone will lead and make disciples, but they should.

We need to push, challenge, and deploy disciples to lead the world to a better place. We need to push them to be agents of change. We need to show them the power they have to change the world. Nathanael made an incredible connection that changed my understanding of 1 Peter 3. He was teaching on wives submitting to husbands. He framed it well by keeping Peter's words in context with the entire book. Peter was not saying it was fair for women to live in a culture where they were not seen as equals. He was teaching the same truth that he had been teaching in chapters one and two: wherever you find yourself, live excellently for God. Peter taught new Christian women that they could be agents of change. Their excellent living in a lousy environment might even lead to their husbands' salvation. Then Nathanael moved to verse seven and blew my mind.

In the same way, you husbands must give honor to your wives. Treat your wife with understanding as you live together. She may be weaker than you are, but she is your equal partner in

God's gift of new life. Treat her as you should so your prayers will not be hindered.

He made the obvious point that men should honor women like women honored men. Then he said, "But do you see what he says to husbands? He tells Christian men that they are to fix the bad culture. They are to be agents of change and treat their wives the way God wants. They are to fix the problem by treating their wives as equals." Incredible. Powerful. We can lead our world to a better place. We can be agents of change, bringing the love and truths of God to those around us. We need to raise up godly leaders for their own good and for the good of all those around them. We need to help them become what God designed them to be. We need to help them become the leading light to the world.

We also need to push, challenge, and deploy disciples to make other disciples. There is no better way to learn to make disciples than to make a disciple. You never learn more than when you are teaching. You never learn more about your discipleship practice than when you make disciples. Making disciples in sustainable discipleship is not about checking off a box. Making disciples is part of being a disciple. It is part of the sustainable-discipleship journey. It is a step on the pathway, and making disciples makes me a more complete disciple. It cements truths. It teaches me more about application. It causes me to consume, process, and produce truth. Making disciples is about me being made a disciple. It is part of my individual, personal journey in following God. Making disciples is powerful for disciples. We need to push disciples to make disciples in the second year of discipleship two—for their own good.

We also need to prepare disciples to make disciples before we deploy them. Use the fourth quarter to reveal the secret sauce, the burger, and the "how" you make disciples. Teach them everything you know, along the way, in context with each moment. Begin to prepare them by modeling and revealing how the process works. Use the last months of the fourth quarter to read and review this book as part of your extra-biblical reading. *Sustainable Discipleship* will give them the practicals they need to make disciples. It will also supercharge their experience in discipleship three.

It is important to note that we have lost more disciples at this point than at any other point in the process. We lose them to two challenges for the same reason. We lose them to the 9a challenge, where they simply want to do their own thing. These emerging leaders feel prepared to go out and conquer the world. We often lose the impatient and intolerant at this point. We also lose disciples when they refuse to make time to make disciples. Some say that they are not ready to lead someone else. Others say they do not have the time. Some say they need a break. Whatever the words, the reason for the losses is the same. Money, family, and pride (that horrible unholy trinity) also take their toll at this step in the process. Do your best to challenge, cheer, and coach them through these challenges. Do not lose heart if you lose a disciple or two. You cannot make people follow God. You cannot make people make disciples. Think about it, if God cannot get them to wait or make disciples, can you? You might be encouraged by our experience. Almost every disciple who disconnected at this point reconnected a year or two later as they watched their peers go on to even greater living. Schedules clear up, exhaustion fades, and God keeps challenging them. Do your best to rescue them, keep in contact, pray for them, and wait until they become hungry again.

On a side note, when these disciples return to the process, we do not have them take the step of discipling others. We start them in discipleship three and see how they do with following God. We do not let them lead others until they finish discipleship three.

The fourth quarter is all about moving disciples to the point of "being consecrated" and helping them find a resident place to serve, grow, and learn.

Step Twelve
Supporting Them in Year Two of Discipleship Two

Sustainable discipleship releases disciples to make disciples in year two of discipleship two. The disciples' ability to connect and synthesize biblical truth will grow as they make disciples. The disciples have been sharing their success with other believers. They have been sharing their story, leading unbelievers to become followers of God. You have been pushing a comprehensive discipleship process. You have been advertising the opportunity and value of giving a year to God to become a closer follower. You should have a pool of people ready to start discipleship one. Those people are the people year-two disciples will lead.

If your church is smaller, you may have fewer people in the pipeline. If your church is larger, you may need to transition some of your people from small groups to be part of discipleship groups. You may need to send the disciples entering year two out to recruit three people each. Your goal is to get each year-two disciple to be able to make disciples during year two. There have been cases where we have had to skip this step, but skipping this step is always a last resort. Disciples who have made disciples excel in discipleship three.

Making disciples during year two does not relieve the disciples from residency. Residency continues concurrently with the disciple-making disciples reflecting the lifetime practice of discipleship. We will always be serving God somewhere, and we will still be making disciples amid that service. There is more to life than making disciples. Disciple makers need to remain connected to the body and carrying out the work of the church and Kingdom.

Year-two disciples should only lead discipleship one. Regardless of your church's need, the first step in leading disciples needs to be leading discipleship one. I discourage first-time disciple makers from leading a group larger than three. I prefer that they not lead one-on-one, as it limits their potential to learn through this process. Leading two to four individuals increases exposure to the "aha" and troublesome moments of others. It requires more learning and more prayer. It also reinforces the idea and skill of discipling individuals in a group along the way.

The first support step is to walk the new leaders through the steps of "The Step-by-Step Guide." Review the process with them. Teach the focus, the tone, and the goals of discipleship one. Review the model with them and provide plenty of time for questions and answers. We gather all the current year-two disciples together for a three-hour seminar on how to start and conduct a discipleship-one group. We select a key leader for the seminar. We also include several of our best, most experienced disciple makers in the process. These leaders provide color and commentary. These champions help answer questions and leverage the power of a variety of leadership styles and experiences.

The second step is to design the groups, assign new disciples to their leaders, and help the leaders prepare for the assessment meeting. You need to be available all along the way. You will assist with book selection. You will provide support, answering more difficult Bible questions behind the scenes. You will offer tips and tricks as the new leaders face challenges and opportunities.

You need to check in often at the beginning of the process. I talk weekly with those I deploy to make disciples. I ask them about their group to ensure that the leaders have made a good assessment of the individuals. I ask them what their next steps are going to be. I ask them how the group is interacting. I ask them if they are staying focused on truths that can apply. I ask leading questions, like, "So how will you apply Torrey's book to their lives?" and, "What are the big truths in Deuteronomy?" I also make myself readily available to answer little and big questions.

You are responsible for how well the individuals in discipleship one are being discipled. You are responsible for the success of the process. You are on call all year long. You are discipling those who are discipling others. You are mentoring, modeling, and answering. You are challenging their work.

Most importantly, you are making sure that these new leaders are taking care of themselves. You need to make sure that they are practicing good soul care. You need to make sure they are resting and taking time for their personal relationship with God. You need to help them over the exhaustion of the first quarter as they adjust their schedules. You need to keep them encouraged as they "fake it until they make it." You need to cheer them on as they learn to make disciples. The second year of discipleship two is easier for you. Be aware that it is not easier for the new leaders. Take care of them well. You are still discipling them.

17

FINISH DISCIPLESHIP WELL WITH DISCIPLESHIP THREE

At a young age winning is not the most important thing... the important thing is to develop creative and skilled players with good confidence.

— ARSENE WENGER

W elcome to the final year in the process of making sustainable disciples. You are getting ready to complete a generation. The disciples in this group may be your first generation of disciples. What a privilege to complete the process. You have more mature disciples thriving as they follow God. By the end of discipleship three, you will release new leaders to carry and expand the work of ministry. God may even lead them to start new ministries. The dream is coming true for individuals and the Kingdom of God.

Your discipleship-three group will move from residency into self-sustaining leadership. They will teach. They will be servant leaders. They will expand the team of Kingdom leaders. What they become is even more important. They will become servant minded and kingdom minded. They will be prepared to thrive personally and lead in God's work. Your greatest privilege will be releasing them prepared, confident, and skilled to live their best life ever.

They were taught God's truths and guided to apply those truths in discipleship one. They learned to learn and connect direct truths in the first year of discipleship two, and they made disciples in year two. Discipleship three will expand their experience of God. They will be exposed to a wide variety of followers, beginning with the very first generations of Christianity. They will explore the more mystical concepts of God and following. They will learn to test and synthesize all they have learned. They will begin to make indirect connections linking one truth to a new truth.

Disciples coming to discipleship three have passed the step of "being" consecrated. They are all in. They are in residency—leading, serving, investing somewhere in the body of Christ. They have been tested. The disciples will be on their third or, ideally, their fourth cover-to-cover reading of God's words. You will be amazed at what they know and how capable they are to apply the truths. If they made disciples in the last year, they will excel even more. They will have emptied their lives into others, and God will have taught them much.

The disciples are not the only ones who have grown. You have grown. You have completed discipleship three or covered all of the material yourself. You should "be" different than when you started discipling. You know, even more, how the process works, and you have seen God transform lives. Your confidence should be contagious.

If this is your first time leading discipleship three, you are going to have to reread the Bible. You will need to read the extra-biblical books. You will need to give attention to the focus and tone of discipleship three. You need to know the dangers inherent in this phase. There are more dangers in discipleship three. Prepare yourself to guide disciples through them. If you have completed several cycles, you will be more experienced. You might simply review the works and methods.

You need to give attention to the method of biblical reading and review for this phase. You need to be proficient in the process before you attempt to lead the disciples through it. The Holy Spirit longs to bring to mind all that we have learned. The Holy Spirit broadens our experience as we connect direct truths. God's word increases in transforming power when we begin to connect indirect truths. There is power in expanding and synthesizing truth. His Word becomes even more capable to save us in our immediate environment. We need to be experienced in listening to the Holy Spirit as we read and think upon God's words to us.

This chapter is designed to give you a simple step-by-step guide to launching your first discipleship-three effort. It is written from the perspective of group discipleship, but the steps are virtually the same for one-on-one discipleship. These steps are the steps that we can guarantee. These are the steps we use every time we start a new discipleship group. This is how we do discipleship three.

Step One
Review the Model

My review of sustainable discipleship is very different as I prepare for discipleship three. I focus on the big picture of the entire discipleship process. I do a whiteboard review and chart the whole process. I have found there are several reasons that I need to see the process in its entirety:

- I need to be reminded of why I make disciples;
- I need to remember how to make sustainable disciples;
- I need to be reminded of the secret sauce;

- I need to remember the successful methods; and
- I need to own the vision because I will pass the vision on in discipleship three.

The disciples need that vision as they are released to live out the practice of discipleship. They need that vision as they are released to lead. They need to know the biblical models. They need to see the big picture. They need to understand the value of a lifetime practice of following. I need to remember these things so that I can pass the torch.

I need to face the terrible state of discipleship and become an agent of change. The essence of making disciples is introducing people to God, who loves and understands them, helping them understand who they are and what they can be, helping them apply God's transforming truths, and releasing them as prepared, confident, and skilled to live their best life ever on earth.

Discipleship three is all about adding skill to the preparation and confidence of disciplineships one and two. This phase releases them to the practice of discipleship. Sustainable discipleship keeps disciples focused on the core truth: Being always comes before doing.

Sustainable discipleship has a predictable path. I need to refresh my thoughts on that path so that I can communicate it well in discipleship three.

- Being convicted leads to repenting, which leads to being taught.
- Teaching leads to being enlightened, which leads to being called.
- Being called leads to serving, which leads to learning to learn.
- Learning to learn naturally leads to being prepared, which leads to that moment of consecration.
- Being consecrated, abandoning oneself to following, leads to residency, which leads to leadership.

- Leading opens the door to becoming servant driven, which expands to seeing the bigger picture and becoming Kingdom minded.
- And then we send. We go to the whole world.

The "bes" are the most important part of following. The two biblical models reveal this truth.

I need to remember the four foundational components to making sustainable disciples:

- The fuel for transformation are God's words.
- The process is intentional.
- The definition must be simple to keep us focused.
- The focus is on individuals.

I need to remember that discipleship takes time. I need to remember the cost. The disciples are headlong into a life of abandonment. The process will fade into a lifetime practice, but the practice will still take time. Disciples will need to invest time every day in "being" followers. They need to talk to God, meditate on His words, and apply His truths.

Sustainable discipleship is comprehensive. It is much more than the formal process. Making sustainable disciples invades our vision, pulpits, and events. Discipleship is done along the way, every day, every minute. Practicing discipleship is the same. Discipleship needs to move from weekly meetings to intentional, private, scheduled time with God. The life of discipleship needs to invade our lives, along the way, every day, every minute.

I also need to be very aware of my role throughout the process. I taught and guided. Then I guided and helped disciples learn to learn. I helped them connect the dots of God's character, calling, and commandments. I helped them connect themes and truths throughout the Bible. In discipleship three, my role transitions from a guide at the beginning to a peer at the end. I will not be their leader at the end of this phase. I will be a peer disciple. This is the natural process of sustainable discipleship, and I need to embrace it. I need to give that "you are going off to college" speech all year long.

Step Two
Establish the Objectives

Discipleship three is a twelve-month process guiding disciples through the next four steps along the pathway:

- Lead
- Be Servant Driven
- Be Kingdom Minded
- Send

The Focus of Discipleship Three

Discipleship three most often begins at the step of residency and focuses on the disciple synthesizing and connecting the truths of God in a manner that prepares him to teach or lead others. The first "be" in this phase is the disciple becoming servant minded. He will be ready, willing, and able to do whatever great thing God gives him to do. The second "be" is the disciple becoming kingdom minded. She is a prepared, confident, and skilled believer ready to live the best life ever and share that same life with others. Her perspective is far bigger than her life, her church, or her town.

Discipleship three adds practical skills to the life of the follower. Learning how to leverage our spiritual gifts is practical. Applying wisdom is practical. Both allow disciples to be able to do life, leadership, teaching, and so much more. Discipleship prepares followers to live their best life ever with God. Discipleship helps them consume God's truths, learn to learn, and apply those truths. Discipleship three continues to build confidence while it adds skills through experiential learning.

Discipleship three also adds mystical and historical components to the journey. These components are leveraged to move the discipleship from the formal process to lifetime practice.

Discipleship three is a relentless push. The model works. This phase works. Disciples will succeed, but they need encouragement. They will need mentoring in time management and decision-making. They also need some good, old-fashioned cheering on.

The Tone of Discipleship Three

The tone of discipleship three is one of a deeper spiritual life and a deeper understanding of scripture. A deeper understanding of theology. A deeper understanding of the skills needed to live and lead. There is a mystical component to discipleship three. Much of the reading exposes the disciple to various traditions and cultures of Christianity. These mystical and varying traditions should always be tested against scripture. Critical thinking is essential in this phase.

The Followers of Discipleship Three

Discipleship three will have a narrower spectrum of followers than other phases. These followers get the plan. They have conquered the challenges and pitfalls of group discipleship. They have led others. They will quickly assimilate and will immediately practice intimacy and transparency. Your discipleship-three group will be comrades. There is a unique *esprit de corps* among them. But they are likely to be tired as well. Time is tight, as disciples are

- in residency, learning on the job how to do whatever it is that God is calling them to do in the body,

- learning to synthesize and teach God's truths, and
- preparing for their own future discipleship practice.

Followers in discipleship three may also face the challenges of emerging leadership.

The Bible Reading Focus of Discipleship Three

The disciples will read the Bible cover to cover using a daily reading plan for the third time. There are no days off. Disciples are pushed to read daily instead of cramming it all in the day before their meeting. Disciples are encouraged to use the same Bible containing their highlights from discipleship one. This allows them to be reminded of their previous answers and observations. It also allows the leader to focus them on the passages that are not yet highlighted. If disciples use a new version of the Bible for discipleship three, they need to transfer their previous highlights.

The Bible reading focuses on disciples expanding truth, synthesizing truth, and being able to teach others truth. Ask the disciples to pick a new color for highlighting. Direct them to ask three questions:

- What do I know about this passage?
- What do I not know about this passage?
- What do I need to know about this passage?

The goal of discipleship-three Bible reading is to get the disciples to think "bigger" about their observations. Thinking bigger expands the practice of connecting truths. The method of connecting truths in discipleship two connected directly related truths. For example, people were saved in the Old Testament by following the law. People were saved in the New Testament by faith. But following the law meant that people had to believe in God (faith). The connection is that salvation has been by faith since the beginning of time. There is a direct connection between tithing in the Old Testament and the New Testament. There is a direct connection between Abraham giving a tithe to Melchizedek and God's future law of the tithe. Both were thankful offerings of 10 percent. Thinking bigger extends beyond these direct connections. Thinking bigger connects the first truth to the next related truth until no further truth relates. Thinking bigger connects indirect truths. Thinking bigger is powerful for fueling personal transformation, teaching others, and leadership.

Jesus thought bigger when He said,

> *"You have heard that our ancestors were told, 'You must not murder. If you commit murder, you are subject to judgment.' But I say, if you are even angry with someone, you are subject to judgment! If you call someone an idiot, you are in danger of being brought before the court. And if you curse someone, you are in danger of the fires of hell. So if you are presenting a sacrifice at the altar in the Temple and you suddenly remember that someone has something against you, leave your sacrifice there at the altar. Go and be reconciled to that person. Then come and offer your sacrifice to God."*

> — MATTHEW 5:21–24

He tied the selfish gain of murdering someone with the selfish gain of being hateful to someone. He tied the contempt of murder to the contempt of hate. He also provided a pathway out and showed the real problem: we need to live at peace with each other. When we are not at peace, we need to be reconciled. He tied in the idea that it is better to obey than to sacrifice. Disciples could even extend this bigger thinking to the truth that we are to share what we have with those in need. Giving is so much bigger than the tithe. John wrote,

If someone has enough money to live well and sees a brother or sister in need but shows no compassion—how can God's love be in that person?

— 1 JOHN 3:17

That truth leads to the next indirect truth, connecting truths about giving to love. When we love, we share, and love proves that we are living the new life.

If we love our brothers and sisters who are believers, it proves that we have passed from death to life. But a person who has no love is still dead.

— 1 JOHN 3:14

Us loving one another gets bigger when we see that truth led to the next truth: we can only love because God is love and has shown love to us. Again, John writes,

We love each other because he loved us first.

— 1 JOHN 4:19

Which leads us to all the concepts of God's love. For example, the enduring love of God found in the entire Psalm 136 and Paul's correction to the pathway of the Corinthian disciples:

Love never gives up, never loses faith, is always hopeful, and endures through every circumstance.

— 1 CORINTHIANS 13:7

The loving, stern course correction in 1 Corinthians leads to the idea that we need others around us to remind and guide us.

Get all the advice and instruction you can, so you will be wise the rest of your life.

— PROVERBS 19:20

This ties back to the idea of love. Love corrects.

For the LORD corrects those he loves, just as a father corrects a child in whom he delights.

— PROVERBS 3:12

And that truth gets bigger when we tie it to 2 Timothy, where we see that God has given His words to correct and guide those He loves.

All Scripture is inspired by God and is useful to teach us what is true and to make us realize what is wrong in our lives. It corrects us when we are wrong and teaches us to do what is right. God uses it to prepare and equip his people to do every good work.

— 2 TIMOTHY 3:16–17

And 2 Timothy gets bigger when we connect a next truth: because God loves, He sent Jesus to provide salvation. John 3:16–17 teaches us that Jesus did not come to condemn but to save. Saving should be our goal. We should be lifeguards. This truth leads us to our duty and many teachings on judgment, like Jesus's words recorded by Matthew:

"Do not judge others, and you will not be judged. For you will be treated as you treat others. The standard you use in judging is the standard by which you will be judged."

— MATTHEW 7:1–2

The truth about judgment gets bigger when we connect the truths that God is the only one who is capable to judge. It expands when we explore God's judgment and see the connection made in Hebrews:

> *And just as each person is destined to die once and after that comes judgment, so also Christ was offered once for all time as a sacrifice to take away the sins of many people.*

> — HEBREWS 9:27–28

In the same way that we live, die, and are judged once, Christ was offered once for all sin. The next big truth could be the fullness of God's salvation. And all of this can tie back to the contextual truth of our first verse in Matthew, where Jesus told the lawmakers that they needed to embrace the concepts of the law and find salvation in Christ, the only one who could make them righteous.

Thinking bigger is about the indirect connections from truth to more truth. Thinking bigger meditates on all that we have learned to get every drop of application out of what we learn. Disciples are instructed, "Make it bigger," as we ask,

- What other truths does this passage reveal?
- What other truths relate to this passage?

Teaching disciples to expand the immediate truth and context to other truths will result in them synthesizing God's truths cover to cover. Synthesizing truths supercharges followers to understand God and themselves. Disciples no longer apply a single truth at a time. They now see and apply many deeply connected truths at once.

This process of expanding and synthesizing takes time to learn. You need to challenge their connections that stretch His truth. You need to provide course correction when disciples begin to take verses out of context. An exegetical mindset will help them avoid reading truths into verses that are not there. Keep disciples focused on finding truths capable of transforming their lives. As in the other phases of discipleship, you need to allow the Holy Spirit to work. Ask questions and give hints, but allow the Holy Spirit to show them the other truths in their highlights. Let the Holy Spirit expand the indirect connections. Your role is to show them how God can expand and synthesize truth. Your role is to guide them to allow God to make truth bigger.

Discipleship three opens the door to online search engines and research books like *Christian Theology* by Millard J. Erickson. Bible study to find, understand, and connect transforming truths is encouraged. Using a study Bible is discouraged because they usually have a particular focus. Study Bibles tend to create shortcuts to self-study and cross-referencing. The focus of the author's notes can hamper the work of the Spirit to guide the disciple. It can also prevent the disciple from obtaining a broader opinion. Continue to champion the unbiased, inductive, exegetical study of God's word. The Bible is capable of explaining the Bible.

Useful, applicable truths remain the focus of discipleship three. Disciples are encouraged to avoid endless, fruitless arguments and studies. God's truths set us free only if we apply them. Also, it is essential to model and teach the truth that there are things we simply will not understand now, or perhaps ever.

Extra-Biblical Reading and Work for Discipleship Three

Disciples will complete the "How to Study the Bible 102" course within the first four weeks. This course will prepare them for reliable inductive and exegetical study.

Outside reading in the remaining forty-six weeks focuses on biblical doctrine, leadership, and historical texts of the church fathers. We also use books that develop and inspire skills and creativity. No less than eight books will be read in addition to the Bible-study course. It is likely that those you lead will consume far more than eight books.

Some of the reading will expose the disciple to the mystical truths of God and Christianity. The practical and the mystical coincide for every disciple. The practical leads us to stand in awe of the mystical through experiencing the presence of God in and around us. The mystical empowers the practical as we learn with the Holy Spirit as our guide. To get lost in the mystical will lead to a life without bearing, result, or effect on this world. To get lost in the practical will lead to actions that are shallow, meaningless, and ineffective. You need to champion a balance between the mystical and the practical.

We require disciples to read the following books during discipleship three:

- *The Book of Mystical Chapters* (John Anthony McGuckin)
- "Can I Lose My Salvation?" (Doug Burrier)
- *Good to Great* (James C. Collins)
- *Good Boss, Bad Boss* (Robert I. Sutton)
- *Spiritual Leadership* (J. Oswald Sanders)
- *The Great Omission* (Steve Saint)

The sustainable library also categorizes the following books as additional resources for discipleship three:

- *Surprised by Joy* (C.S. Lewis)
- *The Purpose Driven Church* (Rick Warren)
- *Scary Close* (Donald Miller)
- *The Longevity Project* (Howard S. Friedman and Leslie R. Martin)
- *Fresh Power* (Jim Cymbala)
- *Piercing the Darkness* (Frank E. Peretti)
- *The Pursuit of Holiness* (Jerry Bridges)

- *Letters to Timothy* (John R. Bisagno)
- *Deep and Wide* (Andy Stanley)
- *Blink* (Malcolm Gladwell)
- *21 Irrefutable Laws of Leadership* (John C. Maxwell)

There is no break in the outside reading. Disciples are pushed to read as many extra-biblical works as possible. The library also has topical books appropriate for any phase, to address specific needs or to push the group forward. You may choose to build your own library. If so, make sure that it focuses on the tone, the plan, and typical challenges faced in the four steps along the pathway of discipleship three. The group should read the same books at the same time. Pick wisely, trust God, and watch the truth unfold.

On-the-Job Training

Disciples in phase three choose a teaching or service track. You should prepare them for direct or indirect leadership as appropriate. You need to work with your church or ministry leaders to find leadership spots for each disciple. Disciples need to lead a team in ongoing work or to teach regularly. Disciples will serve in this leadership capacity throughout discipleship three. Include time in your weekly meeting for discussion.

Residency and leadership change the disciples' perspective of the Bible. They move from seeing excellent and poor examples of leadership in the Bible to applying those principles to their work, service, family, and life. Disciples should move from residency to leadership during discipleship three. This is a push-and-stretch step that deepens reliance on God and improves the ability to follow and serve in life.

Preparing for the Practice of Discipleship

Preparing someone to transition from the process to a

personal practice of discipleship is a great and risky adventure. Casting vision and discussing how the disciple will continue living their discipleship are essential components of discipleship three.

Ask the disciples to build a list of mentors and peer disciples that they will leverage for their future growth, walk, and journey. Give them access to the "beyond formal discipleship" library.[1]

The Dangers of Discipleship Three

Again, the unholy trinity of money, family, and pride can quickly derail the discipleship process. Point them out as soon as you see them. Save everyone time, and save the disciple from the enemy. There are three dangers specific to discipleship three:

- Getting lost in the mystical
- The 10-11 challenge
- The emerging-leader challenge

Mainstream Christianity tends to move away from searching and understanding the mystical. It is hard to teach deep concepts to a broad audience, and people often get lost in the mystical. People begin to long for that which they do not understand. Getting lost in the mystical and abandoning the practical is a unique danger in discipleship three.

I found Brendon wandering in the five acres of woods behind our church. Brendon was serious about God, had been raised in the church, and was excelling in discipleship. But here he was wandering around the woods with a prayer rope, in a monk's robe that he had made, talking very spiritually. "I just love getting lost in this prayer. I feel God so much. I am connecting to Him like never before. I am thinking about living out here."

"Really," I replied, trying to hide my thoughts.

"Yeah. I think those early Christians who set themselves aside and just prayed were onto something."

"They were, Brendon. I am so glad you are connecting with God. There is nothing better than solitude. There is nothing better than time in the Spirit, but can I ask you a question?"

"Sure!" Brendon replied.

"Aren't you supposed to be at work? Everyone is looking for you."

"Well, uh, yeah, but God comes first. Who can walk away from Him? I think this is my pathway."

"Brendon. How are you going to feed your family? And what about the commitments that you have already made. You said earlier that God gave you that job."

I wandered with Brendon as I reminded him how Jesus said He did what His Father gave Him to do. I reminded him how Jesus returned from His incredible mystical retreats. I reminded him how Jesus brought Peter, James, and John down from the Mount of Transfiguration. I reminded him of Paul's teaching that we can pray without ceasing in every environment.

Brendon was getting lost in the pursuit of the mystical. Yes, God is a mystery in origin, action, and direction. Miracles are amazing. Reaching a point in prayer where you feel a union with God is incredible. Looking into the mysteries of God and thinking mystically will be new to most disciples. God is, however, both mystical and practical. We still need to work, strive, and live in this world. We worship God, not his mysteries. You need to help the disciples stay balanced. I did not want to shut down the mystical in Brendon's life. I wanted to bring it into balance. Looking into the mystical also brings many teachers and many opinions. You should challenge disciples to test everything mystical against the truths of God's word.

The 10-11 challenge is about exhaustion and the enemy attacking. Disciples rarely abandon discipleship at this point. They are all in. The benefits are incredible, they have turned that corner, and they love giving back to others. They are discipling people. They are leading. And they get tired. When you push them to take a Sabbath rest, they push back with, "I love this stuff." When you push them to say no, they push back with an incredible worldview of the lost needing to be found. It is our responsibility to teach delegation and pacing during this challenge. Disciples need to be reminded that the work of God is a marathon. They need to be pushed to have their own walk— after all, this is where all the fun started. Our role is to be their experienced mentor.

My friend Greg is an incredible leader and manager. He gets people. He loves people, and he is not afraid to positively push those we train for leadership. I will never forget the first time he called a young leader a punk. I almost fell out of my chair. We were lined up on a huge porch, relaxing after a long day at a men's retreat. I was three or four rocking chairs away, minding my own business, when Greg lovingly said, "Randy, you are being such a disrespectful punk to Doug." Everyone stayed quiet as this great, young leader replied, "What? When was I a punk? Oh no." Greg went on to explain how Randy had been trying to one-up me all day and then chastised me in front of the group.

"I did not even mean it that way," Randy replied.

Greg affirmed him, "Randy, you are incredible. I know you love Doug. You are becoming such a great leader. But you are getting a little big for your britches."

Greg continued to support, encourage, and lovingly correct Randy's course. He reminded Randy that a student is never greater than his teacher. He taught him that the teacher will always be a part of the student's success. Randy moved down a few rockers to apologize.

I said, "You don't need to apologize, but thanks. You have a great resource in Greg. Man, how much he loves and admires you for telling you that."

"Well, was I a punk?"

"Honestly? Yes. But it happens. We all grow in leadership. You are getting smart. You are going to be a better leader than I ever will be. That's the dream. In fact, you were right in what you said, but it was kind of shaming the way it happened."

"Oh, I am so sorry."

"Really, I am okay. I hope you will always be there to complete me. I hope we will always stand behind each other. If I ever get off track, I want you to call me on it. But we are leaders. We have to lead well together. Maybe next time you could say something quietly, ask why I am doing what I am doing, or assume I know what I am doing. In the worst case, if I am wrong, assume the best about me, have my six, and help me be the best I can be."

"I didn't mean it," Randy continued.

"I know. None of us ever means it. But the devil uses it to destroy church after church, ministry after ministry, and leader after leader. It's good. You want a cup of coffee?"

Emerging leaders can get a little punky. It is a lot like the 4b challenge. Leaders are prepared, confident, and skilled. Sometimes the confidence turns into pride. Emerging leaders can struggle to submit. They often talk too much and counter their leaders in public. And they make decisions out of sequence. Be frank and understanding, but address this head-on. Remind them of Peter's words:

> *In the same way, you who are younger must accept the authority of the elders. And all of you, dress yourselves in humility as you relate to one another, for "God opposes the proud but gives grace to the humble." So humble yourselves under the mighty power of God, and at the right time he will lift you up in honor.*

> — 1 PETER 5:5–6

Many emerging leaders never make it past this danger, leaving the process to begin a cycle of starting new things that they control. Love them though this danger, and share your stories.

Mission Trips and Service Opportunities for Discipleship Three

Again, you should push each disciple to join you for one weeklong mission trip. We have already discussed the bonding, the power, and the opportunities to teach along the way during extended trips. Do not miss this opportunity with those you make disciples.

We do not require service at all special church events during discipleship three. Disciples are challenged to exercise their "best yes." Leaders champion disciples to practice healthy self-care and time-management skills.

Step Three
Develop Your Plan

It may sound redundant at this point, but developing a practical plan is critical. Discipleship three requires working with other leaders to find leadership opportunities. It requires time outside of the regular meetings. You may need to be more flexible on the meeting schedule. You may need to take a week off each month or even meet every other week. Disciples are serving in residency or leading and are studying on their own. If a disciple's focus is teaching, he will need to prepare. If a disciple's focus is serving, he will need time to lead service. Caution should be taken with flexibility. Regular meetings are still the goal.

Making Time

If this is your first time leading discipleship three, you will have to read everything that the disciples read. You will need at least forty-five minutes of uninterrupted time a day to read and prepare. You will need two hours to lead the weekly discipleship meeting. You will need a few hours to answer emails and texts, and have coffee with those you lead. You need to make time for service events, mission trips, and regular service at your church. These are the times where you lead along the way and teach in the moment. Make sure that you plan your time well. Do not overextend yourself. Plan your time one step at a time.

1. At what time, each day, will you read and prepare?
2. What day and time can you hold a regularly scheduled meeting?
3. What months are you available to go on a mission trip or an extended service event?
4. Does your church have a mission trip or extended service event that you can plug your group into? If not, you may have to do a little research.
5. What regular service are you currently doing?
6. What other service opportunities are there—at that time—that your group can join you in?

Pick Your Launch Date

If your church has established a standard plan, your launch date might be just a week or so after the completion of the previous cycle. If you do not have a standard plan, I encourage you not to wait too long between discipleships two and three. Discipleship three can be completed in fifty weeks. Work to keep the launch date of various phases consistent.

When will you launch your group?

Pick Your Meeting Day and Time

Picking your standard meeting day and time is actually picking two or three times that will work for you. If you are launching several discipleship groups with several leaders, you have the flexibility to plug followers into several different times.

If you are the sole leader launching two groups, you will definitely need a few options and need to be flexible.

Meeting on the same day and at the same time is easier. People are creatures of habit. Standard meetings are easy and predictable, and always work best.

What are your best days to meet?
What are your best times to meet on those days?
Are you willing to be flexible?

Pick Your Meeting Place

What three spaces can you access for your meeting?
Is the space quiet or, at least, not disrupting?
Is the space comfortable?
Will you feel rushed?
Does it have a whiteboard?

Pick the Books You Need to Read

Your first discipleship-three group will be more efficient and informative if you stay ahead of those you make disciples. If you are only on your second or third read of the Bible, it is probably a good idea to read it through again. Remember, by the time a disciple makes it through discipleship, he will have read the Bible four times. Stay ahead. Stay fresh.

Be ahead of the disciples in extra-biblical resources too. If you are going to use the "How to Study the Bible 102" course, make sure you complete it before you have your first meeting.

How many times have you read the Bible cover to cover?
Will you reread it before starting discipleship?
Have you highlighted the Bible using the discipleship-three reading focus?
Will you highlight it before beginning?

Have you completed the "How to Study the Bible 102" course?

Have you reviewed the recommended list of books for discipleship three?

What are the first two books that you will require disciples to read?

Set Up Your Standard Meeting Agenda

Discipleship-three meetings will likely take longer than other phases. Here is the agenda that I use for discipleship three.

- Life Update and Prayer (5 minutes)
- Bible Reading Review (55 minutes)
- *The Book of Mystical Chapters* Review (20 minutes)
- Extra-Biblical Reading Review (30 minutes)

The meeting has one additional component: the review of *The Book of Mystical Chapters*. I set aside twenty minutes for this weekly review. You can find more detail on *The Book of Mystical Chapters* in step eight below.

Step Four
Set the Requirements for Discipleship

You know the basic requirements of formal discipleship. Here is Jesus's summary for following Him:

- Love God more than anyone else.
- Deny yourself, and take up your cross.
- Forsake all that you have.
- Count the cost.

We have three basic requirements to begin and sustain a formal discipleship process.

- They need to be able to make weekly meetings.
- They need to make time to read.
- They will be reading the Bible cover to cover.

These are the additional requirements of successful discipleship:

- There is no learning without submission.
- Attending, serving, and tithing are essential.
- We do not chase.
- We do not do lying.

Again, you may wish to add or subtract from these requirements as you gain experience making disciples. Your nation's or society's culture may necessitate changes to the requirements of formal discipleship. Be careful as you make requirements. Do not make discipleship impossible or too hard. Do not adjust the requirements for individuals. Requirements should be the same for the group—for anyone being discipled. Avoid legalism, and make sure that your requirements are biblically based.

Step Five
Recruit Your First Members

There is no recruiting for your first discipleship-three group. You simply carry those who have finished two into three. You might need to recruit in future cycles because life happens. Schedules come and go. New jobs come along. Delays between discipleships two and three happen too. Sometimes these delays are the result of life circumstances. Sometimes these delays are more strategic. It is irresponsible to move a disciple into discipleship three if he has not become consecrated. You will set him up for failure. There are times when it is responsible to guide disciples to exercise better soul care before they move into the busyness of discipleship three.

Review the list of people moving through discipleship. Check in on those in between phases. Talk to other leaders, and see if it is time to get them going on the next phase.

After you have determined your group members, here are the next steps:

1. Pick a day and time for your regular meetings.
2. Pick a place.
3. Pick your launch date.
4. Set a forty-seven-week Bible reading plan.
5. Distribute the information above, and communicate what they are to highlight for the first meeting. I encourage them to focus on the "not previously highlighted" portions of the text for this first week. The initial meeting will be much like a regular meeting, with time to review a week's worth of Bible reading.

I communicate all of this information in a short, inspiring email. I include a pitch that sets the tone and the focus of discipleship three. You may choose to meet with them over coffee or use another method. Disciples entering this phase know the plan. They are excited. They simply need information.

Step Six
Assess Your Group Members

If this is your church's first discipleship-three group, you may be leading the same people you led in discipleship two. There will be little need to assess them. You know them. You are in a groove. They know you. Discipleship three will just pick up where each disciple is on the pathway. Your planning will be simple.

Hopefully, your church's process has grown, and your leaders are strategically mixing up leaders, phases, and followers. Developing a responsible plan begins by determining where disciples left off.

The discipleship-three group assessment is like the discipleship-two assessment. There is no introductory meeting. There is no pitch. You should be determining where disciples left off in discipleship two before the first meeting. Talking to each disciple's previous leader is your greatest asset in this assessment. Disciples are still growing. They might still think that they need something they do not need. They might believe they are further along or further behind where they actually are on the pathway. Their discipleship-two leader can quickly get you up to speed.

Group assessment begins intentionally but casually in the first meeting. It continues throughout the first few meetings, with pointed questions. Observing the disciples in action is your greatest asset.

The main goal of group assessment is to get to know the disciples. Your goal is to understand God's design of, the talents of, the personality of, and the gifts of each disciple.

Step Seven
Your First Meeting

The first meeting of discipleship three is an extended regular meeting. The disciples will pray and review the Bible reading for the week. The extra-biblical time will be used to share the vision and tone for discipleship three. The extended time of this meeting will allow the disciples to get to know you.

The agenda should be well planned, and you should keep to the agenda. I use the following outline for my first meeting:

Open with Individual Prayers (5 minutes)

Disciples will be familiar with praying for one thing that they need in the moment. You may need to interrupt them or remind them at the end, "This prayer time is not for your aunt, your mother, or even what your spouse needs. Just pray for one thing that you need." You may need to rattle the cage a bit or remind them of the purpose of this prayer time.

The Focus and Tone of Discipleship Three (10 minutes)

I use the predictable-pathway chart to remind disciples of their journey. I start a discussion about the focus and tone of discipleship three. I review the three phases of sustainable discipleship and each step within those phases:

- Phase one focuses on repentance and teaching.
- Phase two focuses on learning to learn and connecting truths.
- Phase three focuses on synthesizing truths, leading, and teaching.

I cover the focus and tone of discipleship three discussed above. I set them free to use outside resources. I work to discover and explore their leadership and teaching interests. I introduce the concept of the formal process of discipleship becoming a lifetime, personal practice.

I have also found it valuable to ask them, "Why are you in discipleship three?" We asked this question at the beginning of their journey. Now we use it to help refocus disciples and remind them that we are in discipleship to learn how to follow God.

I cover the three dangers of discipleship three. This is one of the few times where I talk about a danger that has not become a reality. Disciples in this phase are mature. They can handle a warning without it derailing them or becoming a self-fulfilling prophecy.

Getting to Know Each Other (30 minutes)

This section of the meeting achieves two purposes: it allows the disciples to get to know me, and it begins my group assessment of the disciples. I do not keep my agenda secret in discipleship three. Remember, these disciples have already made disciples. They have already read this book. I remind them of what I am doing in each assessment step. I still ask, "What do you want to know about me?" The time is always fun even though they know what is going on. The time begins to build intimacy and relationship. The interaction increases transparency and trust.

This question-and-answer time provides the opportunity for me to ask them the questions that they ask me. It allows me to transition to getting to know each disciple. The back-and-forth movement between my story and their stories allows me to begin to sense who they are. Let the Spirit lead your questions and your answers. Use this time to bond with the disciples and to assess them.

Review of Bible Reading Method for Discipleship Three (15 minutes)

I review the Bible reading method for the first two phases of sustainable discipleship:

- Discipleship One: Disciples were pushed to simply read the Bible. They did not study the text but simply allowed the Holy Spirit to guide them to "aha" and troublesome verses. They were pushed to read it as if it were the first time they had ever read it. The leader affirmed the "aha" moments and

answered the troublesome questions, always helping
disciples find truth to apply.

- Discipleship Two: Disciples highlighted "aha" verses
  and verses raising questions as the Holy Spirit
  worked. No outside studying was allowed. Bible
  reading focused on inductive study as disciples were
  guided to answer their questions by connecting the
  verse in question to other biblical truths. The leader
  helped disciples find applications and make those
  direct connections.

Then I share the Bible reading focus and method for discipleship three. I illustrate how the process has grown from exposure to connection, and now to synthesis. I use examples and
teach the method of "thinking bigger."

I give them the responsibility to research their questions,
always looking for the Bible to answer the Bible. I remind them
that the goal of thinking bigger is a year-long goal.

Reviewing the Bible (50 minutes)

We review each disciple's highlights. Disciples should have
highlighted the following:

- New questions they noticed.
- Connections between a truth they noticed and other
  truths that they have learned.
- New "aha" verses that inspired them or caught their
  attention.

You know your discipleship culture and environment. You
may develop an agenda that works better for you. Whatever you
do, make sure that you pray together, review the Bible, and
remind them of the requirements. Set the proper tone and
expectations for them. Again, I encourage you to speak little

about why you are doing what you are doing. Just do it, and let the results be experienced.

Step Eight
Get the First Quarter Right

Discipleships one and two focused on preparation and confidence. Discipleship three focuses on adding skills to disciples' preparation and confidence. As with the previous phases, the first quarter sets the tone and expectations for the year.

The second through the twelfth meetings form the foundation for thinking bigger. This quarter broadens the disciples' exposure to the mystical. The meetings will cement the three practices of thinking bigger:

- Connecting immediate truths.
- Expanding to related truths.
- Synthesizing truths cover to cover.

There are several practical matters to address in the first quarter. It took time and diligence to shift the disciples' Bible reading from typical Bible study to Spirit-led learning in discipleship one. You probably found that it took much longer to cover the first five books of the Bible. Bible reading should have been easier in discipleship two. Disciples were accustomed to looking for life-transforming applications among their highlights. They learned to make direct connections of truth to other verses in the Bible. Discipleship three adds the skill of making indirect connections while reading the Bible. Teaching and modeling the method of "thinking bigger" is time-consuming at first. You will not be able to think bigger about every one of the disciples' highlights from Bible reading. The process will get smoother as they embrace this skill. Disciples will come prepared, having already thought, noted, and prepared. Your goal is to get them thinking bigger as quickly as possible.

However, not every truth needs to get bigger. Not every truth needs to expand. For example, noticing that God buried Moses is incredible, but it does not really expand. There are no direct or indirect connections to life-transforming truths. Once the disciples begin to think bigger, there is a tendency to try to expand everything. They will begin to suppose things and stretch truths and connections. You need to keep them focused on actual truth. You need to guide them away from allegorical interpretation. Guide them back if they begin to make the error of making everything mean something more. Keep them focused on observing what the Bible actually says about the Bible.

Let the Spirit guide you as you pick and choose which truths to expand. You simply cannot expand every truth in your meetings. Be careful not to do all the expansion work. Guide the disciples to think bigger by asking questions and giving hints. Allow them to see the process of connecting, expanding, and synthesizing. Remember that transformation, not education, is the goal. Thinking bigger should find truths that apply to living and following God. Disciples should be able to adjust their lives to the truths they discover.

The extra-biblical reading also reinforces thinking bigger. Disciples will practice critical thinking and connect learning back to the Bible. Reading *The Book of Mystical Chapters* begins the disciples' exposure to indirect and mystical truth. It is a critical component of sustainable discipleship. I am not sure that we could complete the discipleship process well without it. *The Book of Mystical Chapters* is a collection of three hundred teachings from early church leaders. The teachings are broken into three sections: *Praktikos*, *Theoretikos*, and *Gnostikos*. The early church fathers used this system of teaching as they led disciples deeper in their understanding of God. The book gives a detailed understanding of this ancient system. Here is a brief review of the three sections:

- *Praktikos*: These writings focus on disciplined prayer,
  diving deeper, and thinking about the truths of God.
  The writings are practical in their application.
  Praktikos is instruction.
- *Theoretikos*: These writings focus on contemplation,
  enlightenment, and illumination. Meditating on
  God's truths is instrumental to *Theoretikos*.
- *Gnostikos*: These writings focus on a contemplative
  union with God by encountering the divine God
  behind the truths. Worship and praying without
  ceasing are some of the modern equivalents.
  Gnostikos is about the experience.

You may notice a similarity between this ancient practice
and sustainable discipleship. The practice reflects both the
predictable pathway and the biblical models of discipleship.
Discipleship one is about being convicted, repenting, being
taught, and becoming enlightened. It is about the beginning
practices and truths of following. Discipleship two begins to
think about the whole of God's word and to connect truths. It is
contemplative as the learner learns to learn. Discipleship three is
about thinking bigger, experiencing a transformed life, understanding God, and assuming leadership. Paul illustrates the same
pattern in Romans, chapters six, seven, and eight:

- Romans 6: Leave the old ways and live the new life.
  He introduces the idea of us being crucified with
  Christ. He teaches about grace abounding where sin
  exists. He teaches basic, beginning truth.
- Romans 7: Understand the new ways and the truths
  of God. Paul addresses concepts like "Does sin exist
  where we have no law?" and "Why do we do the
  things that we do not want to do?" He explores the
  more intricate connections of the flesh, sin, and
  salvation.

- Romans 8: Nothing can separate us from the love of
  Christ. Paul addresses concepts like God's eternal
  promise to conform us to the image of Christ. He
  discusses the spiritual power of our relationship with
  God. He moves from practice and understanding to
  being united with God.

Did you know there are three ways to sin? God leveraged
His power to help me overcome sin when He showed me this
truth. And I have spent years sharing this truth with anyone who
would listen.

- We sin when we do a "don't." You see this in Romans
  6 and throughout the Bible.
- We sin when we don't do a "do." You see this in
  James 4:17[2] and throughout the Bible.
- We sin when we do a "doubt." You see this in
  Romans 14:23[3] and throughout the Bible. Even if
  we guess right, we are not following Him when we
  guess.

The "three ways to sin" reflects the progression of maturity
the ancient fathers found. It reflects the same progression that
Paul illustrates. The first steps in conquering sin are very practical and based on not doing what is wrong. The second step
requires that we learn what is right and begin to think about
how we adjust to God's truths. It requires that we know and do
what is right. The third step requires something more mystical:
faith. We have to learn to synthesize God's truths and listen to
the Holy Spirit for direction in those matters not directly
addressed in scripture. We have to think bigger about the character and desire of God to find direction.

Maturing in our faith and walk with God is a distinct
process. Sustainable discipleship reflects this growth process
throughout the three phases. Discipleship three begins to add

the mystical along with the skills. Disciples move from being taught and learning to living out a relationship with a God who is not seen. To do this, they must further understand how to be spiritually united with God. We leverage *The Book of Mystical Chapters* as a catalyst. It is an excellent aid to the process, but it is not scripture. It is a collection of teachings based on the ancient fathers' understanding at that time. It is not infallible. I cannot connect all their teachings to clear, simple, biblical truth. I do not defend all of their perspectives. But *The Book of Mystical Chapters* is an excellent aid to discipleship three. It causes the disciples to focus on and synthesize truths about their immaterial relationship with God. It champions critical thinking as they test the concepts against scripture. The teachings will stretch them and light a holy fire that needs to be lit in each of us. A fire that believes in the miracles of God, believes in communicating with God one-on-one, and believes in the work of the Holy Spirit.

We ask the disciples to read one writing each day throughout the year. We require that the disciples find a Bible verse related to or illustrating the truth of each writing. We read, review, and look at each of the writings and verses during *The Book of Mystical Chapters* review each week. In essence, we are practicing the truth of not turning away a prophet but, instead, testing what they say. You will be amazed at the more profound thoughts and lives that develop throughout the year.

Discipleship three pushes a different way of thinking. Many of the extra-biblical books are secular and can seem disconnected from the process of discipleship. We use some pretty crazy books to champion the challenge of thinking bigger. Erica struggled with the challenge while reading *The Art of War* by Sun Tzu. This classic volume was written by a Chinese military strategist in the fifth century BC. His genius observations and strategies have endured for generations, being applied to everything from modern warfare to business. Tzu's truths are also conceptually applicable to spiritual warfare and leadership.

"I just don't get how this applies," Erica said in exasperation. "I feel stupid."

"Let's take one, for example. How about Sun's strategy that you should never set out to kill the enemy or destroy the enemy's city? How can that apply to leadership?"

"Uh, I . . ." You could hear Erica giving up.

"Okay, so let's say that there is someone wrong in the church, and they have begun to create chaos and division. You have to face it. You have to fix it. Most everyone can see that they are wrong. You could simply call them out and shame their approach and win the battle. But that would destroy them and might scare others who are newer. Is there another way to win that doesn't destroy?"

"Um . . ."

"It's okay. Let's think about this another way. Why did Jesus come to earth?" I asked.

"He came to save us. He came to restore us to a relationship with God," she replied.

"Great. You are exactly right. Do you remember what John 3:17 teaches?"

"Oh, I have this one. He came to save, not to condemn," she answered.

"Right. And in James, it teaches us to rescue one another from sin and prevent a world of trouble for each other. Do you see how that applies?"

"So we shouldn't destroy them but somehow save them?"

"Right! God is always about reconciliation and restoration. There are times you might have to defeat the enemy, but what if you could come up with a strategy that reflects God's heart and love for all people? What if you could find a way to win the person, or at least try to win the person?"

"Okay . . ."

"Sun Tzu recognized that people and cities are valuable assets. In fact, they were the things to be won in war, not things to destroy in war. There is an incredible, biblically consistent truth in that. Does that make more sense?"

"Yes."

Erica needed to learn how to connect what seemed distant and draw out applicable truths. It is irrelevant whether those truths were from *The Art of War* or from another resource. Erica was learning to see God's truths play out in the world around her. She was learning a discipleship mindset of always looking for a way to learn, teach, and apply. This mindset will help her as she teaches her children along the way.

Your goal is to use extra-biblical reading to push, strengthen, and add skill to the process of synthesizing biblical truth into real life. Your goal is to help the disciple constantly think about God's truths. They should be listening to the Spirit for "aha" moments where they see God's principles in play around them.

You should also ensure that every disciple is in a one-year residency within the first quarter of discipleship three. It is critical that disciples teach, lead, and interact as leaders with others. Leading forces us to produce. Leading forces us to think. Leading forces us to apply God's truths in a way that following does not. Residency, and then solo leadership, is critical to the success of discipleship three. Disciples need to see the bigger picture and become servant minded.

You also need to reaffirm the disciples to evangelize. Remember Bill's weekly question, "Who did you share your story with this week? How did it go?" Make time to push this Kingdom-minded principle. Work diligently to get disciples to embrace the responsibility of sharing their life story.

The first quarter sets the stage for discipleship three. It also sets the stage for the future practice of independent discipleship. The first quarter begins the transition to being a self-sustaining disciple of God.

Step Nine
Plan That Trip

The service projects of discipleships one and two have super-charged the disciple-making process. Each required self-sacrifice and immersed disciples in challenges. As you plan service projects and mission trips in discipleship three, you need to push the disciples to take leadership roles in the service projects and mission trips during discipleship three. Leading is entirely different than following and will provide new opportunities for disciples to apply God's truths. Use these events strategically as you prepare and train the disciples. Step out of the lead, and stand beside them. Guide them as they lead.

Step Ten
Your Second and Third Quarters

The second and third quarters of discipleship three bring increased ease in biblical and extra-biblical review. These quarters bring depth as disciples progress further through *The Book of Mystical Chapters*. You will learn new truths and applications along with the disciples. You will also notice a natural progression toward peer discipleship. Embrace this trend.

You should increasingly allow disciples to speak into each other's lives. You should ask, "So, Bob, what do you think about Tim's verse? How would you expand it?" Allow other disciples to chime in with bigger thoughts while keeping the group on track. This type of interaction is the future for disciples. This type of interaction is the dream of sustainable discipleship. Disciples will need you less and less. Their success becomes your success as they follow God with less guidance. Your role will shift from the guide to the facilitator and then to a peer. Disciples will push into your life. Allow them. Be honest. Treat them as peers, being intimate, honest, and transparent about your challenges and walk with God. Entrust them with your life, and model the trust they will need for the future.

Also, be careful that as your relationship changes, you continue to be the leader. Keep pushing them. Keep them reading. Make sure that interaction does not derail completing the Bible review.

Step Eleven
Planning Their Future in the Fourth Quarter

If you have followed the sustainable-discipleship process, disciples have already read this book. They are familiar with the idea that the process is ending and that the practice is beginning. They know the secret sauce. They know the plan. They know the "secrets." Four years is coming to a close. Soon, they will be released as prepared, confident, and skilled followers of God. You need to begin to prepare them for the practice of discipleship. You need to remember that they have not lived the practice. You need to guide them to the practice that you have been living. You need to teach it, push it, and model it. You need to warn them of the challenges that come with the end of a formal process.

The fourth quarter begins a process of evaluating their personal, corporate, and service life. You need to ask these questions:

- Will they disciple?
- Will they lead?
- Will they teach?

You need to remind them that all those "dos" will quickly fail if they fail to "be followers." Help them take a look at their personal life. Help them set a schedule that provides for soul care, time with God, and continued learning. Warn them of the dangers of being overinvested. Talk to them about their dreams and gifts. Help them find where God is working in their life and ministry. Push them to join Him there.

You also need to prepare them for the disconnect that happens as discipleship three ends. Do you have lifelong friends from high school or college? I do not. I graduated and moved on. I do not keep up with the close comrades of my graduate work. We all moved on. I never missed any of them in the rush of marriage, kids, and building a future. Oddly, I really miss the guys from discipleship. I met with them weekly for years. Greg and I spent four years together, every single week, and then we did not. Greg's kids and business kept him busy. Leading a church and writing kept me busy. I lost my guy time with mature, peer followers. I lost my time with Greg. We had to really work to fix it. We had to make time between all our family and discipleship relationships to meet up. We had to work to reconnect. You cannot always give. You have to restore and receive. Being in ongoing discipleship relationships is critical to being a sustainable disciple.

I also have to be very intentional to make time for phone calls and lunches with those great men who helped make me a disciple. Phil lives far way in Mexico. We are both busy, and he has many "Dougs" in his life. I have to schedule time to talk. I keep him up to date through text. I plan breakfast a couple of times a month with Doc. These men, who disciple me, are critical to me continuing to grow and learn. They are my teachers even though we have become peers.

You need to prepare those you make disciples for the changes in your relationship. You need to make time for them, and you need to push them to have other peer-disciple relationships. Provide creative ideas from your practice and resources from your experience. We have a continuing-education library for disciples transitioning to the practice of discipleship. We stay in touch. Whatever you do, use the fourth quarter to help each disciple come up with a plan for their practice of discipleship. It is critical that you release disciples well.

Step Twelve
Pushing Them to the Kingdom

Discipleship three carries the disciples through leadership to becoming servant and Kingdom minded. Discipleship three releases disciples prepared, confident, and skilled to live their best life ever on earth. Discipleship three is also the beginning of the process to launch disciples into the world. Your church may not have enough leadership opportunities. You may not need four new teachers. However, the world and the Kingdom always need more leaders and teachers. The world and the Kingdom need sustainable disciples to make other disciples. There is an endless need in the world and the Kingdom.

Kids are different. Some cannot wait to get out of the house. Others can never imagine being away from home. I am the latter when it comes to our church community. I have dreams. There are things I would love to do and new ministry adventures that tempt me. But I cannot imagine not being in community with the followers at Three Taverns Church. I cannot imagine not growing, serving, and reaching others with this incredible community. The problem is that the entire world is waiting to hear the Gospel. There are millions of people who could live a much more abundant life if they could have the privilege of following God. Sure, I do my part here in our community. I do my part in the world. I lost count after fifty short-term mission trips supporting incredible ministries. The challenge for me is to ask, "Will I go?" Am I willing to step out into the deep water and trust God if He calls? Am I willing to even hear the call?

Your Kingdom challenge might be different. Those you lead will face different Kingdom challenges. Your goal is to get them thinking about the Kingdom of God and their role in that kingdom. We need to push them to make themselves available to God and get them thinking about what God needs. Your goal is to get them to answer the question, "Where is God working in the world?" Your goal is to get them serving where He has needs. They need to be deployable. They need to reach their immediate world, making disciples. They need to be open to serve around the world and to serve in other ministries. And we need to be willing to let them go. We need to be willing to release them to new adventures. We need to release them to God's work near and far.

Growing the church and having incredible leaders are vital to us. It takes courage and sacrifice to send your leaders out. It takes less courage when you are always making disciples. It takes bravery and faith to free your people to leave and serve in other ministries. It takes less bravery when you and I are Kingdom minded. Success is anything that builds up the Kingdom. Sustainable disciples spreading discipleship in other churches is success. Sustainable disciples starting other churches is success. Sustainable disciples leading in other ministries is success.

Not everyone will be called to go. God will continue to develop and build stable leadership in your community as He makes disciples. Doing will get done because of who these followers become. Your goal for those who stay is that they evangelize and make disciples in your community. Your goal for those who stay is that they send help, people, and support to those God sends out. If they do not go, then they send others.

But how can they call on him to save them unless they believe in him? And how can they believe in him if they have never heard about him? And how can they hear about him unless someone tells them? And how will anyone go and tell them without being sent? That is why the Scriptures say, "How beautiful are the feet of messengers who bring good news!"

— ROMANS 10:14–15

Discipleship is so exponentially powerful. The average church will have exhausted the need for discipleship by its fifth or sixth cycle. The work of making disciples, however, never ends. The world needs to hear, see, touch, and feel the love of God. People need to see what can be. The church needs the reformation that real discipleship can bring. Help the disciples dream, plan, and scheme how they will live out their calling to make disciples. Challenge them to have a plan. Hold them accountable. Help them find needs and opportunities inside and outside your community. Celebrate and support them if God calls them to go. Strategically plan to send disciples out into the world. This is what Jesus did. Become a training center for people to live their best day and for them to help others live their best day. It is precisely what Jesus did.

The fields are white for harvest. Intentionally, send them out. Send out prepared, confident, and skilled disciples. Send them out near and far to live well, to change the world, and to make disciples wherever they go.

18

OUR PRIVILEGE

After all, who is Apollos? Who is Paul? We are only God's servants through whom you believed the Good News. Each of us did the work the Lord gave us. I planted the seed in your hearts, and Apollos watered it, but it was God who made it grow. It's not important who does the planting, or who does the watering. What's important is that God makes the seed grow.

— 1 CORINTHIANS 3:5-7

People need help becoming followers. We get the privilege of doing just that as we make disciples. We have the privilege of guiding people to and teaching them to apply eternal truth. We have the privilege of helping them learn to learn. We have the privilege of exposing them to the Holy Spirit and walking with them through life-transforming moments. We have the privilege of helping people see God's original design for humans and His model for exploiting that design. We get to make disciples.

We also have the responsibility to walk along the way, never abandoning the one learning to follow. We have the responsibility to provide hope when the inevitable challenges come. We have the responsibility to "get their six" when the enemy attacks. We have the responsibility to guard them from the unholy trinity of destruction. We get to make disciples.

How cool is that? There was a day when we could never have made a disciple out of anyone. We did not have a clear destination, and we could not articulate a biblical way to "make a disciple." But we have grown up a bit.

We have an easy model built on God's word. We have the experience of others to help us repeat their successes and avoid their failures. We have a simpler answer to the question, "What is discipleship?" Discipleship is making disciples, and

Making disciples introduces people to God, who loves and understands them, helps them understand who they are and what they can be, helps them apply God's transforming truths, and releases them as prepared, confident, and skilled to live their best life ever on earth.

We understand the discipleship pathway and the fourteen steps that happen very naturally along that pathway. We know there are seven "be" and seven "do" steps linked together, where "be" (who we are) always pushes "dos" that then transform us to another "be."

- Being convicted leads to repentance.
- Repentance results in needing more information and leads to being taught.
- Being taught allows us to become enlightened and connected to God.
- Being enlightened leads to being called.
- Being called opens the opportunity to serve, and serve requires that we begin to learn.
- Learning results in being prepared.

- Being prepared leads us to a choice of consecration, which leads us to be consecrated.
- Being consecrated leads to a life that grows in independence and living out God's truths with confidence and skill.
- Residency leads us to solo leadership and solo living as we are released prepared, confident, and now skilled.
- Leadership brings us humility and leads us to being servants.
- Being a servant leads us to being Kingdom minded.
- Being Kingdom minded leads us to go and send to the world.

We have faced the truth that making disciples takes time. Four years may seem like a huge investment, but it feels like you just started yesterday when you complete the formal process and move to a lifetime practice of discipleship.

We have learned from example and scripture that the goal of discipleship is the transformation of individuals. We are only guides. God is the one who transforms. We also know that God's transformative work is fueled by His truth and His Spirit.

We have learned that disciples are found one at a time and that making disciples is done hands-on and along the way. We know the seven core practices that are always part of making sustainable disciples. We not only have the privilege to make disciples, we are ready to make disciples. We are prepared. We are confident that God will empower His call and His methods. We are skilled.

After all, we have been made disciples, and who better to make disciples than disciples? Who better to change the world than disciples? Who better to give the gift of peace and a greater life to others?

There is no one better than you. In fact, God is counting on you and me to spread the cure, to give the answer.

"Everyone who calls on the name of the LORD will be saved."
But how can they call on him to save them unless they believe in
him? And how can they believe in him if they have never heard
about him? And how can they hear about him unless someone tells
them? And how will anyone go and tell them without being sent?
That is why the scriptures say, "How beautiful are the feet of
messengers who bring good news!"

— ROMANS 10:13–15

We have the ability, we have the responsibility, and we have the privilege to solve an age-old, ongoing problem. We can make disciples. We can provide the everything answer by creating a comprehensive discipleship culture where we formally and informally make disciples. We can make disciples from our stages and pulpits. We can make disciples at our events. We can make disciples as we serve together. Even more powerful, we can launch a formal discipleship process that will leverage the secret sauce to sustainable discipleship.

Making disciples is entirely about who someone is and becomes. It is not about what they do or how they do it. Doing is the natural result of being.

My church has the privilege of being five generations deep into the discipleship process. We have people who are steady, strong, and honest. We are broken, humbled, and thriving individually. We have also seen that discipleship is the everything answer—providing innovation, support, creativity, leaders, teachers, and sold-out followers of God. Our community is headed toward Paul's dream of the church being fully equipped and living in true unity.

We would not be where we are today without taking that first step of discipleship: making disciples. The people would not be who they are today without investing the time to become disciples. What we enjoy is the result of us simply committing ourselves to God's great commission to be and make disciples.

What we enjoy is the result of working within God's methods and models for discipleship.

There is no greater joy than watching self-sustaining disciples thrive in their lives. There is nothing more amazing than watching them make new disciples. God's plan has the exponential power to save our world. And He has entrusted us with that power. If we make disciples, they will be made. If we do not, they will not. We are privileged to participate with God. There is no better work than to lead someone to follow God in every moment, in every thought, every day. There is no greater privilege than to release people prepared, confident, and skilled to thrive with God as they live their lives. I pray that you will give heed to His ways of making disciples. I pray that discipleship will invade your every moment and thought. I pray that you will join me in this sacred work, for it is the only work God specifically told us to do: go and make disciples.

SUSTAINABLE DISCIPLESHIP

RESOURCES

Sustainable Discipleship Library

Get access to our Sustainable Discipleship Online Library to see reviews and discover strategies for extra-Biblical books. See how we use them, use the library yourself, or learn to customize your own library at: Sustainable-Discipleship.com/resources

Live Workshops

Clarify discipleship and create a discipleship strategy for your organization by registering for a Live Workshop. You can also schedule a Private Workshop for your team or Host a Workshop for your city. Learn more at Sustainable-Discipleship.com.

Inspiration and Design

Let us inspire your team, evaluate your process, or help you launch a sustainable discipleship plan. We would love to help. Email us at team@sustainable-discipleship.com.

Speaking

Doug is a high-energy, creative speaker. He thrives unlocking the secrets of how to make and be disciples. To learn more, email speaking@sustainable-discipleship.com.

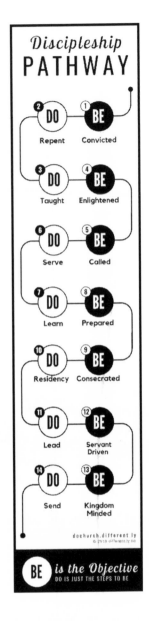

You can download this infographic, the Forty-Seven Week Bible Reading Tool and find other free resources at: Sustainable-Discipleship.com/resources.

NOTES

1. The State of Discipleship

1. The State of Discipleship by Barna Group, © 2015 The Navigators
2. To measure this metric, the study quantified a wide range of activities including attending Sunday school or fellowship group, meeting with a spiritual mentor, studying the Bible with a group, or reading and discussing a Christian book with a group.
3. Matthew 28:16–20.
4. The apostle. The guy who wrote Romans and 1 Corinthians. Credible.

3. The Burger

1. Frank, Alex. "The 10 Most Popular McDonald's Menu Items of All Time." *Spoon Media Inc.* n.d. https://spoonuniversity.com/lifestyle/mcdonalds-most-popular-items.
2. I work with two incredible groups of people who are my team. The incredible minds at Different.ly (our decision science consulting firm) and the discipleship team at Three Taverns Church relentlessly pursue the philosophy of discipleship.
3. Smietana, Bob. "LifeWay Research: Americans Are Fond of the Bible, Don't Actually Read It." *LifeWay Research.* April 25, 2017. https://lifewayresearch.com/2017/04/25/lifeway-research-americans-are-fond-of-the-bible-dont-actually-read-it/.
4. 1 Peter 3:15.
5. Deuteronomy 6.
6. I will share what we have learned about optimal group sizes in "Using Group Discipleship" section.
7. Customization is easy and achievable and makes a world of difference. We will explore customization in the section "What Is Discipleship?"

4. Two Irrefutable Discipleship Models

1. 1 John 2:7.
2. Segal, Marshall. "Make Disciples: The Life-Changing Ministry of Why." *Desiring God.* September 21, 2016. https://www.desiringgod.org/articles/make-disciples.
3. "The Tipping Point Chapter Three: Summary & Analysis." *LitCharts.* n.d. https://www.litcharts.com/lit/the-tipping-point/chapter-three-the-stickiness-factor.

4. Ephesians 6:4.
5. John 21:25.
6. Matthew 10:5–9.
7. "History of The Navigators." *The Navigators*. n.d. https://www.navigators.org/about/history/.
8. Matthew 28:19–20.
9. Romans 10:15 and Matthew 5:14, to name a few.
10. Matthew 9:9.
11. Luke 19:1–10.

5. "Be" Comes before "Do"

1. My first-person adaptation of John's teaching in 1 John 4:19.

6. The Everything Answer for Churches

1. I attend Three Taverns Church in north Atlanta. It is one the coolest, small, strong communities that I have ever experienced.
2. Paul spent some twelve or more years following Christ, being discipled, and preparing before his ministry began.

7. What Discipleship Is

1. You can find this pathway in the chapter "Leverage the Predictable Pathway" as we explore the sustainable-discipleship model in detail.
2. This is the step of "consecration" along the discipleship pathway. See the predictable pathway.
3. Again, see the steps along the discipleship pathway later in this book.
4. Prayer ropes date back to 3 AD, when they were used by Desert Fathers to help structure prayer. There is no rule on what or how to use a prayer rope. It is just a tool to help structure prayer. For more information on prayer ropes, do a search or check out "Prayer rope." *Wikipedia*. Last edited July 9, 2019. https://en.wikipedia.org/wiki/Prayer_rope.
5. Coleman, Robert. *The Master Plan of Evangelism*. Grand Rapids: Revell, 2010.
6. Of course, not his real name.
7. John 3:17.
8. James 5:20.
9. Crucify yourself and quit what is not right (chapter 6), strive to do what is right (chapter 7), and then mature to running on the Spirit's moment-by-moment guidance (chapter 8).
10. Nee, Watchman. *Sit, Walk, Stand*. Carol Stream: Tyndale House Publishers, Inc., 1977.
11. Not his real name even though this is a real story that we see repeated again and again and again.

12. It was interesting that all five men's experiences lined up perfectly with Barna's research on the state of discipleship.

13. Sustainable discipleship started out as a series of answers for those who were beginning to disciple others. It evolved into a loosely constructed manual for the third generation of disciple makers. Now five generations deep, our leaders have pushed me to document the concepts, truths, and methods that we learned, were taught, and discovered along the way. Leaders and churches we have coached have asked us to put it down in writing for their evolving leaders.

8. The Evolution of a Plan

1. Credit goes to Malcolm Gladwell's *The Tipping Point*, where he describes that moment when everything changes, when things go viral, and when things take off. Gladwell, Malcolm. *The Tipping Point*. New York: Back Bay Books, 2002.

2. Titus 2:3–5.

9. Plan on Four Years

1. Clabaugh, Jeff. "If education counts, Americans have never been smarter." *WTOP.* April 3, 2017. https://wtop.com/business-finance/2017/04/education-counts-americans-never-smarter/.

2. Norris, Floyd. "Fewer U.S. Graduates Opt for College After High School." *The New York Times.* April 25, 2014. https://www.nytimes.com/2014/04/26/business/fewer-us-high-school-graduates-opt-for-college.html.

3. If you have never been in a discipleship relationship, you may want to discover the practice and value of being a disciple before you begin making disciples. It is difficult to lead someone to a place you have never been.

4. *The 21 Irrefutable Laws of Leadership* by John C. Maxwell. Maxwell, John. *The 21 Irrefutable Laws of Leadership: Follow Them and People Will Follow You.* New York: HarperCollins Leadership, 2007.

10. Deploy Comprehensive Discipleship

1. Interestingly, this was the exact solution God gave Moses through his father-in-law, Jethro, when the first God nation was established. See Exodus 18:13 ff.

2. *Fresh Wind, Fresh Fire* by Jim Cymbala is great testimony to this point. Cymbala, Jim. *Fresh Wind, Fresh Fire: What Happens When God's Spirit Invades the Hearts of His People.* Grand Rapids: Zondervan, 2003.

3. "Us": the team at Three Taverns Church.

4. One of my favorite examples is Jesus speaking to Thomas (John 20:24–29). A classic example is the Lord's Supper.

11. Leverage the Predictable Pathway

1. The 20/80 rule says that 20 percent of the people will do 80 percent of the service, giving, and work in a church.
2. The stories in this paragraph are real, but the names are not.
3. Reeves, Keanu. *The Matrix.* Warner Bros., Village Roadshow Pictures, Groucho Film Partnership, 1999.
4. Luke 14:27, paraphrased.
5. Year three is the second half of discipleship two.
6. Year four begins the formal process of discipleship three.

12. Use the Seven Core Practices

1. See the section on critical thinking in this chapter.
2. This target is for our preferred group size of four: one leader and three participants. The target for larger groups is two hours.
3. 1 Timothy 3.
4. You can find this library on Three Taverns Church website. "Thrive." *Three Taverns Church.* n.d. https://threetavernschurch.org/discipleship-books/.
5. Adapted with permission from RIBBI Mexico. RIBBI. *RIBBI Red de Iglesias Bautistas Interdependientes.* http://www.ribbi.org/threetaverns.html.
6. "Our Concept and Definition of Critical Thinking." *Foundation for Critical Thinking.* n.d. https://www.criticalthinking.org/pages/our-concept-of-critical-thinking/411.
7. "Socratic method." *Wikipedia.* Last edited on June 26, 2019. https://en.wikipedia.org/wiki/Socratic_method.

13. Customize the Process

1. I talk in detail about our role as people who formally make disciples in the next section, "Understand Your Role."
2. Based on John 5:17; 19–20.
3. This method is covered in detail in the chapter "Launch Your Discipleship-One Group."
4. The formal assessment is different for each phase of discipleship. You can find details in those chapters.
5. This principle is not only helpful but mandatory for sustainable discipleship that is conducted one-on-one. Trust us. Trust history.
6. 2 Samuel 11:2.
7. Titus 2:2–3.

14. Understand Your Role

1. Russ, Eric. "Biblical Basis for Discipleship." *Discipleship Defined.* n.d. http://www.discipleshipdefined.com/resources/biblical-basis-discipleship.
2. "The Shabbat Laws." *Chabad-Lubavitch Media Center.* n.d. https://www.chabad.org/library/article_cdo/aid/95907/jewish/The-Shabbat-Laws.htm.
3. Again, Phil Brown with RIBBI Mexico helped us put language to these challenges that we experienced again and again. I cannot count the times that Phil has championed me or pushed me saying, "Do you see it? Money, family, and pride derail discipleship again!" Phil is a genius disciple-maker.
4. Dever, Mark. *Discipling: How to Help Others Follow Jesus.* Page 91. Wheaton: Crossway Books, 2016.
5. Segal, Marshall. "Make Disciples: The Life-Changing Ministry of Why." *Desiring God.* September 21, 2016. https://www.desiringgod.org/articles/make-disciples.
6. Rarely, if ever, do co-leadership. It is confusing for those who follow. If you must co-lead to train or because of schedules, make one leader the leader and the other leader the helper who rarely speaks when the leader is present. Co-led groups are dangerous. Did I say rarely?
7. Thackeray Ritchie, Anne. *Mrs Dymond.* Page 342. London: Smith, Elder; 1885. This quote has often been attributed to a Chinese, Italian, and other proverb, but this is the first occurrence in written literature.

15. Launch Your Discipleship-One Group

1. Laurie, Greg. "The Requirements of Discipleship." *Harvest Ministries.* n.d. https://harvest.org/know-god-article/the-requirements-of-discipleship/.
2. Romans 7.
3. See the "Recruit" and "Assess" sections of this chapter.
4. Tithing is one of the "16 Key Topics in Christianity."
5. The State of Discipleship by Barna Group, © 2015 The Navigators
6. Smietana, Bob. "LifeWay Research: Americans Are Fond of the Bible, Don't Actually Read It." *LifeWay Research.* April 25, 2017. https://lifewayresearch.com/2017/04/25/lifeway-research-americans-are-fond-of-the-bible-dont-actually-read-it/.
7. Bill Sizemore gave me these words as he championed us to stay centrally focused on evangelism as a healthy practice for all those who follow.
8. Dever, Mark. *Discipling: How to Help Others Follow Jesus.* Wheaton: Crossway Books, 2016.
9. Matthew 7:13–14.
10. Barna.

16. Continue Leading Disciples in Discipleship Two

1. John 14:26.
2. 1 Timothy 3:9.

17. Finish Discipleship Well with Discipleship Three

1. We maintain this sortable library online.
2. Remember, it is sin to know what you ought to do and then not do it.
3. But if you have doubts about whether or not you should eat something, you are sinning if you go ahead and do it. For you are not following your convictions.

Made in United States
Orlando, FL
05 May 2022

17523988R20200